D1476063

NO LONGER PROPERTY OF
SEATTLE PUBLIC LIBRARY
NO LONGER PROPERTY
SEATTLE PUBLIC LIBR.

THE COMPLETE
RIB
DAG PIKE
manual

Published by Adlard Coles Nautical
an imprint of Bloomsbury Publishing Plc
50 Bedford Square, London WC1B 3DP
www.adlardcoles.com

Copyright © Dag Pike 2013

First published by Adlard Coles Nautical
in 2013

ISBN 978-1-4081-8012-9
ePDF 978-1-4081-8014-3
ePub 978-1-4081-8013-6

All rights reserved. No part of this
publication may be reproduced in any
form or by any means – graphic, electronic
or mechanical, including photocopying,
recording, taping or information storage
and retrieval systems – without the prior
permission in writing of the publishers.

The right of the author to be identified as
the author of this work has been asserted
by him in accordance with the Copyright,
Designs and Patents Act, 1988.

A CIP catalogue record for this book
is available from the British Library.

This book is produced using paper that
is made from wood grown in managed,
sustainable forests. It is natural,
renewable and recyclable. The logging
and manufacturing processes conform
to the environmental regulations of the
country of origin.

Designed by Austin Taylor
Typeset in Grotesque MT

Printed and bound in India
by Replika Press Pvt. Ltd.

Note: while all reasonable care
has been taken in the publication
of this book, the publisher takes
no responsibility for the use of the
methods or products described
in the book.

THE COMPLETE RIB manual

DAG PIKE

THE DEFINITIVE GUIDE TO HANDLING AND MAINTENANCE

ADLARD COLES NAUTICAL

BLOOMSBURY

LONDON · NEW DELHI · NEW YORK · SYDNEY

PUBLISHED IN ASSOCIATION WITH BARRUS Est. 1917 AND PANTAENIUS Yacht Insurance

CONTENTS

The rise of the Rigid Inflatable Boat (RIB) has been one of the most dramatic developments to take place in recent boating history. Most changes in the boating world take place in a slow, step-by-step way, but within just a few years the RIB had taken it by storm. What makes it more amazing is that the RIB started life as a rescue boat in the commercial sector, and then went on to embrace every part of the market.

The RIB was developed from the inflatable boat, so its arrival was not quite a sudden Eureka moment. However, the inflatable was developed primarily as a practical, portable boat that could be deflated and folded up. The RIB turned that idea on its head and replaced it with a less portable concept that embraced most of the good features of the inflatable and the best of the modern sports boat. Add a few bells and whistles such as the saddle seat, and the RIB became what was probably the most seaworthy and practical boat for its size anywhere in the world.

You might expect that would be enough to ensure its success in the commercial and military sectors but what no one expected was the way in which the RIB was adopted in the leisure market. Perhaps this was a reflection on the design excesses of some of the sports boats at the time, maybe there was a latent demand for a boat that was both practical and safe, or maybe people were just excited by something different that they could use as a fun boat. Whatever the reason, the boating public took to the RIB like a duck takes to water – and the rest is history.

It is interesting to note that it was also the leisure market that started the trend towards larger RIBs. So many people, including me, thought that the RIB was only viable in smaller sizes, where its extraordinary capabilities really stood out. In larger sizes the advantages were not so apparent (which was not a problem for leisure users, but was for the commercial/military sector). But as soon as it became clear that the RIB was the perfect boat design when you needed to go alongside other vessels at sea, and had an authoritative appearance, then first the military and rescue people adopted the concept, and now most commercial operators use all sizes of RIB as their boat of choice.

All of this is despite the fact that a RIB is more expensive to buy and maintain than a matching hard hull, so the benefits must outweigh the extra

cost. I do wonder how many people actually try to quantify this, but the RIB has now become the standard by which other boats are judged.

Appearance has become a very important factor in RIB design in the leisure, commercial and military sectors, and it is starting to compromise other aspects of the design. To make them look good, the tubes are inflated so hard that they bounce rather than absorb impact shock loadings. The result is a harsh ride, to the point where many operators now demand the fitting of sprung seating to protect their crews. This in turn can add weight to the boat in the wrong place, making the ride even livelier. Reducing tube pressure is essential to a smooth ride, but sensitive driving also helps. Hull design is also a major contributory factor and the lessons we learnt from the early days of RIBs are being largely ignored in the search for performance and style. We seem to have entered a vicious circle of development that does not have an easy solution, and need to go back to the basics of RIB design to find answers to the various problems now facing RIB operators.

Despite this, RIBs are now so good that crews tend to drive them to the limits rather that nursing them through the waves. There is sometimes a macho culture amongst RIB drivers that can lead to less than skilful driving. RIB crews have now become the weak point, rather than the boat and its engine: this is a tribute to modern RIB designers and builders, but does show that the time has come for a major rethink about RIB design and driving.

Today the RIB is everywhere and there are probably more RIBs being built than any other category of boat. You can see them in every harbour, where they are used as yacht tenders, stand-alone sports boats, harbour patrol boats and serious cruising boats. Thrill-ride operations almost invariably use RIBs as their 'go anywhere' boats and in nearly every country around the world the military now operates RIBs.

I am proud to have played a small part in the development of the RIB, even if was mainly to show what didn't work. I am proud of the way that the RIB has advanced boat design and development into a whole new world of capability. After 50 years of existence, the RIB is set for world domination, and its place in maritime history is now assured – hopefully for all the right reasons.

PART ONE

A HISTORY

OF THE RIB

1 EARLY DEVELOPMENT

THE FIRST STEPS on the road to developing rigid inflatable boats (RIBs) were taken when we were trying to solve a problem. During the 1960s there was a growing number of casualties around Britain's coasts involving small boats, surfers and swimmers, and the large all-weather lifeboats were not well-suited to rescue work. The lifeboat society in France (Societé Nationale de Sauvetage en Mer) had introduced the flat-bottomed inflatable boat as a small rescue craft that could operate off open beaches. The French had a fleet of 5-metre Zodiac inflatables and a year or two later the Royal National Lifeboat Institution (RNLI) introduced its own inflatables based on that Zodiac design.

IMPROVING THE INFLATABLE

The 5-metre outboard powered boats did a wonderful job of inshore rescue work and were welcomed by the traditional lifeboat crews as a supplement to their all-weather, but slow, traditional lifeboats. However, the virtually flat fabric bottom meant the crews were in for a harsh ride through wave impact, even though the inflatable structure of the boat absorbed some of the shocks. Furthermore, the shape of the hull made them susceptible to a high level of wear and

← The RNLI inflatable
rescue boat from which
the RIB developed

↙↙ These inflatable rescue
boats had a tough life
operating from open beaches

↓↓ The author on a sea trial
with the first RIB developed at
the RNLI depot at Boreham Wood

11

tear, particularly when they were launched and recovered from open beaches. However, their flexible nature and ability to absorb some of the wave impact was noted, plus the inflatable tube also made a good built-in fender for boats used for rescue work at sea.

I got involved with these rescue boats when I joined the RNLI as an Inspector of Lifeboats in 1962. Initially I introduced the craft to new lifeboat stations and trained crews to use them, before managing all maintenance and development of the inshore lifeboat fleet.

The RNLI built up a fleet of over 100 inflatable inshore lifeboats. Since many of the new lifeboat stations were operating from open beaches, the boats were being dragged across rough sand and shingle during launch and recovery operations. This was causing the bottom fabric to wear out quickly, particularly in the area around the wooden transom, and it was becoming a major maintenance headache. In an attempt to overcome it, we cut out the rear section of

the floor fabric (about 1.5m) and replaced it with a piece of flat plywood braced rigidly to the transom. The plywood was able to stand up to the harsh conditions and as a bonus it also improved the boat's performance by creating a hard planing surface. This semi-RIB solution also allowed the boat to be deflated and rolled up for easy transport when a replacement had to be sent to a lifeboat station.

This modified boat was an improvement, but sadly it did not solve the wear and tear problem entirely. Instead of it taking place around the transom, it was simply moved further forward to the point where the fabric was attached to the plywood bottom. We had to go back to the drawing board. Why not replace the entire bottom of the boat with plywood so there would be a hard, robust surface to stand up to the wear and tear caused by beach launches? We did this, constructing a plywood base roughly in the shape of the original fabric bottom, and took it out on sea trials. This was probably

the first full-scale RIB ever built. It worked beautifully in calm water but once we hit waves the plywood bottom structure started to break up. We quickly realised we were trying to put a rigid structure into a boat that was designed to be flexible – something had to give. Unfortunately this was the rigid plywood bottom, because the longitudinal pressure in the boat was now being transferred from the inflatable tubes into the wood, which was just not strong enough for the job. We were left with a heap of broken plywood and a boat returned to its original form – and at that point we gave up.

That could have been the end of the RIB. However, one of the RNLI inshore lifeboat stations based at Atlantic College in South Wales had been facing much the same severe wear problems on the fabric bottom when launching and recovering its boats on stony beaches. Its initial solution was to attach longitudinal plywood strips to the bottom fabric, which would flex to a degree and at the same time offer some protection to the fabric. This led to its senior students

starting a project to discover a better long-term solution. This work was carried out with the blessing of the RNLI, who funded some of the development work.

Like us, the students' first thought was to replace the bottom of their rescue boat with a plywood sheet glued to the tubes. That worked, but it gave a harsh ride, so they persevered with the concept of a fully rigid hull bottom, introducing a V-shaped cross-section at the bow with the plywood section tapering aft to a flat profile. This was a similar solution to the one we had tried, but in their case it worked, probably because the stress on their shorter boat was less than we had found when trying to construct the same thing on our 15-footers. The students worked on a couple of larger prototypes and then developed prototypes X-1 to X-3 with a funding agreement from the RNLI. This work was being carried out at around the time the deep vee hull was starting to make an impact on the small boat market, and the suggestion was made to design a deep vee hull that would fit into the inflatable tube.

It would have sufficient depth to insert
strong longitudinal stringers, ensuring the
hull shape was strong enough to take the
strain. This development resulted in the
first working RIB with the hull form we
know and love today.

THE ATLANTIC 21 CONCEPT

A number of prototype hulls were built
and tested (mainly based on quite small
hull designs) and as progress was made a
couple of the more advanced designs with
deep vee hulls showed promise. In 1966 two
later boats underwent trials on an RNLI
inshore lifeboat station. A further series of
prototypes were designed and built by the
college in 1968 and 1969. I think in all there
were something like 20 prototypes built at
Atlantic College, but it was in 1969 that the
college designed and built the 21-foot RIB
Psychedelic Surfer in which John Caulcutt,
Graeme Dillon and Simon d'Ath took part
in the first ever Round Britain Powerboat
Race. This boat drew on the considerable

RIB design experience amassed at Atlantic
College and it was completed in a few
weeks, just before the race started. Because
the race rules stipulated a minimum length
of 21 feet, the available tube had to be
lengthened and *Psychedelic Surfer* became
the largest RIB of the time and the first to
have a twin outboard installation. It was
ground-breaking stuff, and to everybody's
amazement the boat went on to finish this
tough race in good order, and to attract a
lot of attention in the process. *Psychedelic
Surfer* demonstrated just what a rigid

inflatable might be capable of and its design went on to form the basis of the Atlantic 21 inshore lifeboat that was used very successfully by the RNLI for many years, and which became the cornerstone of their inshore fleet.

Psychedelic Surfer had demonstrated that a RIB with a higher length/beam ratio worked better in waves than the shorter boats. But while these prototype designs held together under the strain of operating in waves, the best solution for a rescue RIB design emerged slowly; the addition of a deep vee hull increased the draft of the boat, which required long shaft outboard engines. This deeper hull caused problems when launching it from an open beach, as the boat had to be taken into sufficient depth of water for the engine to be started. This led to

the vee of the hull being truncated to take a few inches off the depth.

The next stage was to modify the shape of the inflatable tube to create a longer, leaner and more sea-kindly hull shape.

While this RIB development work was happening at Atlantic College, I was transferred from inshore lifeboat maintenance and development work at the RNLI depot in North London to being responsible for all lifeboat stations in Wales and the Bristol Channel. Of course, that included Atlantic College and I became a regular visitor there to check on the developments. This particular race boat design became the famous Atlantic 21 inshore lifeboat and was transferred to the new RNLI inshore lifeboat base at Cowes on the Isle of Wight. From there the Atlantic 21

← Students launching the
RNLI Atlantic 21 at the College

↓↓ An early RNLI Atlantic 21
in rough seas

↓ An early Atlantic 21 now resting
quietly in a transport museum

15

concept was finalised and the craft entered service in 1972. This was probably the most seaworthy boat for its size ever built and with minor modifications it remained in service for over thirty years.

Now that the seagoing capabilities of the craft had been resolved, the crew had become the weak point of the system and part of the success of the Atlantic 21 concept was in resolving the driving position. Atlantic College had been working on the saddle seat idea, which enabled the driver to securely locate himself at the helm thus leaving his hands free to control the boat and giving the crews a more comfortable ride. The RNLI had also decreed that all its lifeboats should be capable of being righted after a capsize, and while the crew of small inflatable rescue boats could manually right their crafts, the Atlantic RIBs were too large and heavy. The self-righting system was therefore developed, comprising an inflatable bag mounted on an arch at the stern, and the crews trained for the job.

OTHER PIONEERS – FLATACRAFT AND AVON

The RNLI were not the only organisation looking at the RIB concept to develop a new class of boat. Flatacraft was one of the first to bring the idea to the leisure market. Tony Lee-Elliot is convinced that his brother Edward was already building his first RIB in the autumn of 1966, based on the design of

↓↓ The first Flatacraft RIB
on Lake Windermere with
Ed Lee-Elliot driving

↓↓ Early Avon Seariders
changed the face of
leisure boating

↓ An early Avon Searider
resting quietly in a field
in the Scilly Islands

16

A HISTORY OF THE RIB

a Tinker Tramp sailing inflatable the two of
them had rented. After building an inflatable
boat that wouldn't get on the plane, the
brothers realised they needed to add a hard
bottom if the boat was going to perform.
Their first RIB was 11.5 feet long, with
parallel tubes and a spray cuddy, and was
powered by a 33hp Evinrude outboard. They
went on to build a 14.5-foot RIB powered
by a 50hp Evinrude in 1969. The Flatacraft
RIB was unique in that it had a small
transom at the bow as well as a full sized
one at the stern, which simplified the tube
construction. Like the Avon model, it was
self-draining, with the floor of the cockpit
above the waterline.

The Flatacraft company was launched
in January 1972 and while Lee-Elliot admits
Avon was ahead of them in producing RIBs,
he lays claim to building the first commercial
forms of the craft. In fact, that 14.5-foot RIB
was the first to circumnavigate the British
Isles when the Royal Marines borrowed it
to evaluate RIBs in 1972, although
Flatacraft was not allowed to publicise
the fact at the time.

Meanwhile, on the Isle of Wight, the Galt
brothers were working on the RIB concept
using tubes supplied by Avon (Avon had also
supplied tubes to Atlantic College in the
early days of RIB development). At that time,
Avon was building its remarkable Redstart
and Redcrest inflatable boats, which were
transforming the yacht tender market
(because they could be deflated and stowed
away on board and inflated when needed).
Eventually Avon teamed up with the Galt
brothers and their designs evolved into
the famous Searider range of RIBs.

These were unique in having a rigid hull moulded from glass-reinforced plastic (GRP, or fibreglass), the first commercial RIBs to be made from this material. When the boat was at rest in the water this rigid section would flood through a hole in the transom and the water would drain out as the boat came onto the plane. The logic behind this idea was that the entrained water would improve the stability of the boat at rest, transforming it into a stable platform, and then drain away as it came onto the plane. However, the weight of water in the hull made the acceleration sluggish and if the boat was left afloat, seaweed and barnacles tended to grow inside the ballast space (when it was out of the water, you could always recognise an early Searider that had been left afloat by the smell of rotting vegetation). The first Avon Searider RIB was exhibited at the London Boat Show in 1969.

↓↓ An early Atlantic 21 with its flat bottom section in the deep vee hull

↓ Self-righting sequence from an early Avon advert

Atlantic College had patented the concept of the RIB and they vested this patent to the RNLI. This meant in those early days Avon had to pay a royalty to the RNLI for each RIB it built (the RNLI was asking for £3 per boat). Meanwhile Flatacraft refused to pay the royalty, stating it had built its first RIBs prior to the Atlantic College patent, which meant it was exempt. This was proved to be the case, thus demonstrating Flatacraft was in the RIB business before its competitors, but Avon was arguably the first to sell RIBs commercially.

Each of these early RIBs was mostly outboard-powered using a single engine of around 40 or 50hp clamped onto the transom. The Atlantic 21, because of its larger size, was able to have a twin outboard installation, thus improving its capability

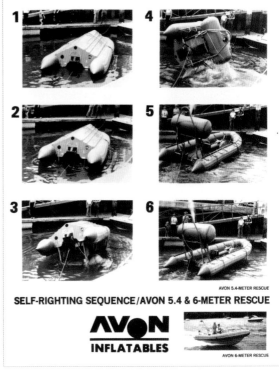

SELF-RIGHTING SEQUENCE/AVON 5.4 & 6-METER RESCUE

AVON INFLATABLES

and reliability on arduous rescue missions.

Because of disasters such as the Sea Gem rig collapse on 27 December 1965, which occurred during the early days of North Sea oil exploration, the authorities demanded each fixed installation out at sea should have a standby vessel in attendance, which would go to the rescue in the event of an emergency. Most standby vessels were redundant trawlers required to carry rescue boats on board, which could be launched in an emergency. RIBs were chosen for this role. I was involved in these operations, both in training the crews to operate their new, fast rescue boats and in developing launch and rescue systems that would allow rescue boats to be launched and recovered, even under adverse conditions.

Avon was the one of the first to meet
the demand for North Sea rescue boats,
initially with its Searider designs and later
with larger crafts intended to meet more
stringent safety requirements. However,
there was one major problem with the
use of outboard-powered RIBs: standby
ships had to carry petrol on board, which
concerned the officials who set the safety
standards because of the increased risk
of fire. Consequently, the demand grew for
rescue boats powered by diesel so the fuel
for both them and their mother ship would
be compatible. This posed a new challenge
for all RIB builders entering the developing
market.

One of those early pioneers was David
Still Marine, based near Chichester in the UK.
This company had developed a range of larger
RIBs using an existing sports boat hull as the

rigid section and adding the tube above.

It set about developing a RIB that would
incorporate a diesel engine. The available
high-speed diesels were still large and
relatively heavy at the time, so the challenge
was to install this weight into a relatively
small RIB. By using a shallower vee than
normal to give the hull a better load-carrying

jet RIB. During much of this pioneering RIB development, David Still Marine was working with Watercraft, which was a major builder of traditional lifeboats.

Avon came up with an 8-metre version of a diesel RIB shortly afterwards, again designed as a North Sea rescue boat. In fact, the early diesel RIBs were no smaller than 7 metres in length and as other builders came into the market, stern drives were used as an alternative propulsion system, although many of the existing stern drive units were not capable of handling the high torque of the diesel engine. It was to be several years before diesel-powered RIBs became commonplace and it was the advent of lightweight, high-performance Yanmar diesels that really made the diesel RIB a viable proposition in smaller sizes.

capability, the first diesel-powered RIB became a reality. The diesel engine was coupled to a water jet, creating another first in the history of RIB development: the water-

RIB DEVELOPMENT IN AMERICA AND EUROPE

The first RIB to be built in North America is thought to have been constructed at the sister college to Atlantic, located in British Columbia. Built in the mid 1970s, it was a 21 footer, similar to the Atlantic 21, and this and later boats were loaned to the Canadian Coast Guard (CCG) for operational use as rescue boats. The CCG also employed Avon Seariders for summer use on inshore rescue boat duties in the later 1970s and used them as tenders on some of their patrol boats.

While RIB use was expanding rapidly in Europe, the concept did not enthral the US market. I recollect giving a paper in New Orleans in 1982 on the use of RIBs as workboats and most of the audience looked bewildered and could not really grasp the idea of what an RIB encompassed. It took many years for the transformation to take place, triggered mainly by the US Coast Guard and the military starting to use the craft.

One of the first commercial RIB builders in North America was Hurricane, the company that later became Hurricane Zodiac. Even when the RIB became commercially available in the US it took a long while for the concept to filter through to the general public. I recall taking a RIB on a long promotional voyage from New Orleans to Miami. One day we went up the Suwanee River in Florida to refuel and arrived at a small fuel dock on the river. It was lunchtime,

↓ You can see the beginnings of the
modern-day RIB in this Avon sports boat

and eventually the attendant came down scratching his head. 'Ain't never seen a boat like that before!' he said, and then after a pause, 'Ain't going to sink, is it?' That was the late 1980s, when RIB use was expanding rapidly in Europe.

British builders led the world in the early RIB designs. Famous names like Delta and Humber arrived on the scene in the 1980s, but most of the output from early British builders was aimed at the commercial and military operator or the serious leisure user who wanted a 'go anywhere' type of boat or a dive boat. Avon and Flatacraft catered for the lower-size part of the market, where the RIB was being used as a yacht tender or as a fun sports boat, although the craft was still something of a novelty to leisure users.

Serious leisure users, however, developed the art of RIB cruising, which was really a progression of the Raids or Camping la Nautique (during which a fleet of inflatables cruised in company during

the day and camped on beaches at night) pioneered by Zodiac inflatable users in the Mediterranean. I participated in one of the pioneering RIB cruises in the 1970s, during which we launched three boats under the Severn Bridge in the Bristol Channel and set out to cross the Irish Sea, round the Fastnet Lighthouse, and then head back along the English Channel to Poole via the Scilly Isles.

It was a big adventure, and the boats were sabotaged in Ireland because the locals thought we were the authorities come to clamp down on illegal drift net salmon fishing. We made a 150-mile open sea passage from the Fastnet to the Scilly Isles and we had thick fog as we entered the English Channel, but cruising with three Delta RIBs (which gave us an added measure of safety), we succeeded in our mission. Apart from the run-in with the Irish locals, we didn't encounter any problems – a tribute to the RIB's reliability.

Design and colour

I remember the 1970s and 1980s as a time of considerable experimentation in RIB design and construction. While British builders pioneered RIB development, it was the Italians who advanced RIB style. Builders such as Novamarine and Novarania introduced stylish white tubes, consoles and arch masts. They matched curved inflatable tubes to curves in the console, seating and masts to create a harmonious whole that was far removed from the harsher practicalities of the early RIBs. Their use by the military and the Special Forces had already enhanced their macho appeal among adventurous boaters, but when the Italians introduced fashion into the equation, the scene was set for an explosion in the RIB leisure market.

The quality of the fabric used on many early RIBs, however, was poor and there were constant problems with porous material in the RFD tubes; it was not uncommon to find a multitude of tiny bubbles appearing when they were covered in soapy water. This was mainly caused by wicking, where air entered the cut edge of the fabric along the tiny channel formed in the internal fabric and then escaped through the outer layer of rubber. This could only be detected once the tube had been made and inflated. Because of this design fault, we had to reject several boats. Furthermore, neoprene rubber was poorly applied to some of the early fabrics and it would also delaminate at the glued joints when put under stress. This is where Avon had an edge – it was using good-quality fabrics, which meant its boats did not have to be pumped up every time they went to sea.

It was the introduction of Hypalon rubber, or CSM, coatings that led not only to a much improved quality of fabric, but also to the introduction of colour. Neoprene rubber was one of the first of the artificial rubbers to be developed during World War II when natural rubber supplies were hard to acquire, and in fact it boasted much better durability. Hypalon rubber came later, and what made it particularly special was it could be dyed without leading to a deterioration in the fabric. However, its air-holding qualities were not quite as good as neoprene, so designers took to using a combination of neoprene (both on the inside and outside) and an outer coating of Hypalon on their fabrics.

Hypalon transformed the appearance of RIBs almost overnight. Prior to its introduction most RIB tubes were black or grey and you could only liven up their appearance by applying fabric patches, such as the orange we applied to rescue boats. Suddenly RIBs exploded with colour. White

of the major outboard manufacturers adding RIBs to their portfolios, enabling them to sell the complete package.

Tube experimentation

Some commercial users, however, were not convinced by the RIB's inflatable tubes, thinking them too vulnerable in the harsh commercial environment. This led to the development of foam-filled tubes, where the foam interior was shaped to match the requirements, and then covered with a hard-wearing polyurethane skin to create a more durable design. They maintained a small

tubes were like a breath of fresh air to the leisure market, and when combined with the Italian's stylish consoles and arch masts, the RIB quickly became *the* boat to own, displacing the conventional sports boat.

As RIBs progressed in style they also became available in smaller-sized, outboard-powered craft. These mass-produced designs met the market demand for a better yacht tender than the pure inflatable and also created a new market in starter boats for couples and families that could be carried on the roof of a car and launched virtually anywhere. Many in the industry believed the inflatable would dominate this sector, but it transpired the ability to fold the boat wasn't a priority for most leisure users, since they did not relish the chore of inflating it before each use. The small RIB, however, could be used on sheltered waters; provided a safe, stable platform at rest; and ensured enough performance to satisfy this growing market's needs. A higher demand increased outboard sales, which led to some

degree of flexibility so they could absorb shock loads, which worked well in fendering, but some of the variable geometry characteristics of the inflatable tube were lost (another of the compromises made in RIB design).

Another new tube type was constructed from cylindrical plastic fenders attached along the top of the hull, forming a tube of sorts. The idea here was that if one fender was damaged, it could be replaced in isolation. However, the construction lacked resilience and consistency in shape along its length, meaning it got caught up when going alongside other structures.

At this time, most RIBs were still mainly hand-built, and this labour-intensive construction caused production of many of the smaller-sized RIBs to be moved to countries where labour costs were low. Even with production running at perhaps several thousand units per year, it was proving difficult to automate many of the production processes, particularly the tube manufacture. Consequently, designers began using alternative materials such as PVC and polyurethane, which could be heat-welded rather than glued. Today, PVC tubes are found on many smaller RIBs and they work fine; however, if they are damaged they are difficult to repair and the material has a short life expectancy.

Avon had originally entered the RIB business to expand its extensive rubber business, which was mostly centred around car tyres. A competitor, Dunlop, also started RIB building to grow its product base. Its contribution to the market was a revolution: the first catamaran RIB. This design had an inflatable tube down each side of the

boat and, because they were identical and interchangeable, the boats were cheaper to manufacture and easier to build. However, the catamaran hull did not capture the market's imagination, because it was outside the mainstream of design.

During this time of experimentation, a variety of hulls were also introduced. Barrus claims to have been involved in the first rigid aluminium-hulled RIB. The material worked well and certainly appealed to the professional side of the market, which was more familiar with aluminium than Glass Reinforced Plastic (GRP). Some aluminium RIB designs also incorporated the material into the tubes so that now the whole boat was rigid once again, with the tubes simply providing additional buoyancy and stability at rest. Other 'RIBs' were constructed from polyethylene, a more or less rigid plastic used frequently in pipework. They were formed from tubes cut from sections of a longer tube and welded together with heat, with sheet plastic used for the centre hull.

↓↓ The author navigating on a
Round Scotland RIB race

↘ Rounding the Fastnet Rock
Light on an early RIB cruise

↘↘ Simple saddle seating
married to the helm console

A HISTORY OF THE RIB

These were rugged workboats but, like the aluminium designs, they lost many of the RIB qualities because the tubes did not change shape under wave impact.

SUMMARY

When we first started building RIBs fifty years ago we were simply trying to solve a problem with the existing inflatable boats. What started as a solution to a problem turned out to be what is perhaps the biggest revolution in motorboat design since Ray Hunt produced his first deep-vee hull. The RIB was never the cheapest solution, it was never the easy option, but its capabilities and its sea-keeping convinced most users it was a sound choice. Today, few people need or use the craft to anywhere near its

full potential; rather, they are content it exists as a sensible, practical everyday boat with a good margin of in-built safety. In the commercial and military sectors, the RIB has become the boat of choice for a great many operators and even in the US, where RIBs were very slow to catch on, it has gained huge headway in all markets.

Throughout its 50-year existence, the RIB has challenged boat designers, and traditional designers and naval architects still seem to find it difficult to understand the craft and its features and benefits. Most of the early designs were produced by the builders themselves, signalling a return to basic design techniques used in boat construction for the past 2000 years, in contrast to modern conventional boat design that tends to follow set rules and predictions. The early RIB builders were themselves RIB users, and they discovered what worked and what didn't through trial and error. Today's RIBs are the result of that long and often hard-won practical experience, which perhaps explains why they are some of the best and most seaworthy boats in the world.

LOOK AROUND ANY HARBOUR today and you will see RIBs being put to a wide variety of uses. There will be tenders taking crews to and from yachts moored in the harbour; safety boats escorting sailing dinghies from the local sailing club; the harbour master and/or police patrolling the waters; sports RIBs launching to enjoy a day of fun on the water, or perhaps a picnic or an afternoon's waterskiing along the coast; dive boats taking enthusiasts out for a day underwater; rescue boats carried by working boats entering the harbour; and finally lifeboats and inshore lifeboats may even be RIBs. Virtually every sector of the boating market is covered by the RIB, and they are increasingly moving into the larger sizes, where they have become lifeboats, patrol boats and pilot boats. Perhaps the only sector the RIB has not infiltrated is the angling market, since fishing hooks would not be compatible with inflatable tubes.

SMALL RIBS AND TENDERS

RIBs are seeing their greatest growth in the yacht tender sector of the market, where they come in a wide variety of sizes, ranging from around 2 metres up to the massive 10-metre RIBS used for superyachts. There is little to differentiate between RIBs operated as tenders and those used as small family boats to spend a day on the water or perhaps to reach less crowded beaches. The same follows with larger superyacht tenders, since there are considerable similarities between these and the more stylish, stand-alone sports boats.

The small RIB tender or dayboat is often restricted in size because it is usually carried on board a yacht or in the garage of

↓ A small RIB tender with a pressed aluminium rigid hull

↓↓ An aluminium hulled diesel-powered cruising RIB

a motor cruiser (in fact, most sailboats still need to tow their tenders). Because of this, some can be as small as 2 metres in length (big enough to carry several people) and most are compact enough to fit on the roof of a car, which can accommodate a

maximum length of about 3 metres. Transporting the boat in this way is far preferable to towing it by trailer and the inflatable tubes are much kinder to a vehicle's gloss finish than a hard boat.

Small RIBs are at the price-sensitive end of the market and many models are therefore semi mass-produced using PVC-proofed fabric, rather than the more expensive Hypalon. PVC works well for this size of RIB, where life expectancy may be around ten years and design and construction are kept as simple as possible. The rigid part of the hull is usually moulded in GRP, although several builders are pressing the hull into the desired shape from a single piece of aluminium, ensuring rigidity through the introduction of double curves. Some boats

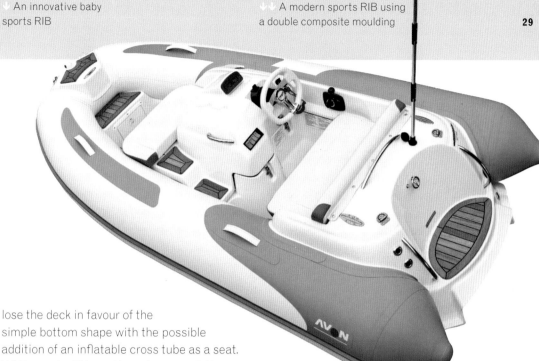

lose the deck in favour of the
simple bottom shape with the possible
addition of an inflatable cross tube as a seat.
While most will be outboard-powered, they
can also be rowed. Indeed, most small RIBs
have paddles or oars as an optional means
of propulsion when the outboard refuses to
work. Simplicity is the name of the game
with these very basic RIBs and there are
few, if any, frills.

The next step up in the RIB tender
market is a more dedicated design including
an interior created from a separate
moulding, which may incorporate a helm

console and seating. This is often the tender
of choice for motor cruisers, since those
just 9 metres in length are now regularly
equipped with garage storage. However, the
profile has to be kept quite low due to the
lack of headroom space, which provides a
considerable challenge for the designers.
Petrol engines – either outboard or inboard
– are the norm and keep the weight down,
and these RIBs are fast enough for planing
speed and make for exciting boating when
used as stand-alone sports boats. With most
mother ships using diesel power there is
now a demand for diesel-powered tenders,
and we are now seeing this fulfilled in
tenders as small as 3.5 metres long. Water-
jet propulsion is often used in conjunction
with diesel power to create an exciting and
flexible performer. These compact tenders
are a great illustration of how RIB design

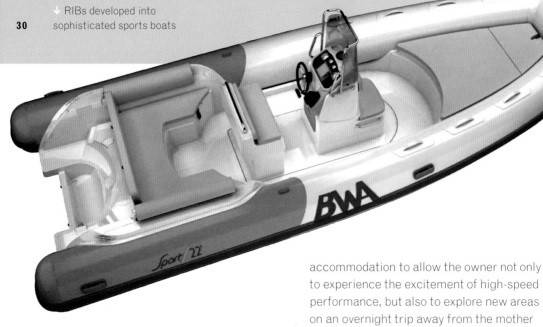

has been developed and refined to meet a specific market requirement.

Moving up the ladder, the dedicated RIB superyacht tender market is relatively new. Here cost is often secondary to style and performance, meaning these crafts represent some of the most exotic RIB designs ever developed. They are fully custom-built to exacting standards; a well-designed and aesthetically pleasing tender allows the owner and his guests to arrive at a prestigious yacht club in style. The inflatable tube provides good fendering alongside the pristine finish of the mother yacht, while the styling and colouring of the two can often be matched. Furthermore, some superyacht owners look to their tender to be more than just a taxi to shore – it can also provide an escape from the formality of the yacht. Consequently, weather protection is often a requirement and luxuries such as air-conditioning and advanced sound systems can be catered for. Tenders up to 12 metres long can be carried on the larger superyachts and these may have cabin

accommodation to allow the owner not only to experience the excitement of high-speed performance, but also to explore new areas on an overnight trip away from the mother yacht. Still, most larger tenders are required to fit into compact garages on board so they demand a low profile. However, some will follow along behind or may even be towed, meaning few limitations on style and design, while performance and seaworthiness are paramount. All larger tenders are diesel-powered to ensure total compatibility with the mother yacht.

RIBs in the leisure sector are growing in size, with several Italian builders offering them up to 20 metres. The current record is

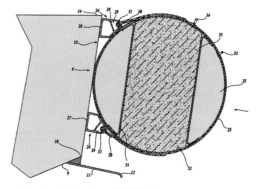

↑ A patented design of RIB tube with a foam air combination

↓↓ Perhaps the ultimate in sports
RIBs, this Fabio Buzzi 55 footer
developed for offshore racing

31

RIBS TODAY

held by Italian builder Heaven, which has produced a RIB superyacht with a length of 24.5 metres. You have to ask why – I did sea trials on this super RIB and, sure, it behaved like a RIB sports boat, with quite exciting performance, but a conventional motor yacht of this size gives more internal and open deck space (this RIB even had three bathrooms, which must be a record of sorts). There have been reports stating that the Americans have created the largest RIB in the world. They claim to have fitted a 110-foot-long crew boat with a tube around the hull so it could act as a support boat for an America's Cup challenge. It seems this market will grow and grow.

SPORTS RIBS

The sports RIB is a close relation of the large yacht tender and because many builders supply both types of craft, there is an interchange of ideas between the two

concepts. There are two schools of thought in relation to sports RIBs. In the first, owners rate style as highly as performance, and this is where the sports RIB can take the best of what the large tender has to offer in terms of design features, such as teak decking and dedicated seating. Furthermore, there are no restrictions to height, they extend up to 20 metres in length and powerful outboards create even more space inside the boat. Some of the more extreme Italian designs challenge the motor cruiser for innovation, taking the RIB in a new and exciting direction.

The second school of thought in relation to sports RIB design harks back to the craft's origins, and owners who fall into this category are after a more professional-looking RIB. To that end, these boats often retain the orange or black colouring of the professional craft, while seaworthiness is more important than style (although image is still an important consideration). Owners

of this type take RIB cruising seriously and will often cruise for several days in some of the more challenging regions of the world. Clubs in Britain, Belgium, France, Greece, Scandinavia, Italy, and many other countries organise adventure cruising in company for support and safety, while some clubs focus on family cruising.

RIBs made an early impact in the leisure market when they were used to take diving parties out to dive sites. Indeed, builders like Delta were originally formed to specifically build dive RIBs, before they moved on to building a range mainly for professional use.

As a dive boat the RIB ticks all the boxes. It can provide quick transport out to the dive site and creates a stable platform when at rest. The low freeboard makes it easy to depart into and climb on board from the water and because it is an open boat, there is space for air bottle stowage and dressing

for the dive. The dive boat sector has now become a specialised part of the RIB market and many of the major builders offer dedicated designs in this field.

The ultimate RIB cruise

Alan Priddy was the first person to go around the world in a RIB and now he is heading out there again, this time with the aim of setting a record speed for the circumnavigation. His boat is a RIB, but is unlike anything you have seen before; it features a long, relatively narrow hull close to 80 feet in length and the inflatable tubes are fitted like a STAB (see pages 37-38) extending for just about half the hull length from the stern to add extra stability in rough seas.

PROFESSIONAL RIBS

There was a time when there was a distinct line between professional and leisure RIBs, but today the lines are blurring. However, the standards for professional RIBs still tend to be higher, particularly in some of the details, such as the electric wiring. Failure is not an option for these crafts, and not only do they put in a lot more hours than their leisure counterparts, but they tend to be used in more arduous work environments. They are therefore designed to meet increasingly stringent health and safety requirements covering noise levels and shock mitigation. Boats are becoming more capable, allowing them to operate in ever more extreme conditions where the crew become the weak point and the shock loadings the limiting point for operation in rough seas.

Professional RIBs can be divided into two main groups: those operating mainly in harbours, such as harbour patrol boats and police RIBs, and those operating in the open sea where speed is an important factor, such as military and rescue services.

Open sea RIBs – military and rescue

Out in the open sea, the challenge is in obtaining the best ride characteristics for the RIB hull, the layout and seating, and providing electronic systems for navigation and communication. Military RIBS often require guns and crew protection to be fitted, and in all cases the inflatable tube offers good protection when the boat has to go alongside another vessel at sea. It would be fair to say the RIB has transformed the focus of many military and para-military operations in that the mother ship has become just that: a means to get the RIB near to the action so it can be used in close-up operations. Launch and recovery systems also come into reckoning here, and will often be the limiting factor in when and how the RIB can operate.

Much the same applies to the demanding

world of search and rescue, for which the RIB was originally developed. Today, search and rescue work demands speed in adverse conditions and the ability to go alongside at sea and to recover casualties from the water, all aspects a leisure RIB operator would normally avoid. Again, the need to provide comfort and safety for professional RIB crews has challenged designers to come up with suitable solutions, especially with regard to how the craft is driven. When it is

↑ A full plastic moulded 'RIB' that would lack many of the qualities of the conventional RIB

↓ The ultimate accolade - a RIB design used as an all-weather lifeboat in Holland

A HISTORY OF THE RIB

designed and driven well, the RIB is without doubt the most seaworthy craft of its size.

Rescue boats are also carried on board ships, mainly in the offshore oil sector, but also increasingly on board passenger ships of many types, where they are used for man-overboard recovery as well as for herding liferafts in an abandon-ship situation. RIBs operating from safety ships in the offshore oil arena have a demanding life, since they are launched frequently on exercise and routine transfer duties (which is great because the crews become familiar with their use). Those carried on board passenger ships, however, are far less effective, partly due to crews rarely launching and recovering them, but also because launch and recovery is fraught with danger due to the very high stowage location of the boats. This is certainly an area for future development.

Moreover, there is also an increasing use of larger RIBs and now they are accepted as all-weather lifeboats, RIBs are being built in sizes closer to 20 metres in length. I remember forecasting many years ago that RIBs would never get larger than perhaps 9 metres because the stress on the inflatable

tubes would be too high on anything more. However, today there are 18-metre lifeboats complete with the equipment and capabilities of conventional lifeboats – and they work. The tubes might be used mainly as a fender when going alongside rather than as a variable geometry component of the boat (because the heavy-duty tubes will not deform in the same way as lighter tubing on smaller RIBs), but overall they are functional and their crews very happy.

Large rescue RIBs of 18 metres have been built to be carried on board mother ships and while these are functional, they do place heavy demands on their launch and recovery systems. The Dutch builder No Limit Ships has built several very large RIBs for both the commercial and the leisure market and as this book is being written, it is building a 24.8-metre one for survey work in the open waters of the North Sea, which will be the largest fully-developed RIB in the world.

Safety boats

The safety boats used to escort dinghies when they are racing are generally smaller RIBs that will operate mainly in harbours and under conditions less extreme, since dinghy races often won't go ahead in difficult conditions. Cost is a factor, because sailing clubs do not generally have large sums to spend on them. However, their role is vital and the Royal Yachting Association (RYA) offers a list of safety boat standards and guidelines on how they should be operated.

OTHER DESIGN CONCEPTS

The normal monohull RIB comes in many forms and guises depending on the role it is required to play, but the RIB market has also spawned a variety of alternative concepts, mainly based on alternative designs for the rigid part of the hull. We have already mentioned the catamaran hull pioneered by Dunlop (*see* page 25), and catamaran RIBs are still built, with the attraction being the larger area of deck space they create. One modification of the catamaran hull has seen a foil fitted between the two hulls to generate extra lift at speed and thus allow higher speeds for a given power. The foil also creates a degree of damping in waves. While this RIB concept works, it is never likely to hit the mainstream because most operators favour the monohull as the basic shape of a RIB.

Another concept, developed by FB Design in Italy for its fast patrol boats, has been termed the STAB RIB. The main

feature of this design is the tube, which
extends only roughly halfway along the
sides of the hull from the stern. This still
provides stability at rest and fendering when
coming alongside, but the weight and cost
are considerably reduced. Willard Marine
in the US offers a similar system on its fast
interceptor RIBs.

RIBs were not designed to fly voluntarily,
although they sometimes do when driven to
excess. In Italy, however, one enterprising
designer produced a real flying RIB. The
craft had a folding wing mounted on the hull,
made from something like a microlight fabric
wing, and it was propelled by means of an air
propeller at the stern. It would actually take
off from the water and fly, but because of the
high cost and safety issues, it never became
a commercial proposition.

Small hovercraft RIBs have also been
developed, mainly for leisure use, although
they could find application as a 'go
anywhere' craft for disaster and flood

relief work. The hovercraft, with its inflated
skirt, is to all intents and purposes a RIB,
and its ability to make the transition from
water to land and to operate over difficult
terrain gives it a unique capability, although
it does have limited ability in rough seas.
The RNLI already operates small hovercraft
as rescue boats in some areas of extensive
mud and sand.

RIBs with wheels are another concept.
Many small tender RIBs can be fitted with
a pair of wheels at the transom so they can
be easily moved on land, but New Zealand
builder Sealegs has taken this idea one step
further and fitted its RIBs with powered
wheels that can be lowered down as the
craft approaches shallow water, enabling it
to be driven onto dry land. The system works
– this RIB does plane and wheeled RIBs
are being offered commercial – but both
weight and cost is considerably increased
and performance can also be compromised.

↘↘ An amphibious RIB capable
of operating on land and water

↓ The ultimate experience -
a flying RIB developed in Italy

However, the Sealegs RIBs offer a good solution to those who have a house or boat storage near the water and need to simplify launch and recovery from an open beach.

Building on the idea of wheeled RIBs, we have recently seen the development of a RIB with caterpillar tracks. This model is designed to service wind farms built in shallow water, for which there is a requirement to travel over sandbanks to gain access. It can also be used in a rescue, should there be an emergency.

Then there is a whole new generation of RIBs that can operate without any crew on board, thus reducing the concern for shock mitigation. These drones were initially developed for military requirements and have incorporated some quite sophisticated designs with the addition of armaments and remote control operation, but the market is expanding beyond that niche. They could have a role in survey work and monitoring sea and atmosphere parameters, and they may also prove useful for monitoring fishing operations and in other surveillance. Perhaps with the introduction of these specialised crafts we are seeing the future of many marine operations.

PART TWO
RIB

HANDLING

3 WHAT MAKES A RIB WORK?

WHY IS A RIB so much better than comparable boats? It is a frequently asked question, but there is no easy answer. What the RIB concept has done that others have not is bring together many elements of boat design and merge them into a complete whole. This has created not only one of the most seaworthy boats for its size, but also one of the most practical and exciting.

The starting point in RIB development was the inflatable boat, which had already existed for many years and had proved itself in several applications, including as a day sports boat and a rescue boat. However, it also had limitations: mainly its flat-bottomed hull shape. By the time the RIB was developed the deep vee hull was a tried and tested solution for small boat hull design and when merged with the inflatable, these two technologies formed a craft that opened up a whole new era of boat design.

However, the RIB was more than just a combination of two existing technologies. The addition of the saddle seat and helm console made the relationship between the boat and its driver much more intimate and allowed it to be driven much harder in adverse conditions. The self-draining nature of the hull and the low freeboard, plus the additional buoyancy of the tube, also enabled the RIB to operate in conditions where conventional designs could be at risk.

As we have seen, the RIB did not have an easy birth. The fact that Atlantic College built at least ten prototypes before it got it basically right shows how the evolving concept required fine-tuning before it could take up the mantle of a good working design. This may be because early RIBs were based on modifications to existing inflatables, which were trialled on water, rather than in painstaking detail at a drawing board. It is doubtful whether any boatbuilder could afford the luxury of constructing so many prototypes to perfect its design, but the fact that the RIB was largely a student project meant that it wasn't limited by commercial demands, thus allowing it to develop over time and in many exciting directions.

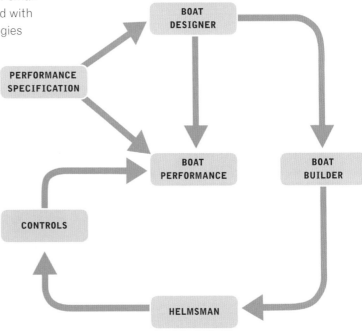

↑ The various ways that the builder, designer and helmsman influence the performance of the boat

THE VARIABLE GEOMETRY HULL – TUBE DESIGN

No one hull performs optimally, and every boat design is a compromise to find a middle road on which it will operate under most required conditions. However, one new concept introduced with the development of the RIB was the variable geometry hull; in effect, a hull that could change shape under the impact of waves and thus adapt semi-automatically to changing conditions. The tube on the pure inflatable incorporated this shape-changing technology to absorb some of the shock loadings from wave impact, but the effect was largely cancelled out by the virtually flat bottom of the boat, which offered little or nothing in the way of cushioning. By combining the inflatable tube with a deep vee hull, the shock-absorbing qualities of the hull were dramatically increased.

Tube pressure

Variable geometry has been the dream of boat designers for a long time and over the years there have been attempts to introduce hulls where the shape can be changed by means of large flaps or other surfaces. The conventional transom flaps found on many fast boats are a form of variable geometry; however, nothing can do the job as automatically as an inflatable tube can. The shock-absorbing qualities of an inflatable tube vary considerably with the air pressure inside it. A relatively soft inflation allows the tube to change shape so that in effect the

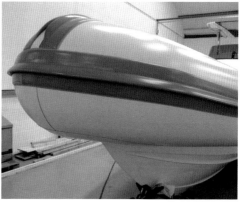

overall hull shape alters, helping to establish a near optimum shape of hull to absorb the impact of a wave. It was this new concept that contributed to the RIB's excellent rough sea performance.

In theory this was a revolutionary invention. However, an inflatable tube's shock-absorbing quality is quite sensitive to pressure and this can affect the results of the variable geometry. When the tube pressure is too high, its whole character changes and instead of adapting to oncoming waves, the tube starts to bounce. Think here of a tennis ball being dropped – yes, it does change shape at the point of impact, but there is an almost equal and opposite force that drives the ball away from the surface it hits. A hard inflatable tube acts in the same way; instead of absorbing wave impact, it induces a 'bounce effect', making the impact worse, increasing

the boat's motions and slamming it into waves rather than damping them out. With advances in the strength of tube materials, most RIBs operate at quite high pressure so that any wrinkles in the tubes are removed, for aesthetic purposes. However, this is very much to the detriment of the variable geometry effect that made those early RIBs such great performers.

This bounce effect can also cause the boat to bounce from side to side, creating a very uncomfortable lateral motion, which the saddle seating does not resist and the steering can often exacerbate. Since the boat is moving forward, it is not always easy to identify this lateral bounce factor, yet it has been responsible for much of the adverse commentary regarding RIB performance.

I recollect that we undertook many trials to establish optimum tube pressure

performance, during which we found that a pressure of approximately 2psi kept the tube in reasonable shape while still retaining the variable geometry characteristics. However, most modern RIBs use pressures of double this figure, which accounts for many hard and uncomfortable rides. Nevertheless, you can tell when tubes are at roughly optimum pressure simply by feel. If you punch it and it feels hard, the pressure is too high; if it gives comfortably, it is about right. However, keep in mind that tube pressure is sensitive to temperature, which is why they can go rock hard when a RIB is left out in the hot sun, and why the pressure is likely to drop quite a bit when it encounters cold water. On some RIBs there is an automatic pressure relief valve that will release the pressure if it gets too high. What it can't do, though, is allow air to enter again when the tube becomes cold and you find that it is soft and soggy when you come to use the boat.

Fundamentally, though, these are not such serious problems as they may sound, since very few RIBs are required to operate under really adverse sea conditions. However, if you do start to use your RIB in challenging seas, think about reducing the tube pressure to produce a more comfortable ride.

Tube location

Another characteristic that defines the variable geometry inflatable tube is the way in which it is attached to the boat and its location. When it is attached to a relatively small landing area at the side apex of the rigid hull (usually by the cockpit deck), it is is free to roll in towards the centreline of the boat under wave impact. This is another of the RIB's hull shape-changing phenomena, and even when the tube pressure is high it will be partially effective. Of course, you will not get this rolling-in in the transom area because the transom itself will prevent this, but it can be an effective variable geometry characteristic of those RIBs designed for operating under adverse conditions (most

→ The left diagram shows a smooth flow of water away from the hull whilst an angle flow (right) can lead to a harsher ride

rescue boat designs adopt this concept) and it should help to reduce tube bounce.

Look around at a variety of RIBs and you are also likely to see a variety of tube heights. If the tube is too low and partially in the water at rest, it could well cause unnecessary drag when the boat comes onto the plane, leading to sluggish performance. If it is too high and well clear of the water at rest, you lose the stabilising effect and its becomes more of a fender than a stabiliser. Furthermore, in the case of rescue boats, if the tube is quite high at rest a casualty in the water could disappear under it, making recovery more difficult. Therefore, the optimum should be a tube that is just above the water surface at the stern when the boat is at rest. At this height, any tilting of the boat starts to immerse the tube on the lower side, thus stabilising the hull, and when the boat comes onto the plane, the tube should be well clear of the water, reducing drag. (Bear in mind that you must establish tube height with all crew and any other equipment on board, since a four-member as opposed to a three-member crew can make quite a difference).

Tube shape

On the earlier RIBs the inflatable tubes were the same diameter throughout their whole length, since the techniques for making tapering tubes had yet to be developed. This made for quite a blunt entry at the bow, even when the two side tubes met in a vee at that point. RIBs with a squared-off bow create more internal space and keep the tube well clear of the water, but problems start when operating in waves (particularly in following seas), in which the bow can drop down after coming over a crest, immersing the tube. The additional buoyancy is great for preventing the bow from submerging, but the resulting spray of water caused by the sudden immersion of the blunt tube usually ends up drenching riders at the helm and can restrict progress in following seas. The modern tapering tube, however, results in a much finer bow shape and a smoother entry in such a situation, although there is the possibility of the bow submerging completely if driving close to the limits (*see* page 97, for more on driving techniques).

The round shape of the inflatable tube does encourage spray to curl on board over

← Testing a RIB in a tank – note
how the tubes integrate with the
moulded section of the hull aft

↖↓ A sudden change in angle at the bows
of these designs could lead to a harsh ride
particularly in following seas

47

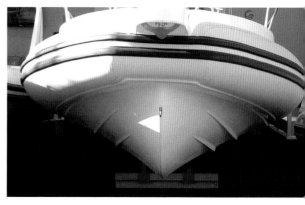

the tube when operating in waves and you
are most likely to encounter this when the
boat is starting to lift onto the plane, or
coming off the plane, when the tubes are
quite low. To reduce this problem, try fitting

rubber rubbing strips along the hull that are
shaped like an inverted V so that they catch
the water rising over the tube surface and
deflect it back down. The rubbing strips only
have a limited effect, but they do help.

Tube attachment

There are many ways to fix the tube to the
rigid hull and they divide into three main
solutions: those where the tube is glued to
the hull, those where the tube is designed
for easy removal and replacement, and
those where the tube is bolted to the hull.

A glued tube can be removed by
gradually freeing the glued seams with
a hot-air gun or even a hairdryer, but the
removal and replacement of this type of tube
is generally a workshop job rather than one

↑ Hard inflation
causes this tube
to adopt the
desired shape

→ Alternative ways
to attach the
inflatable tube to the
rigid hull section

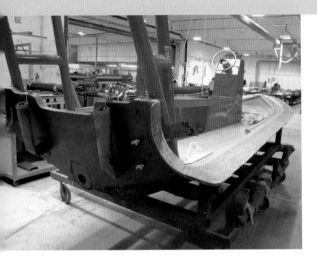

and the rigid part of the hull. There are three main options for the rigid hull:

■ the rigid section is virtually a triangle in cross-section (original design);
■ vertical sides extend upwards from the rigid hull and the tube is fastened to the outside of these sides;
■ the tube is let into the top sections of the rigid hull.

The first and original is still the best solution when you want the RIB to perform in rough seas, and it is where the true qualities of the craft shine through. This position of tube attachment allows the tube to roll in and thus increases the amount of variable geometry available to reduce wave influence. This method is found on many rescue boats and most small RIBs and it offers one of the simplest solutions.

Raising the side of the boat up above cockpit deck level is like having bulwarks attached to the bottom section of the hull and has the advantage of creating a clean, practical RIB interior, with places to attach fittings and fixtures. With this vertical bulwark the RIB could probably operate as a boat without the inflatable tube attached and when this arrangement is used the tube is usually attached at the top and bottom so that when it is inflated it adopts a D-shape in cross-section. Obviously, there is no roll-in effect with this type of tube but it is an arrangement that can create a practical RIB for certain commercial operations. However, the bottom of the tube will not present a smooth transition with the rigid section and this can increase slamming in waves.

that can be done in the field (furthermore, it is usually only professional users that need to replace tubes in the field. A naval ship carrying a RIB as a sea boat might well carry a spare tube on board).

The second solution is what is described as the 'sail track system', where there is a channel that is either moulded into the hull or attached to the outside of the hull and a rope or shaped edge flap slides along this channel to hold the tube in place. The tube is slid into place when deflated and once inflated it is locked firmly into position.

The third system, which is rare today, is to literally bolt the tube in place using studs attached to the hull that match up with a flap, or flaps fitted to the tube. This system also allows the tube to be replaced while in the field, but it is a slower and less elegant solution than the sail track system.

The relationship between tube and hull

We have covered tube pressures, location, shape and attachment and now it is time to look at the relationship between the tube

↓ Attaching the tube to the
hull in inflated condition

↓↓ A modern double moulding RIB hull ready
for tube attachment with a slide-on 'sail track
system' moulded into the hull

49

The third option has the tube fitting into a curved opening moulded into the side of the hull. This type of attachment might use glued or sail track fixings, and it integrates the tube neatly into the hull shape. However, a tube mounted in this way is less effective as a stabiliser because there is only a relatively small change in buoyancy when it starts to become immersed. This type of tube installation is usually found on cabin RIBs and those where there is some form of covering over the front of the boat. A modern RIB concept with top and bottom hull mouldings will have this form of tube and the STAB tube is usually attached in this way.

Another aspect of tube design that has to be considered is the relationship between the tube and the rigid hull, and here we see enormous variations. In many cases the junction between the rigid hull and the tube forms an inverted V in cross-section, often just above the chine line of the rigid hull. The shape of the round tube attached to the vertical side of the hull naturally forms this inverted V and this can lead to a harsher ride when waves slam up into it. Of course, the tube will distort to a degree to absorb some of this wave impact, but even then the ride can be harsher than if the tube was attached in such a way as to allow the water emanating from under the hull to flow freely upwards. With any fast boat hull, the water flowing away from under the hull needs to be given a relatively free-flowing path if the boat is going to have a

soft ride. When the water gets trapped and is forced into a considerable change of direction, as can happen with an inverted V, it can react almost explosively. The main impact of this unhappy marriage between the rigid and inflatable parts of the hull will occur towards the stern as the boat rises and falls in the waves, but it can also be considerable towards the bow when operating in following seas. This sort of wave impact can put a particularly heavy stress on the tube fastenings to the hull and in cases when a boat is being driven very hard in adverse conditions, it has been known for the tube to part company with the rigid hull and peel off backwards over the main hull. This question of the relationship between the tube and the hull is one that often seems to get overlooked in RIB design, but careful consideration can mean the difference between a comfortable ride and a harsh one.

LENGTH/BEAM RATIO The length/beam ratio of the RIB is another consideration. Because many of the early RIBs continued to use the format of the pure inflatable boat, the length/beam ratio was low. However, this is not the best shape for higher speeds in rough seas and when longer, leaner hull forms were introduced, the performance increased dramatically. You can only get a higher length/beam ratio on larger RIBs and the improvement in performance is often put down to the larger size of the craft, but the finer hull shape cuts through the wave crests cleanly and the boat is much less likely to want to contour the waves and contribute to an uncomfortable ride.

Tube construction

Tube construction has changed a lot over the years, and there have been quite a few alternative ways of making the tube to withstand the perceived stresses of operation. The basic RIB tube is made up of a single layer of fabric glued with a longitudinal seam to form a tube shape. Baffles are usually inserted along its length so that it is split into sections that are inflated individually, so that if one compartment gets damaged the RIB still remains viable. These are usually conical in shape, which allows them to be reversible and helps to equalise the pressure between compartments. Each compartment has its own inflation valve, which is usually located inside the boat, out of the way.

INTERNAL BLADDERS When we had the poor air-holding quality fabric of some of those early RIB tubes we tried to use

⬇ Alternative types of tube construction:
(1) fully inflatable, (2) combination inflation and
foam, (3) tube with inner bladder, (4) foam tube,
and (5) division of the tube into compartments

⬇ Rear cone construction
formed around a hard centre

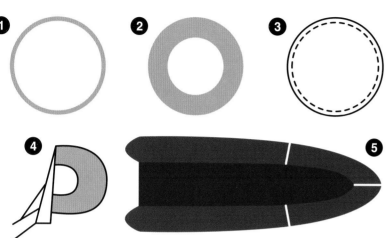

⬇ Constructing tube baffles
around a wooden former

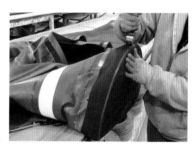

bladders inside the tubes, so that the bladder was the air container and the tube dictated the shape. However, this was not a huge success because it proved very difficult to fully deploy the bladders inside the tube, since there was no escape for the air trapped between the bladder and the outside fabric. On the other hand, Naiad Design in New Zealand has used tubes with bladders right from the time it started building RIBs many years ago, and it continues to use this method today. Naiad believes that with a bladder there is the added protection should the outer skin get punctured, and it has solved the problem of trapped air by having pressure-relieve valves fitted in the outer skin so that the bladder can fully inflate.

On some military RIBs a bladder is fitted but not inflated. Should the outer skin then get punctured by a bullet or otherwise damaged, the bladder can be inflated so that the tube more or less maintains its integrity.

Alternative tube concepts

Concern about the vulnerability of the air tube has led to some alternative tube concepts. A tube formed from three layers has been tried on very large RIBs. The inner layer, which is rather like a bladder, is the air holding tube. This is then covered with a layer of flexible foam, perhaps 2cm thick, which helps to keep these large-diameter

⬆ The tube on a STAB RIB attached
with a slide-on system

tubes in shape while retaining a degree of flexibility. Finally, the outer layer covers this foam and is abrasion resistant. The chances of a puncture getting through all three layers and allowing air to escape is reduced considerably.

Another type of bladder/foam tube was developed by Zodiac for use on some of its military and commercial RIBs. This version has a relatively small-diameter bladder at the centre of the tube which when inflated gives the tube rigidity and shape. The main part of the tube is constructed from foam with an outer, abrasion-resistant covering.

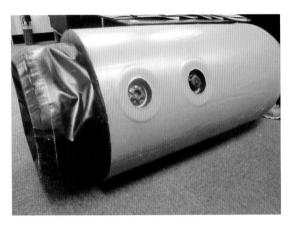

Full foam tubes are constructed from resilient foam that deforms on impact when coming alongside, but which virtually maintains shape under wave impact, and they can vary considerably both in shape and in texture. Some foam tubes are literally little more than an enlarged fender around the area where the deck and the hull are joined, but others take on larger proportions and are often D-shaped, which can create quite a sharp transition between the vertical hull sides and the

tubes that can be susceptible to wave impact. One of the features of foam tubes is that their form is not dictated by the inflation of the tube, but can be made in virtually any shape the designer considers to be appropriate and so they can be used to enhance the overall hull shape. They offer the same improved stability, provided that they are suitably designed, and they give good and durable fendering. It is the perceived durability that is the attraction, and they are very popular on ship-borne rescue boats, many Coastguard craft, some lifeboat designs and on commercial RIBs designed for arduous duties. Boats fitted with this type of foam tube are not really rigid inflatables, since there is nothing in the way of variable geometry, so some of the RIB characteristics are lost. However, because the hull and tube shape can be very similar, they do fall into the RIB category.

Foam tubes have their place in the RIB sector, but several hybrid tubes have been

developed (pioneered by Delta) to match
the characteristics and shape required for
seaworthy performance. These can be a
combination of foam and inflatable sections,
perhaps an inflatable foam tube around
the bow to provide the variable geometry
on wave impact and a foam section along
the sides of the hull where the fendering is
required. This can be a solution for arduous
alongside work, such as that required on
a pilot boat, but this sort of combination
does demonstrate how the tube shape and
characteristics can be fine-tuned for any RIB.

Another hybrid tube solution is found
in those RIBs in which the inflatable tubes
run up each side of the hull: close to the
bow they are replaced with a solid section
of hull moulding. This removes the challenge
of trying to construct the tube to fit the
compound curves found at the bow and it
can create a better-looking boat. The hard
section at the bow also provides a mounting
point for fairleads and anchoring points, or
even a capstan on larger RIBs.

We have seen how polyurethane fenders
were used to form the RIB tube in the past
and this solution does do away with the need
to inflate the tube. It is possible to cover
such fenders with an outside skin to create
a more integrated look and a similar solution
has now been developed by MST for a series
of RIBs built for the Netherlands Navy. Here
the basic tube was formed by inflatable,
shaped sections based around a combined
foam and Hypalon material, with squared
off ends, and perhaps four of these sections

forming one side of the tube on the RIB. These were then held in place by a wrap-around piece of Hypalon fabric that was attached to sail track channels in the hull, with the whole structure tightened and held in place by a lace-up system. This solution was adopted to allow any damaged sections of the tubes to be easily replaced with spare sections carried on board, an important consideration when naval vessels might be operating a long way from support.

Alternative tube materials

Alternative rigid tube materials include aluminium and large-diameter polyurethane piping. The aluminium tube format was used on some large whale-watching RIBs built by Naiad in New Zealand, where the tubes were added to provide additional stability when at rest or going slowly when the whale-watching passengers might all be on one side of the boat. The aluminium tube idea has also been used to good effect on some small leisure RIBs, but it is certainly not widely applied.

Polyurethane large-diameter piping falls into a similar category because this material

does not distort under impact and does not require inflation. There are three or four builders using this type of construction and the design has become more sophisticated, with curving tubes used to enhance the shape. Early on the construction was simple, with the appropriate lengths of pipe cut off and heat-welded together to form a sort of RIB shape, with the bottom of the boat made from sheets of that same material. Today's builders have perfected the art of curving the pipe into a graceful shape and this hard-wearing tube is now married to an aluminium rigid hull. This type of construction creates a rugged workboat that can stand up to a lot of knocking about, which has proved useful on fish farms and construction sites as well as for more general use.

FABRICS AND ADHESIVES

The key to the modern inflatable is the fabric from which it is constructed and the adhesive used to join it.

Tube fabrics and construction

The fabrics used on the very early inflatables were derived from cotton and natural rubber, and they had limited strength and a very short lifespan, unless they were carefully looked after. It was only with the development of new synthetic rubbers during World War II that the inflatable became a viable proposition. Most RIB builders today obtain fabrics from specialist manufacturers who have made an investment in the expensive machinery needed to produce the high quality demanded. It is the fabric quality that largely determines the life of the RIB, and even with hard use, a ten-year life span should easily be possible, and 20 years could be feasible for a leisure RIB with less intensive use (although the inflatable tube might need replacing – there are specialised RIB builders and tube manufacturers who can offer this service).

Today there are three components incorporated into modern inflatable boat fabrics:

■ the base fabric, which gives the fabric its strength and stretch characteristics;
■ the main air-sealing inner skin, which can be one of several materials;
■ the outer skin that forms a secondary air barrier. This outer skin has to be abrasion-resistant and resistant to attack from ultraviolet light (sunlight) and contaminants such as oil, fuel and battery acid.

It is not easy to combine all of these characteristics into one material, which it why it is usual to find different materials used on the inside and outside of the fabric. A fabric may be made up of anything from three to five layers of rubbers or plastics applied to the base fabric.

Today, reinforcing fabric is almost exclusively made from polyester, but Kevlar has been used for some applications where light weight and high strength are paramount. The nylon used in the past had a considerable stretch, which was beneficial in having the air tube adopt curved shapes, but it was not easy to design the RIB to exacting dimensions because this stretch would vary with pressure. Polyester has limited stretch and this enables the cut sections of the fabric to be made up with

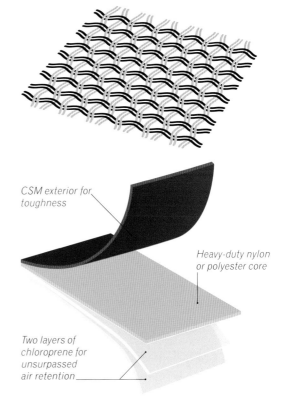

CSM exterior for toughness

Heavy-duty nylon or polyester core

Two layers of chloroprene for unsurpassed air retention

a high degree of accuracy. In fact, modern computer design programs can allow for stretch in the material so that the final tube is an extremely accurate shape when inflated. By designing the tube on a computer, the cutting instructions can be sent directly to automated cutting machines that not only cut the fabric to shape but also buff the sections of fabric that will be glued once the tube is assembled. The computer also 'nests' the cuts pieces, which means that it arranges all of the pieces to be cut in the best way so that minimum waste is generated. This is essential, since tube fabric is very expensive.

This computer design and cutting is about as far as automation goes in tube construction using Hypalon and neoprene, with the rest of the tube construction process being done mainly by hand. The areas to be glued have to be buffed to remove any oxidised layer on the surface and to create a slightly rough surface for

the glue to grip. Precise application of the adhesive can be achieved by outlining the area to be glued with masking tape; once the two surfaces have had the required layers of glue applied, they are brought together and a roller is used to eliminate any air from the glued seam. Modern gluing techniques produce a highly reliable seam that should stand the test of time (*see* pages 250-259, for more on gluing techniques and repairs).

While it is the base material that provides
the strength for the inflatable tube fabric,
the glue connection is between the surfaces
of the coating or proofing. This proofing also
provides the air tightness. It is primarily the
inner skin of the fabric that provides the air-
holding because this skin is being pressed
against the base fabric and not being peeled
away, as could be the case with the outer
skin. Neoprene is normally used for this
inner skin because it has good air-holding
properties and it is cheaper than Hypalon.
There may be two layers of neoprene to
make up the inner coating on the fabric.

The coating on the outside acts as a
secondary air seal and it has to be resistant
to abrasion and various contaminants. It also
provides the colouring for the finished boat.
There may be a layer of neoprene applied first
in order to fill the fabric weave so that this
weave does not show on the finished surface,
and then the outer layer is finished with
Hypalon. Ultraviolet light in particular can

have a strong influence on many rubbers and
neoprene and Hypalon are both reasonably
immune to this, which accounts for their
long life. Of these two rubbers Hypalon has
marginally better characteristics in terms
of abrasion-resistance and resistance to
chemicals and sunlight, although to a large
degree they are both virtually indestructible.
Hypalon tends to be a more difficult rubber
to glue, partly because of its shiny finish,

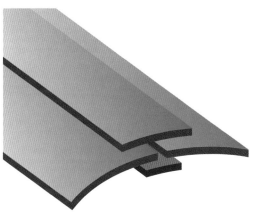

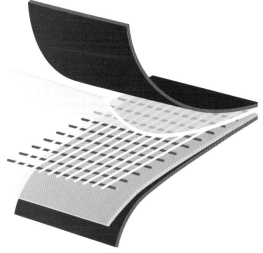

↑ The make-up of
a seam on thermo-
bonded fabric

→ The make-up of
polyurethane RIB
fabric

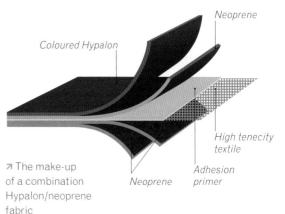

Neoprene

Coloured Hypalon

High tenecity
textile

Adhesion
primer

Neoprene

↗ The make-up
of a combination
Hypalon/neoprene
fabric

but with modern adhesives this is not a major problem. In fact, it tends to be the favoured proofing for the fabric's outside skin, but this is largely because of its cosmetic appearance – it has a better surface finish than neoprene, being smoother, slightly shiny and easier to clean. It is also available in a wide range of colours and has particular appeal in the lighter and brighter colours, which are found on many modern leisure inflatables (one of the latest developments in Hypalon-finished RIB fabrics is to have a textured finish, such as crocodile skin). In the early days of inflatable boat manufacture, black was the only viable colour for neoprene rubber, because it required a proportion of carbon black added to it to get the necessary strength characteristics. Hypalon is much more flexible in terms of colour and although the preferred colour for the majority of modern boats is still a very practical grey, it is possible to get good-quality rubbers in a wide variety of colours, including whites and bright yellows (red and orange are the most popular colour after grey, since they stand out at sea).

COATING TECHNIQUES There are two main techniques used to coat the base fabric with the rubber compound. The first of these is called 'knifing' – the fabric is passed under a straight or knife edge, which stretches the full width of fabric, with the rubber coating forced down behind this knife edge so that it spreads the coating evenly. Each side is done alternately and more than one layer can be added if necessary.

Where the first coat on the fabric is neoprene and a second coat of Hypalon is added afterwards, the material has to go through the calendaring process twice. One problem with adding neoprene in this way is that the bond between the neoprene and its Hypalon coating is not always as positive as it could be. Mixing the two rubber compounds together at the calendaring stage seems to be the preferred method, but different manufacturers use different proportions of the two rubber compounds. There are some manufacturers who use Hypalon as the only material for coating the base fabric and with improved methods of gluing, this rubber is becoming the preferred type of inflatable boat fabric.

The problem with knifing is that it doesn't necessarily provide a good bond between the base fabric and the rubber. You want the proofing material to permeate the weave of the base fabric so that it will form a bond with the proofing on the other side, but knifing does not provide the sort of pressure required for this to happen on a reliable basis, and in the early days there were cases of delamination with the fabrics made by this process.

A much better process, and one used for virtually all modern fabrics, is 'calendaring'. Here, the fabric, together with the coating rubber compound, is passed between rollers at a carefully measured distance apart. By passing both through the rollers at the same time the coating is firmly impregnated into the fabric, resulting in a very positive bond. Calendaring is very much the preferred process, but the machinery required is much more expensive than that used in knifing. It is worth checking when you buy a boat which process was used for manufacturing the fabric; any reputable RIB builder will use calendared fabric.

ALTERNATIVE MATERIALS AND FABRIC QUALITY Fabrics using a polyester base but proofed with PVC or polyurethane can also be used in RIB building. Both of these proofing materials work well and are probably as impregnable to contaminants and as abrasion-resistant as Hypalon, but experience with PVC does suggest that it has a shorter lifespan before it starts to harden and become less flexible. These two, what might be termed plastic, proofing materials have excellent air-holding qualities but they are less easy to glue than the rubbers, and heat – or high-frequency welding is an alternative means of joining them.

It is hard to get reliable information regarding the relative merits of the various proofing materials and each builder will sing the praises of the particular material they use for their boats. The table below shows one opinion of the relative merits of Hypalon, PVC and polyurethane for use on RIBs, but do be aware that this comparison table was produced by the fabric manufacturer Chiorino which specialises in polyurethane-proofed fabrics.

Tube materials for RIBs

The appearance and durability of a RIB is strongly influenced by the characteristics of its inflatable tube. There is a wide range of materials used in the construction of tubes, each with its own set of advantages and disadvantages. To simplify matters, we will divide the range up according to the coating type, which is a common method of differentiation.

PVC AND COATINGS CONTAINING PVC

Advantages

■ *Price: not only significantly lower than Hypalon, but can be fabricated by welding (far quicker than gluing).*

Disadvantages

■ *Performance and durability: this is a generalisation – the PVC materials on the market come from a number of suppliers and there are very noticeable differences in quality. The best-quality PVC can provide a very acceptable level of performance, especially for small/medium sized RIBs. The reputation of the supplier is important here, as with all the other materials discussed.*

■ *Investment needed in welding equipment – only larger companies can afford to fabricate using PVC.*

■ *Although 'polyurethane-based', the recent 'Sharc' material, exclusive to Zodiac and now seemingly withdrawn, is suspected of having a PVC component. Clearly Zodiac will have undertaken extensive testing and were confident of good performance, but only years of real-life usage can provide a definitive answer to durability.*

HYPALON/ CHLOROSULPHONATED POLYETHYLENE *The majority of the materials commonly referred to as 'Hypalon' are actually a generic equivalent, chlorosulphonated polyethylene (CSM). Hypalon is a Trademark owned by DuPont.*

Advantages

■ *Well established; good reputation.*

■ *Performance generally better than PVC.*

■ *No large investment needed in welding equipment, so can be fabricated by the smallest companies.*

■ *Easy to repair.*

Disadvantages

■ *Price: not only more expensive than PVC, but has to be hand-fabricated by gluing. In addition, it has to be abraded prior to gluing, which adds to cost of construction.*

■ *Performance not generally as good as polyurethane, especially with regard to abrasion resistance.*

POLYURETHANE

Advantages

■ *Abrasion resistance about 10 times better than PVC or Hypalon. Results in retaining 'as new' appearance for far longer in demanding usage.*

■ *Easy to clean.*

■ *Polyurethane materials usually have stronger base fabrics than those used for PVC and Hypalon – these are also significantly better at absorbing impact energy. If strength is an important issue for your particular application, ask for the fabric tensile strength and compare.*

■ *Can be fabricated either by welding or with adhesive.*

■ *Available in wider widths than Hypalon, allowing greater freedom in design.*

■ *Welded seams are ultra-reliable long-term in high temperatures.*

Disadvantages

■ *Price: marginally more expensive than Hypalon, although this is off-set by lower cost of fabrication.*

■ *Correct technique of repair not widely known, leading to mistaken belief that polyurethane is difficult to repair. Key requirement is to thoroughly abrade first before using exactly the same procedure as used with Hypalon.*

■ *As welded, sometimes confused with PVC.*

Generally speaking, the fabric used on low-cost, high-volume RIBs is reinforced PVC or polyurethane-proofed material, where cost can be the overriding factor and where a degree of automation can be achieved because of the high number of boats in production. This probably accounts for the poor reputation these materials have acquired in some quarters, but don't dismiss them as being useful only for the cheap and cheerful end of the RIB market. For smaller pure inflatables, PVC and polyurethane are widely used and this trend is extending into RIB manufacture. Moreover, heat- or high-frequency welding techniques can be very effective and they are certainly quicker, cleaner, cheaper and easier methods to automate than using adhesives, particularly when high-frequency techniques are used. The problem with using welding techniques on inflatable products is that the last seams have to be done from the outside because that is the only position in which they can be sealed; but this can be a benefit, since it requires clever and careful design in order to achieve a satisfactory finished product.

While much of the focus of the use of PVC and polyurethane-proofed fabric is on the lower end of the RIB market, we are now seeing some major manufacturers of quality

Zodiac®'s comments on tube fabrics

Where are the buoyancy tubes produced (what plant and for which model type)?
Zodiac® offers PVC and CR/CSM buoyancy tubes which answer its qualification standards.

PVC models are mainly suggested on rigid inflatable boats less than 21'4" and on tenders. This fabric choice is linked to price logic; PVC is a much more affordable material than CR/CSM and better resists abrasion. The PVC buoyancy tubes are mainly thermobonded PVC – this process guarantees better sealing as an industrial homogeneous quality in our Ayguesvives plant in France.

CR/CSM models are offered on our rigid inflatable boats from 16'5" and on most of models up to 19'8". This fabric is also suggested on our range of Jets (Avon brand); our range of Yachtline and on some tenders. The CR/CSM is in demand from some markets. It has a good resistance to UV and to hydrocarbons.

Is Zodiac® continuing to perform the resistance and ageing tests on coating fabrics that are used in its buoyancy tubes production?
The product's quality is at the heart of Zodiac®'s philosophy. Zodiac® benefits from an internal laboratory certified by Bureau VERITAS, the mission of which is to test and qualify fabrics, but also all the elements that are components of the products sold in our brands (stainless steel, polyester, saddler...). The qualification standards applied to PVC or CR/CSM fabrics are particularly strict. Fabrics must resist extreme temperatures and external conditions of use based on an intensive use for five years. These tests may take nine months to complete for the qualification of a new fabric. Here is a short description of the different tests undergone:

boats starting to use these materials. Like so much in the RIB sector it is the quality of the materials used that counts and, as we have seen, there are cheap and high-quality fabrics, the latter tending to have a much stronger fabric base and a higher density of proofing. However, when you find RIB builders with the reputation of Zodiac in Europe and Wing Inflatables in the USA using both PVC and polyurethane fabrics, this could point the way to the future, at least for the higher-volume builders. Part of this move towards the use of the so-called plastics may have been accelerated because DuPont, the originator of Hypalon,

has now stopped production of this rubber over concerns about the chemicals used in its formulation. However, other companies have stepped into the breach, so Hypalon is still widely used (marketed under the name of CSM, which stands for chlorosulphonated polyethylene).

It is something of a confusing picture for the RIB buyer, but both materials are equally viable, provided that the right quality of material is used. You need to know the denier of the fabric used; anything over 1000 is moving in the right direction. Below is Zodiac's take on using PVC in its boatbuilding.

■ *The **Weather Ometer** reproduces the different conditions that may take place during external exposure of the fabric. It simulates various day/night cycles; the sun, thanks to a light reproducing the UV solar spectrum, both visible and infrared; and the rain, thanks to a sprayer. These cycles of several hundred hours allow us to see if the fabric deteriorates under these conditions.*
■ *Fabric alteration is measured with an **infrared spectrometer**, which analyses the fabric composition after these exposures.*
■ *Other samples of fabric are exposed to **external and natural conditions** in a special station developed for this role.*
■ *Fabric resistance is measured with different **dynamometers**, which proceed to **tear tests, stretching tests, breaking tests** and **grip tests**. Other tests also measure the resistance to abrasion.*

**What are the terms given by Zodiac®
to the fabrics (e.g. Strongan, Duotex)?**
The term 'Strongan' is for the PVC coating used by Zodiac® and the term 'Duotex' is the Panama (2 x 2) weaving type. The textile base is composed of polyester threads resistant to putrefaction, that are inserted with two 'weft' threads and two 'chain' threads. This gives it exceptional resistance, allowing us to get a particularly robust product. Therefore Strongan™ or Duotex™ are proof of quality for the consumer who is concerned with the fabric of his buoyancy tube. We don't use specific terms for our CR/CSM fabrics.

**What are these fabrics' characteristics
(type, number of decitex fabric, grammage,
material of the textile base, weaving
structure)?**
The grammage corresponds to the weight of the coating on fabric. It varies from 900g/m² to 1500g/m², depending on the fabric. The highest

(continued overleaf)

grammage is dedicated to our rigid inflatable boats. Our fabrics are very reliable thanks to their material, that is to say, polyester resistant to putrefaction from 1100 decitex to 1670 decitex (decitex being the mass in grams per 10,000 metres). The weaving structure is variable from 9 x 9cm² to 12 x 12cm² (the weaving is a panama type: two 'weft' threads x two 'chain' threads) that guarantees a very high solidity.

What are the techniques of assembly for the buoyancy tubes within the three brands of Zodiac® Group (thermobonding, cold gluing, etc)?

■ *Assembly by thermobonding (PVC): This technology uses a specific production tool which allows us to weld, with hot air, an inside strip and an outside strip with two edges of one buoyancy tube. It lends an exceptional solidity and durability to the buoyancy tube. The Zodiac® boats have been renowned for this technique, which is still evolving. PVS has been reproached for limiting the number of colours and shapes on buoyancy tubes. The Zodiac® Pro range proved the opposite*

by offering buoyancy tubes in plenty of colours (blue, red, black, grey, white, etc) and with innovative shapes and design. Therefore, the thermobonding technique no longer limits the creativity and still offers the same advantages for rigid inflatable boat lovers (perfect sealing, durability of assembly, etc).

■ *High-frequency welding (PVC): Here, it is a technique of hot assembly (transformation of an electrical energy into a thermal one) which allows the fusion of different elements that comprise a buoyancy tube. This technique enables a perfect sealing of the different compartments of the buoyancy tube. It also allows a durable maintenance of components (transom, etc) and avoids hydrolysis problems sometimes encountered with cold gluing. These elements guarantee the durability of the buoyancy tube.*

■ *Cold gluing (CR/CSM and PVC): This method is used particularly for the CR/CSM that cannot be hot assembled. It is also applied to pieces of PVC that aren't the correct size or shape to receive the thermobonding technique.*

TUBE ADHESIVES Adhesives come in a variety of shapes and sizes, with different adhesive manufacturers using different formulations. Today the companies producing adhesives are able to formulate their products to meet specific requirements, so not only are they reliable, but they can also be specific to the material being glued. The two main categories of adhesive are:

1 those which are a single-part adhesive and can be used directly from the tube or tin, and

2 the two-part adhesive, where the two parts have to be mixed together in carefully controlled proportions before use.

Builders of inflatable boats almost invariably use the two-part adhesive because of its superior characteristics, while the single-part adhesives tend to be restricted to the repair kits that are supplied with inflatable boats, where the overriding requirements are ease of use and the ability to use just a small amount of the adhesive in a particular can or

tube without compromising the remainder. For reliability, though, the two-part adhesives offer considerably higher joint strength, but once mixed they have to be used within a few hours at most (*see* pages 251–2, for more information on gluing repairs).

As far as gluing Hypalon fabrics is concerned, most builders use a Bostik adhesive. The industry standard used to be Boscoprene 2404 which worked very well, but now it has been superseded by improved versions.

The reputation of any RIB builder depends heavily on the quality of the glued seams on the boat and the best builders go to great lengths to ensure high standards. This involves detailed surface preparation before the adhesive is applied and then application of two or more coats of adhesive before the surfaces are brought together. Most tubes are made from overlapping seams and these are sealed with tape

inside and out to reduce the chance of 'wicking' and to give a good finish. The tube construction has to be carried out under controlled conditions, with both temperature and humidity kept within prescribed limits. Because this form of construction is still largely a job done by hand, quality control and experience are vital components of the final quality of the tube.

Inflation valves

Inflation valves come in a variety of forms and some manufacturers make their own, while others buy proprietary products. However, all types of inflation valve share major characteristics, and they all have three components. There is the insert, which is glued or screwed into the fabric of the air tube. This usually comes in two parts, one inside and one outside, and when the two are screwed together a seal is formed around the rubber fabric. Inside the insert

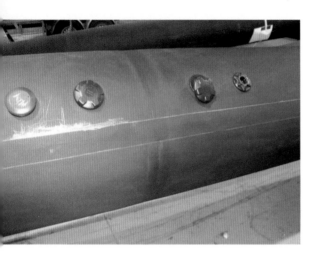

is a screw thread and a landing flange, and the main body of the valve is screwed into this aperture. The main body has a rubber diaphragm flap valve, which deforms to let air in, but the pressure inside forces this diaphragm against the valve body to seal the valve and prevent air leaking outward. It makes an adequate seal during the inflation operation, but if left like this it would probably allow air to escape when the boat is pounding in a seaway. To make a positive seal, a cap is fitted over the valve, which is screwed down against a flexible washer. This valve is usually attached to the flange by means of a small cord or chain to prevent it getting lost when it is unscrewed for inflation. To deflate the boat, the whole valve body is removed, which lets the air escape freely.

There are two principal types of valve, both operating as described above, but one stands proud from the tube and the other is virtually flush. There is a lot to be said for the flush type, which maintains a virtual smooth continuity of the tube, but the protruding type of valve is easier to find and identify and is, therefore, easier to use. When inflating the boat, the valve cap is simply unscrewed and the pipe from the inflation bellows is usually a simple push fit into the valve aperture. After that, the one-way valve allows air to go in but prevents it escaping back into the bellows.

A pressure-relief capability can be built into the valve design so that the pressure is automatically prevented from rising above set limits; alternatively, this can be by means of a separate valve. This is a simple spring-loaded device and it can be a mixed blessing, because while it lets air out if the pressure rises due to an increase in temperature, it will not let air in to compensate when the tube cools, and so you can be left with a soggy tube overnight. With modern, quality tube construction, the requirement for pressure-relief valves is less obvious, except where boats operate in extremes of temperature.

Inflation valves are commonly made of plastic, which doesn't corrode and which can happily cope with the low pressures involved. Both stainless steel and brass have been used for inflation valves, but the cost of these materials is rarely justified. Moulded rubber valves are also used and provide a material which can be more compatible with the tube fabric.

THE RIGID HULL

For the rigid part of the RIB hull, the deep vee hull reigns almost supreme. There are some RIB designs with catamaran hulls and a few more unconventional designs, such as the cathedral hull, but in the main it is the deep vee hull that is almost universal in RIB design.

On small RIBs used as yacht tenders, or perhaps as car-top boats, the V of the hull might be quite shallow in order to accommodate the relatively wide beam without having too much draft; but once you get RIBs over approximately 4 metres, the V becomes pronounced and this is what helps to give the RIB its cushioned ride in waves. A deadrise of perhaps 22 or 24° is normal, close to the sort that you find on offshore racing boats, and this gives the RIB a cushioned re-entry when the hull leaves the water. The high deadrise can be achieved because, in the main, RIBs have a high aspect ratio rigid hull section, where the beam is relatively narrow in relation to the length. This high aspect ratio also improves the performance in waves, allowing the hull to knife through the waves rather than contouring over them, while the inflatable tubes serve to add adequate

transverse stability at lower speeds.

Hull design on fast boats is all about balance. The designer has to find the right balance between the rigid hull section and its inflatable tube, the weight distribution and between propulsion and hull performance. There are many compromises that have to be considered; for instance, there is little point in having a rigid hull section designed for high speed performance and then adding tubes that are set too low so that they introduce extra drag, slowing the boat down. If the tubes are set too high in relation to the rigid hull they will not offer a stabilising effect, meaning that finding this balance of tube height in relation to the rigid hull can be quite critical. Where the RIB has foam tubes, in effect the whole hull is rigid and has to be designed with this in mind. As a general rule, the beam-on foam tube RIBs tend to be wider than those on inflatable tube RIBs and so there can be a reduction in seagoing performance. Finding

↓↓ A hard nosed hull where the bow section is part of the composite moulding and the tubes only run along the sides

the best solution and balance is not easy, but today's designers have experience on their side and have a much better idea of what will work.

The chine

I have always believed that if you want a comfortable ride on a RIB the hull design should always offer the water a smooth flow with no sudden changes in direction, so that the boat and the water flow around the hull are in harmony rather than fighting each other. Of course, you have to be able to generate lift in the planing surfaces of the hull to get the boat onto the plane and to keep it there. The most efficient planing

→ The internal construction of one of FB Design's 'Structural Foam' RIB hulls

surface would be flat, but that would give a harsh ride, and the vee hull is a compromise to both cushion the ride and to act as a planing surface, which is why designers often vary the deadrise to give the boat the desired characteristics. The chine (or angle) of the rigid hull can have a considerable effect on performance, since on boats where the chine is pronounced and where it may even have a downwards hook in transverse cross-section, the sudden change in the water flow away from the hull when it interacts with the chine can add a harshness to the ride. The flat area of the chine itself can add to the wave impact if it is wide, and you can often feel this effect as speed rises and the ride gets notably harsher. Chines can have a good stabilising effect, but a designer can overdo it and this is an area where good balance is important.

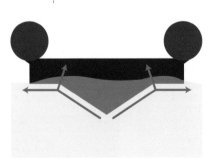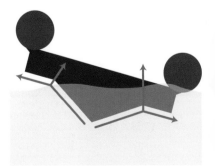

→ How the chine helps to keep the hull upright by generating additional lift when the hull heels over

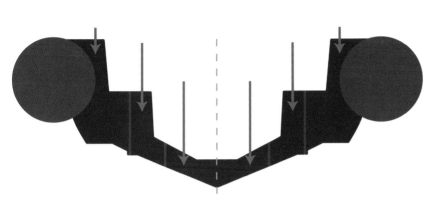

Spray rails

Most RIB hulls have spray rails attached that run from the bow aft. These have three functions:

◼ They help deflect the water away from the hull so that the area of the hull in contact with the water is reduced, thereby reducing friction between hull and water.

◼ They generate lift, since they have horizontal lower edges, which create small, flat planing surfaces.

◼ They help to improve the stability of the hull when it rises in the water and when the chine is clear, because they will generate more lift on the lower side of the hull, thus

helping to keep the hull upright. Spray rails can also improve the directional stability of the hull to make the steering easy and comfortable.

There are many schools of thought about where and how to attach spray rails, some running for the length of the hull to improve stability and some stopping well short of the transom with the perceived benefit of improving the water flow into the propeller.

Stepped hulls

Larger, high-performance RIBs are now using steps in the hull to improve performance. Stepped hulls have been around for a long time, but their application to the deep vee hull is relatively recent. A deep vee hull without steps will generate most of its lift from the rear of the hull at

↓ The way that spray rails and chines deflect the water to generate lift

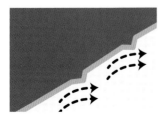
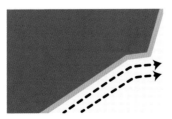

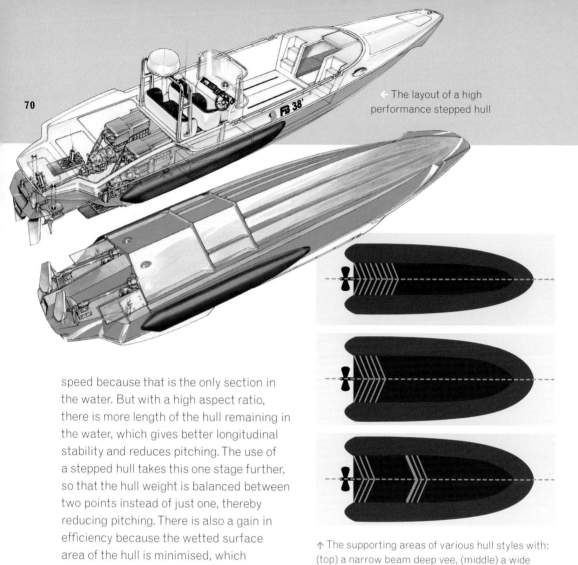

← The layout of a high performance stepped hull

speed because that is the only section in the water. But with a high aspect ratio, there is more length of the hull remaining in the water, which gives better longitudinal stability and reduces pitching. The use of a stepped hull takes this one stage further, so that the hull weight is balanced between two points instead of just one, thereby reducing pitching. There is also a gain in efficiency because the wetted surface area of the hull is minimised, which reduces the friction drag.

↑ The supporting areas of various hull styles with: (top) a narrow beam deep vee, (middle) a wide beam deep vee, and (bottom) a stepped vee hull

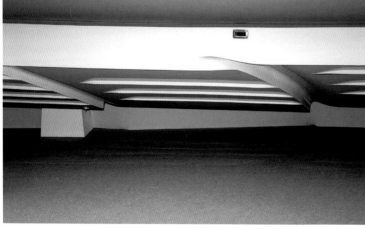

← Steps and spray rails moulded into a composite hull

↓ Saddle seating with: (1) the rear handhold,
(2) the padded seat and backrest, and (3) the
deck toe straps

71

Catamaran hulls

Catamaran hulls have been used for RIBs,
but in this format the tube is simply a fender
because the catamaran hull is inherently
stable. In South Africa there has been a
strong move towards using catamaran
hulls with a foil between them to generate
extra lift. At first this was just a straight foil
between the two hulls of the catamaran,
but developments have seen this foil shape
refined to improve performance, and there
is little doubt that these foil catamarans do
offer higher efficiency. However, catamaran
RIBs tend, overall, to take many RIB
characteristics out of the equation, and if it
is just a fender that is required, why have an
inflatable tube when you can go for foam?

Most RIB users do not require the full
range of characteristics that a RIB can offer
and in most applications the hull design
is not a critical factor, which explains why
there are so many RIB variations on the
market today. However, while the focus
tends to be on the hull design, it can be the
seating, cockpit and helm that matter most.

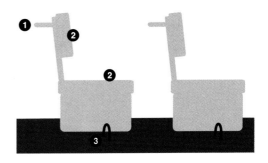

SEATING, COCKPIT AND HELM

Seating

RIB seating has been a focus of design right
from the start and that focus resulted in
the development of the saddle seat. Sitting
astride a saddle seat creates an intimacy
between the driver and the boat that tends
to be lacking in other craft. Such intimacy
replicates the experience of driving a fast-
paced motorcycle, and certainly RIB racing

experience has proved the importance of
this relationship. If the driver is seated or
located securely, he will have a much better
focus on the driving of the boat, making the
saddle seat an almost universal RIB fitting.
The design of saddle seats ranges from the
very simple padded seat on top of a box to
the more complex designs that incorporate
springing, and with seat design there has
tended to be a focus on what the function
of the seat really is.

The seating in a RIB has to perform
two primary functions. Firstly, it should be
able to hold the crew securely so that they
can focus on their tasks. This is particularly
important for the driver of the boat, who
should be able to use his hands to control
the boat rather than having to hold on, but
it also applies to the rest of the crew who
may have to operate radios or navigation
equipment. The second function of the
seat is shock mitigation – the ability to
absorb the impact of the hull in the waves
and so give a comfortable ride.

THE SADDLE SEAT The saddle seat gives
good security in the boat because you can
grip it with your knees and literally hold
yourself in place with your legs. Toe straps

fitted to the deck can afford you further grip and are a useful addition. As far as shock mitigation goes, the padding on the top of the seat helps and, depending on the height of the seat, your legs can help you to brace against the shock loadings.

Saddle seating works well across many applications, but while it supports the body well and gives reasonable location when the boat remains upright, its weakness becomes apparent when the boat lands back in the water at an angle. When this happens, the top half of your body comes under considerable strain to move sideways and the saddle seat does not offer any lateral support. During a sideways type of landing you really need the impact to be absorbed, and when the boat is being driven hard, this sideways impact and movement can be considerable. Ideally, the seat should offer some form of lateral support so that the body remains supported in this situation, but most seating in use today does little to help.

SPRUNG SEATS AND SHOCK MITIGATION Some quite sophisticated sprung seats have been developed in recent years and these are finding application in many military and commercial RIBs, where health and safety regulations demand more consideration for shock mitigation to avoid possible injury.

Designing a sprung seat for a RIB is not easy because it is not only springing that is required but damping as well, so that you don't find yourself going up when you should be coming down. Furthermore, the amount of damping needs to be variable to adapt to different conditions. Consequently,

these seats require quite sophisticated systems and they add not only weight but considerable cost too. Moreover, they still do not provide that vital lateral support, but they are the best current solution to shock mitigation.

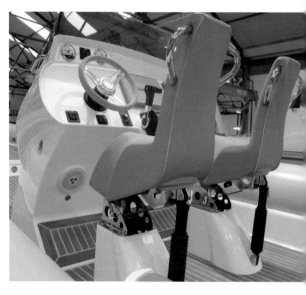

In that case, and for many RIB users, the saddle seat works well overall. The human body can happily absorb the first 3–4 G of any shock loading, so a foam seat is adequate for those users not driving their RIBs hard in adverse conditions. For the hard users, the sprung seat is the next step up. However, it might do as well to look at offshore racing boats to find a better solution. These boats do at least have hip support for lateral location and the better ones have support at the shoulders too. This might be combined with a seat that has a sprung squab (cushion) and which can be raised or lowered so that the occupant has the option of sitting or standing. While this could be a better overall solution, it would still only work in larger RIBs of 12 metres or more.

Clearly there is still much scope for developing suitable RIB seating, and I would prefer to see seats incorporating progressive foam, rather than mechanical springing, as the medium for shock mitigation, plus some form of upper body support.

However, this question of shock mitigation is not just one of seating. The hull design can have a considerable influence on wave impact level, while the way the boat is driven is also a factor. One of the problems with RIB design is that each aspect is considered in isolation rather than trying to find a more holistic solution.

Cockpit

RIBs have traditionally been open boats, with seating and control consoles installed on the open deck. This deck is usually set at a level that is above the waterline when the boat is at rest, enabling it to be self-draining. This was considered to be important in early RIBs because boats were operating from open beaches where a quantity of water might be shipped over the bow when launching in surf. This needed to be cleared quickly to allow the boat to get onto the plane, meaning some early RIBs had an open transom with just a central mount for the engine.

Today, surf launching may be of low importance for most operators and drain holes in the transom provide the simplest solution. Where the deck may be at or below the outside waterline at rest, these may be

fitted with 'elephant's trunks', fabric tubes that can be tied up to stop water entering and released to allow a free flow of water out of the boat when it is on the plane and draining is required. One-way valves are another option, but rarely prove to be fully watertight against water coming in.

Setting the height of the cockpit deck is important. If self-draining is required there

is little choice but to set the level relatively high. This also means that the crew is mounted high and the centre of gravity is raised, which can lead to the boat having a livelier motion. A higher seating position will also accentuate the lateral motion imposed on the crew and they will feel more vulnerable (you certainly feel more intimate and a part of the boat when sitting lower).

INTEGRATED COCKPIT DESIGNS

The concept of the open cockpit RIB is now being challenged by a new generation of RIB designs that incorporates a more integrated interior, which includes a top moulding that integrates snugly with that

of the hull. The seating also tends to be moulded in, so that more conventional styles of seating combining bucket and bench seats have to be used. These are fine for RIBs that might be used as yacht tenders or family boats, and they at least give the RIB a more integrated look that is akin to the sports boat concept rather than the more spartan RIB of tradition. However, they do need handholds or other means of security for the occupants, many of whom may not be familiar with the motions of small boats. This is particularly important for passenger-carrying RIBs, where only basic seating is so often provided for the occupants. Saddle seating may be used on many of the so-

called 'thrill-ride' boats and that offers some stability, but the lack of lateral support and possibly adequate handholds can mean that passengers are vulnerable to injury if the boat encounters a larger-than-average wave or if they relax their grip. Handholds in a RIB need to be rigid so that they can be used both for pushing and pulling. The soft type of handhold is not suitable because you can only pull on them and they can chafe knuckles quite severely where the skin rubs against the tube fabric. The rope handholds used to simulate the lifelines of old are equally inadequate, meaning that the moulded rubber varieties are probably the best solution.

Helm

When considering the internal layout of a RIB, one of the first questions is whether the helm should be located at the front or the rear of the boat. There is no doubt that the ride is more comfortable towards the stern because the vertical motion of the boat is smaller here. If the helm is forward, the crew or passengers located aft are likely to be more comfortable. However, this arrangement means that the helmsman cannot see the passengers or crew and will not be aware of how they are faring, and because the helmsman will be much more in tune with the potential movements of the boat and be better able to anticipate them, he could be unaware that he is giving his passengers a rough ride. If the helm is aft, at least the helmsman will have a much better idea of how the passengers and crew are reacting, but then he will be in the prime location for comfort. The priorities,

therefore, will differ depending on the use of the boat: any military/commercial RIB, or those used for serious cruising, is likely to have the control console amidships or forward, while on passenger-carrying RIBs it will be aft. Many yacht tenders have the helm in the middle to optimise the space within the boat.

Self-righting system

The self-righting system is an innovation found on many rescue boats and military RIBs. It was originally developed to meet the requirements of RNLI inshore lifeboats, and in the event of a capsize it gives the crew a better chance of survival, as well as the possibility of gathering themselves and going on to complete the rescue. To achieve self-righting, buoyancy has to be introduced at a point where it makes the boat unstable when it is in the inverted position. This is usually achieved by means of an inflatable air bag attached to the top of an arch mast at the stern of the boat, where it largely compensates for the weight of the engine(s). This air bag can be inflated automatically if the RIB capsizes, but normally it would be crew-activated so that there is time to ensure that every crewmember is free from the inverted boat, where they would be vulnerable to injury if the boat rapidly righted itself.

While it is usual to locate the righting buoyancy bag on the arch mast frame, several RIB builders have developed systems that do not need the rigid frame. This type of alternative righting system can be required when the RIB has to fit into a low headroom 'garage' or when it has to be

RIB HANDLING

air transportable, which limits top height. These alternative systems use only a shaped buoyancy bag that is stowed at the stern, which when deployed forms a semi-rigid inflatable arch.

Self-righting on cabin RIBs can be achieved by adding additional buoyancy on the cabin roof, rather than by using an inflatable system. This limits maintenance and it may well greatly reduce the chances of the boat capsizing in the first place, because the buoyancy of the wheel house will start to create a righting force as the boat turns on its side and the cabin becomes immersed. (The testing of self-righting systems is always done with a crane that pulls on slings fitted to pull the boat right over. It would be interesting to measure how much righting force there is when the boat is over at 90° or so, and to see if it would come back up without capsizing. If it would, it could simplify the whole self-righting system.)

In a cabin RIB with self-righting, the crew could have a rough ride as the boat goes over and it is essential that they are strapped into their seats. It is also imperative that all doors and windows on the cabin are closed to prevent any ingress of water.

Righting the boat this way is only one part of the system because there is little point if the engines will not start afterwards. Engines are usually fitted with a cut-out switch that automatically stops the engine before it is fully inverted. Then both intakes and exhausts have to include a form of sealing to prevent water entering the engine. The systems become complex and they must be engineered in such as way as to prevent them operating accidentally (*see* page 220, for more information). Batteries should also be of the sealed type and fuel tanks need a breather seal. A lot of pioneering work on these inversion proof engines was carried out by EP Barrus, a company that has specialised in developing and adapting both

outboard and inboard engines for certain
applications.

The whole requirement for making RIBs
self-righting is quite complex, and while you
can argue that it gives the crew one more
survival chance in extreme conditions and
so is demanded by certain health and safety
requirements, preventing capsize in the first
place might seem to be a better approach.
We will look at the mechanics of capsizing
in more detail in Chapter 11, but it could be
argued that when a RIB capsizes it is the
fault of the crew rather than the boat.

This level of sophistication does
demonstrate how RIBs have developed
into very complex craft required for
demanding applications. Standard designs
that are well proven will meet most of the
demands in the RIB sector, but there are

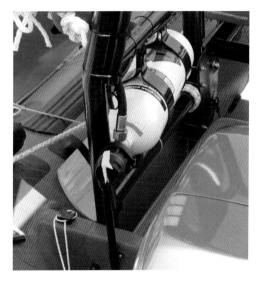

still RIB builders who can meet any specific
requirement, from sophisticated superyacht
tenders to military craft.

4 RIB CONTROLS

ONE OF THE JOYS of driving a RIB is the way in which it responds to your every command. RIBs are the most seaworthy boats in the world and much of that is down to the way you can drive the boat in rough seas. At the helm of a RIB you become part of a partnership where man and machine are in harmony, and the experience has been likened to riding a horse or a powerful motorcycle.

To achieve this level of harmony and control there are two requirements. Firstly, the controls of the RIB must be designed and located to allow you to get the response you need for delicate and positive control, and secondly, you, the driver, need to be firmly located in the boat to allow you to provide that positive control. When you watch many RIB drivers operating in lively seas you can see them using the steering wheel more as a handhold than as a control and sometimes this happens with the throttles. You will never get the delicate control that you need if you are gripping the controls tightly to secure yourself in the boat. From this it is easy to see how essential good and secure location of the driver is to operating the controls properly.

Many RIB drivers are happy to bumble along and take the easy option of reducing speed to make the ride in waves more comfortable but, surprisingly, you can actually have a worse ride in many cases because the boat starts to contour the waves rather than ride across them. However, there are many people who take pride in driving their RIB to the best of their abilities and want to get the best out of it. Then there are those who have no option but

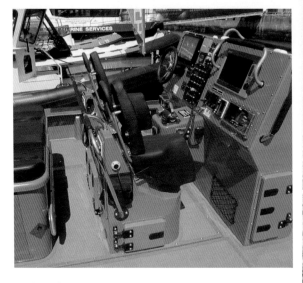

to drive fast in adverse conditions, such as rescue boat helmsmen and sometimes the military and commercial operators. They need to make every inch of fast progress when the going gets tough and this chapter on advanced driving is aimed not only at these groups, but to those who want to learn.

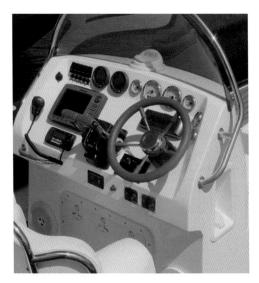

FAST-ACTING CONTROLS: STEERING AND THROTTLE

Steering

Mostly, controlling a RIB requires a series of delicate touches on the controls, rather than the more brutal movements that are often used. Think of it as being like riding a horse, where you need to coax the animal to do your bidding. This particularly applies to the steering, where quick and violent movements of the wheel can produce a much rougher ride in lively conditions. To understand this you need to realise how the deep vee hull that is the basis of most RIB designs behaves when the wheel is turned.

For the full cushioning effect of a deep vee hull to be felt, it needs to be upright so that each side of the vee provides the same amount of cushioning when it is cutting through waves or re-entering the water. On a hull with a 20° deadrise, when the hull is heeled over by perhaps 10°, you will get an effective deadrise of 30° on one side of the hull and just 10° on the other. That 10° deadrise is very shallow for a small hull that is operating in waves and it will offer little in the way of cushioning should the boat choose that moment to impact with the next wave. It means that with the hull heeled over, you present an almost flat surface to the water on impact.

Movement of the steering wheel by perhaps half a turn will angle the outboard or stern drive leg by perhaps 10°, which

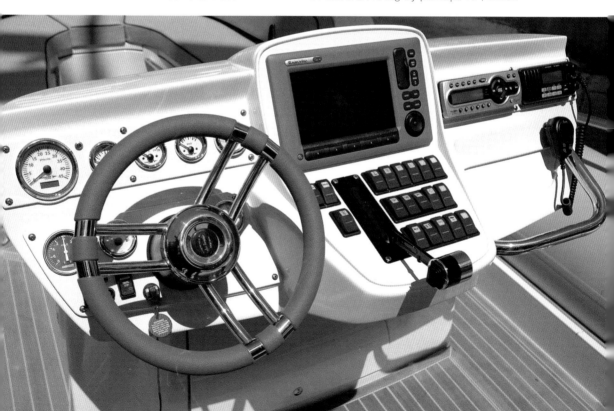

is enough to make the boat heel over by a similar amount, depending of course on the steering ratio that is employed. The boat invariably heels over in the direction in which the wheel is turned and so you end up with the shallow vee side of the hull impacting with the waves more than is necessary, resulting in a rougher ride. In a worst-case scenario, where the driver swings the wheel first one way and then over-corrects and swings it the other way, the boat can end up rocking from side to side in a very unpleasant and seemingly uncontrollable way. Combine this with inflatable tubes that have been pumped up too hard so that they bounce rather than absorb the shock of impact and you can find the RIB bouncing from side to side on the tubes even though it is maintaining a relatively straight course. Your passengers will not take kindly to this unnecessary treatment, all because you are being over-enthusiastic with the steering wheel!

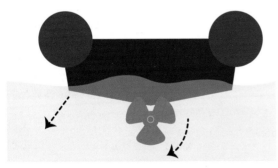

Speed can be a factor in the amount of heel that is created through this type of steering-wheel use, and the faster you go the more sensitive the heeling movement of the boat will be in reaction to the steering wheel movement. On fast boats you need

to just caress the steering wheel, moving it in small increments of just 5 or 10° at the most. Rather than trying to correct each and every alteration of course as you impact with the waves, it is much better to let the boat have its head and most of the time it will come back on or near the course of its own accord, without the need for steering corrections. Even when the RIB does wander more than you would like, bring it back on course by using small movements of the wheel, which pays off in a more comfortable ride.

It is not easy to adapt and use this lighter touch on the steering because the natural reaction is to grip the wheel tightly in lively seas in order to feel in control. You do need to be sitting or standing securely if you are going to use the light touch, and again it is a natural reaction to grip the wheel hard to help balance against the movement of the boat even when you are secure. Sometimes I find myself having to force my hands to relax on the steering wheel, but the benefits quickly become clear. This heeling effect under steering is likely to be more noticeable when the boat is outboard or stern drive-powered when the actual thrust of the engine is used to affect the steering. You can get the same effect with a water-jet drive, but it is not usually so pronounced. This means that the steering effect for this type of dynamic steering of only a few degrees of helm will be much stronger than would be the case with the rudder steering that might be found on a larger RIB.

On most RIBs the steering ratio, i.e. the number of turns of the wheel from lock to lock, has to be a compromise. You want

⬇ A beam wind will have more effect on the bow than the stern, so the helm is used to correct this, causing the hull to heel

81

quick steering response at low speed when you are manoeuvring in harbour, and yet out in the open sea you want a much slower response on the wheel so that you can achieve the delicate touch you need to avoid unnecessary heeling. It would be great to be able to switch ratios but this is rarely possible, so the steering response has to be a compromise. One way to achieve the ideal is to switch from wheel steering at sea to tiller steering in harbour, and that can be done with some water-jet installations.

It is quite reassuring to feel a fast RIB heeling into a turn, since heeling tends to counteract the centrifugal force that wants to fling the boat and its contents outwards in the turn. However, RIBs will also heel even when driven in a straight line when the wind is on the beam, and once again this can produce a harsher ride, because one side of the hull vee is at a flatter angle to the water than the other. This heeling into the wind effect is caused by the wind putting pressure on the weather bow and trying to blow the bow of the boat downwind. The bow of the RIB will often be clear of the water at speed while the stern remains immersed, and so the bow wants to pivot away downwind. You counteract this wind pressure by putting the helm over towards the windward side, and of course that causes the boat to heel that way, creating the heeling into the wind phenomenon. This heeling can be corrected by lowering the windward flap, which will serve to bring the hull upright. Lowering this flap will have an effect on the steering because it will create more drag on the windward side of the hull, so you will need to correct this with a degree

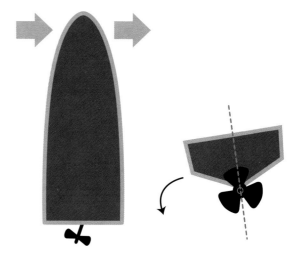

or two on the steering wheel. The slightly lower flap will also bring the bow down a small amount but the overall benefit of an upright boat will result.

Steering will be a lot easier if the RIB has good directional stability, i.e. if it will maintain a set course with only small amounts of correction on the steering wheel. A hull with a deeper deadrise, over 20° perhaps, will normally have good directional stability, but if you find the boat tending to wander about and be less sensitive to steering corrections, you may find that trimming the outboard or stern drive leg out will improve things because this will lift the bow and trim the hull more by the stern. Too much trim could have a negative effect on the steering and it is a question of trial and error to find just the right amount – something that may not be easy to do when running in waves (it is better to find the right settings in calm waters). You will also find that RIBs with dynamic steering tend to have reduced directional stability because of

the much stronger steering effect of
the propeller or jet thrust. (*See* pages 87-9
for more on the effects of power trim.)

Throttles

The throttle lever is the most important
control in a RIB when you are operating in
waves. Obviously you can use the throttle
to control the speed of the boat so that, in
turn, you control the speed of encounter
with the waves, but one other important
benefit of throttle use is that it can also
be used to produce quick and short-term
changes in the trim of the boat. These
short-term changes can be used to help
negotiate the RIB through rough seas in
order to produce a faster and safer ride
in more extreme sea conditions and also
when you want to make the fastest
possible progress in adverse conditions.

When running in waves it is usually
possible to find a throttle setting where the
boat will run more or less comfortably with
enough stability to cope with the larger
waves that come along. Waves come in
all shapes and sizes, and while there is a
certain amount of regularity in any series of
waves, there are always larger and smaller
waves and 'holes' (deeper troughs) among
the wave patterns, which can upset the
progress of a RIB (*see* page 97 for more
information). Therefore, it is best to drive
a RIB on its throttle, using it not only to
control the forward progress of the boat
but also to adjust the trim in the short term
so that the boat is better able to negotiate
larger-than-normal waves.

Offshore racing boats use the throttle
in this way to make the fastest possible
progress. At the speeds at which these race
boats travel, meeting a larger-than-normal
wave could spell disaster and the throttle
man will constantly watch and assess the
waves coming from ahead and use the

throttle to adjust both the trim and the speed to negotiate each wave. This requires intense concentration when travelling at over 100 knots, and is one of the reasons why there is a dedicated throttleman on these boats, but even at the more sedate pace of a fast RIB concentration is needed to make fast and safe progress.

Experiment with the throttle in calm water and you will see the way that that the trim changes when opening and closing the throttle in short bursts. Open the throttle and the bow will lift. Close it and the bow will drop. These changes may only result in a change of trim of a few degrees, but they can make quite a difference to progress if you exploit them intelligently. You will find when experimenting that the changes of trim created in this way take place before there is any increase or decrease in the speed of the boat, which is why the throttle is used in short bursts rather than a prolonged opening and closing.

It may seem against your better judgement and instincts to open the throttle when a higher-than-normal wave crest is approaching from ahead but by doing so the bow will lift and help to ease the boat over the crest. Your natural instinct will be to close the throttle with the approach of a higher wave, but this will cause the bow to drop just when you want it to lift, and while the speed of encounter with the wave might be a shade slower, the results of the encounter could be worse because the boat goes into the wave rather than riding over it. We will look at the way to cope with waves and rough seas in Chapter 5 (*see* page 97), but here I am trying to emphasise that the use of the throttle not only controls the speed of advance but also affects the trim of the boat.

So important is the throttle control in lively seas that you should drive the boat with one hand on the throttle and one on the steering wheel at all times so that your reactions and responses can be as fast

as possible. This in turn emphasises the need for the careful location of the throttle lever, so that it can be used easily and comfortably.

As we have found, active use of throttle control to drive the RIB is necessary in lively sea conditions and when you are trying to make the best possible progress. However, many of the conditions in which a RIB is operated will be less severe or less demanding, and here you can often find a throttle setting that will cope without the need to constantly change it. This will often be the case when cruising and, indeed, when you are making progress without pressure on a longer passage, you will want to find a throttle setting that you do not have to adjust so that you can cruise in comfort.

Both the steering and the throttles are the fast-acting controls in the boat and now we will look at the slower-acting controls that can be used to adjust the trim of the boat to get it running properly and trimmed for the prevailing conditions.

SLOWER-ACTING CONTROLS: THE JOYSTICK, FLAPS AND INTERCEPTORS, POWER TRIM

The joystick

Joystick control is being used on some larger RIBs that have water-jet propulsion and those with stern or pod drives. The

benefits of the joystick are enormous and the level of manoeuvring control is quite amazing, making it possible to position the boat very precisely and to allow it to be moved precisely in any direction. If you need this level of control and instant response, such as might be required on a rescue RIB, the joystick solution is a great way to go.

At higher speeds when on passage, the joystick control acts mainly as a throttle to set the speed, and steering may switch to a form of tiller steering, which may be separate or incorporated into the joystick control system.

There are different types of joystick control that use alternative logic to achieve precise control. One of these allows the joystick to be pointed in the direction you want to travel and then the computer adjusts the drive controls to achieve this. The speed of travel in the chosen direction is adjusted by the amount that the joystick lever is moved in the desired direction. This is a more or less standard format for most joysticks, but extras can be added. This type of joystick does not alter the heading of the boat, so steering can be added, and unless there is a separate tiller or wheel, the steering can be incorporated in the joystick by twisting the handle in the desired direction. This puts all the control into the one lever and the system can be further enhanced by having a push button in the top of the lever that will engage the autopilot so that the boat will maintain a fixed heading. All of this control is virtually in the palm of your hand.

This joystick control will normally be available at speeds up to approximately 10 knots, but above this speed the joystick would normally be switched either manually or automatically to a system of separate steering, with the joystick then controlling the throttles (or in some cases there are separate throttles). Here the steering may switch to tiller or wheel steering; some lifeboat RIBs now use tiller steering – the traditional steering wheel has been removed. I am not a fan of tiller steering for rough sea operations because it is difficult to get the subtle steering control you need – as we have found, you only want a very light touch on the wheel to reduce the chances of the hull heeling over under more aggressive steering, and this light touch is not easy to achieve with a tiller. Furthermore, with joystick control and/or tiller steering in rough seas the helmsman does need to be seated and probably strapped in so that he can achieve the best results with the controls and avoid making inadvertent movements.

With joystick and tiller controls you are putting a lot of faith in the system's computer controls, since it is the computer that translates your commands into actions. There are usually back-up control systems that can be switched on if the computer does not do its job, but in a tight manoeuvring situation you are heavily reliant on technology, and I have seen the joystick control fail at a critical moment when passing through a swing bridge. You have to balance the possible risk of failure against the huge control benefits that the joystick can offer.

RIB HANDLING

Flaps and interceptors

These controls are used to adjust both the longitudinal and transverse trims of the RIB and you will only find them on larger RIBs, say over 6 metres, where the added complication can be justified. They may not be necessary on many RIBs that are used purely for watersports or as tenders where they are not driven to the limits, although there can be a benefit when towing a water-skier, to help get the boat up onto the plane.

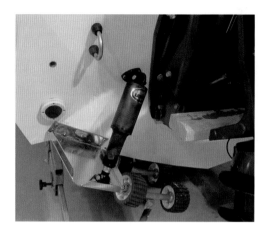

Flaps are hinged plates installed at the bottom of the transom, which can be angled down under electric or hydraulic control to adjust the planing surfaces of the RIB, generating variable lift at the transom. Angled down, they will cause the bow to go down and when raised, of course, the bow will lift and the RIB will run on its normal bottom planing surfaces.

The flaps are used together in this way to adjust the longitudinal trim, but to adjust the transverse trim they are used individually. If you drop the starboard flap it will cause the starboard side of the boat to lift, and the same with the port flap and the port side. Therefore, you will probably only want to use this transverse trim adjustment when running with the wind on the beam when the RIB will tend to heel into the wind at speed, but it can also be used to compensate for

uneven weight distribution. If you do use the flaps individually, they will also affect the steering because the flap that is lowered creates increased drag on that side, tending to pull the boat round into that direction.

Interceptors do much the same job as flaps and are their modern equivalent. Instead of having angled flaps, the interceptor is a vertical plate attached to the bottom of the transom, which can be raised and lowered. When it is raised it is flush with the bottom of the transom and has no effect, but it only has to be lowered a centimetre or two and it will intercept the water flow coming away from the transom and cause the bow to lower. It is claimed that the interceptor has less resistance than a flap when in use, and it makes a more compact

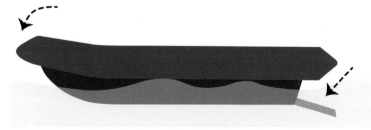

↓ Using the flaps to control
the lateral trim of the boat

↓↓ Graphic controls of a flap control
could be hard to read at speed

↓ A joystick type of
control for flaps

87

RIB CONTROLS

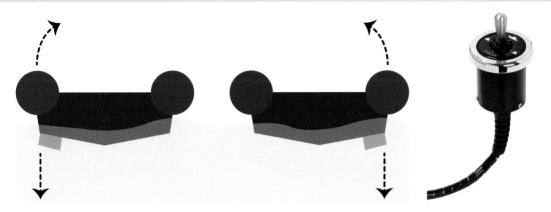

installation on the transom with virtually no projections. Interceptors can be electrically or hydraulically operated and, again, they only tend to be found on larger RIBs.

Both flaps and interceptors tend to be controlled by a rocker switch, although a form of joystick can also be used. There can be some confusion over these switches, some indicating bow down and bow up, others indication flap down and flap up, and you need to be clear which type is fitted to your RIB and what effect movement of the control has. You also need an indicator or dial to show how much flap is down so that you know what is going on at the back of the boat, and these come in many forms: a dial with pointers, indicator lights or mechanical indicators. Without an indicator the only solution is to bring the flaps right up, which provides a datum point for their future operation.

To get a feel for the operation of the flaps and how they work try, them out in calm water and you will be able to see what effect they have when operated together and individually. With experience you will get a feel for the right settings and adjustments when operating in waves. Because flaps are slow acting, you will tend to find a setting that works in the prevailing conditions rather than constantly adjusting them, but you may need to reset the adjustment when you alter course.

Power trim

The power trim is a hydraulic cylinder connection between the drive leg of the motor and the transom bracket, which allows the angle of the drive leg to be altered. This might seem an unnecessary complication but power trim can improve the efficiency of the drive considerably and it can also be used to trim the RIB. Today,

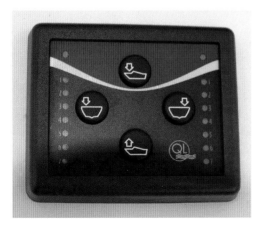

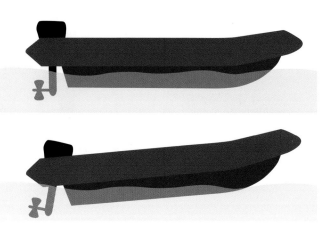

control of power trim is usually by means of a switch incorporated into the top of the throttle lever so that it can be thumb-operated without taking your hand off the throttle lever.

When running at slow speed and when coming onto the plane, the drive leg is kept trimmed in so that the propeller has a good bite on the water. It is only when the boat is up onto the plane that the leg is then trimmed out, and this has two effects. First, by altering the angle of the drive leg the angle of the thrust from the propeller is changed, making it push slightly downwards in relation to the transom. The change of angle may only be a few degrees, but this can be enough to raise the bow by a similar amount, which in turn focuses the planing surfaces of the hull in contact with the water further aft. In effect this reduces the area of the hull in contact with the water and thus reduces the frictional resistance. Flaps could do the same job, but they add resistance of their own so are not as effective.

The second effect of operating the power trim in this way is that it brings the propeller

a bit closer to the surface of the water, reducing the amount of drive leg in the water and getting the propeller to operate slightly in a surface-piercing mode for greater effectiveness. This change may be less noticeable than that made by the change in the hull angle, and the amount of power trim applied needs to be carefully judged. The best way to find the right application of power trim is to experiment in calm conditions when you will be able to clearly see the effect of adjustments. If you have a GPS or log in the boat you will be able to optimise the power trim angle for maximum speed and find a setting that works best.

You might also find that the boat starts to
'porpoise', with the bow starting to lift and
fall, if you have the leg trimmed too far. This
happens because the hull is then planing
on only a small section of the hull aft and
cannot find the right balance and so hunts
up and down.

   You can then use this setting when
running in waves, but in more extreme
conditions you'll find it beneficial to trim
in a little to help keep the propeller in the
water and to ensure that when you open
the throttle you get an immediate response
when the propeller bites. You may also
need to trim in when executing sharp turns
to prevent cavitation (the formation and
immediate implosion of cavities or bubbles
in a liquid) and, of course, as you come off
the plane, the leg should be trimmed right in.

   With experience, you will be able to
look aft to see whether you have the trim
set correctly with a smooth flow of water
from the propeller. Any sign of a rooster tail
from the wake and the trim is probably too
far out. As with flaps, it can help to have an
indicator to show where the power trim is
set and this will allow you to set the trim at a
previously found level. With twin outboards
or stern drives it is becoming common for
the trim of both legs to be adjusted through
a single switch and there should be no real
need to adjust them individually.

   The same hydraulics that adjust the
power trim may also double up as the means
to lift the drive leg right up when beaching,
operating in shallow water or putting the
boat on a trailer. This tilt mechanism will
almost certainly be on a separate switch to
avoid confusion and mistakes and if you do

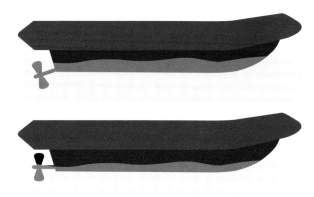

trim the leg up for shallow water work,
you must only use low power.

   Power trim is available on most
outboards over about 50hp and on most
stern drives.

Ballast tanks

Racing boats used to fit bow ballast tanks
that could be filled when underway to help
keep the bow down when operating in head
seas. They certainly helped, and some RIBs,
which had to operate in more extreme
conditions, were built with these tanks.
Today, ballast tanks are very rarely fitted and
the development of the fine bow on many
RIB designs has compensated, because
there is less lift in the bow. Ballast could still
be a useful addition to the controls available
for extreme RIB driving but today it is more
likely to be achieved by having dual fuel
tanks, where you can transfer the fuel from
aft to forward or vice versa. The crew can
also act as moveable ballast, provided there
is seating in the right places, but these days
RIBs tend to rely purely on flaps and power
trim to adjust the trim.

DRIVING POSITION AND CONTROLS

A lot of effort is put into making the driving of cars an enjoyable experience, but with so many RIBs, the ergonomics often leave a lot to be desired and it looks as though the designer has given up when it comes to the helm station, with controls seemingly fitted more for the convenience of the installer rather than the user. However, you will only be able to drive a RIB close to its limits if you have full control, and for this to come into force the layout of the driving position is imperative. The location of the controls, steering, throttles, etc, as well as the relationship between the driver and the controls, are all important, particularly so for those boats working in difficult conditions (rescue boats and military RIBs), but also for leisure RIB drivers, who will want to enjoy a relaxing voyage rather than have to struggle with the controls.

The driver

So what are the requirements? Let's take the driver first and how he is to be located. The concept of standing at the helm has largely disappeared from RIBs, which is sensible because when standing you end up using the steering wheel as a handhold and you are not free to operate the controls correctly (although standing can be an option when you have good body support to help steady you at the helm). Shock mitigation is the focus of much modern RIB seating design, and this is discussed later in Chapter 9 (*see* page 188). Here, we will focus on what a driver requires from his seat.

SEATING Obviously, a seat needs to be cushioned and comfortable, but the main requirement should be that it holds the driver securely, enabling him to have both hands free to operate the controls.

There is no easy solution when it comes to seating. The saddle seat does a pretty good job of locating the driver, provided that

but on a RIB operating in rough seas the constant up and down movement can lead to discomfort because the straps can chafe. The sophisticated sprung seats that are found on many military and commercial RIBs add another complication (these will be considered in Chapter 9 when we take a closer look at shock mitigation, page 188). Therefore, not everybody feels comfortable being strapped into a boat, but the same applied when the law demanded seatbelts be worn in vehicles and we soon got used to it, to the point where you can feel quite naked without a seatbelt.

ANGLE OF THE STEERING WHEEL Now you are seated securely, what angle should the wheel be at in relation to the driver? The options range from almost horizontal,

it has a secure, padded back against which he can brace (*see* pages 71-2, for more information on saddle seats). With a normal seat the driver loses the ability to grip with the knees and feet, meaning there is less ability to brace the body using the legs as partial support. However, to compensate, the back is usually shaped to provide this lateral support at both the hips and the shoulders (although this side section may interfere with the ability to use the controls freely). On some larger RIBs the seating is shaped like a half round section and the squab may be hinged to allow a sitting or standing position. Overall, the saddle seat with a shaped back is probably the best compromise.

One way to secure the driver is to use a seatbelt, and I have used a four-point version with some success. You certainly feel secure and free to operate the controls knowing that your body will stay in place,

↓ A comfortable driving position on a small RIB

↓↓ The location of the ahead range on this angled throttle control could make it difficult to achieve sensitive control

like the wheel of a truck, to the vertical of tradition. Much will depend on whether you have power steering fitted, which will make the steering light and easy to use, meaning steering with a more vertical wheel could work. Many prefer the steering to be a bit stiff on a RIB so that you do not turn the wheel inadvertently due to the movement of the boat, and a horizontal wheel angle allows you to pull on the rim to turn the wheel. This would be my choice, but it does mean that you need to tuck your knees in under the wheel to operate it easily.

The steering ratio is also important. As we saw at the beginning of this chapter, a light touch on the wheel can help to produce a smoother ride. That light touch is easier to achieve if the steering has a ratio that requires at least two turns from lock to lock and possibly more. Then, any inadvertent movement of the wheel has only a minimal effect on the steering. However, such a steering ratio can make manoeuvring at slow speed more difficult when you want to be able to switch from hard over to hard over with perhaps just one turn of the wheel.

This is important with outboards and stern drives where you steer with the drive thrust and where you want to set the angle of the drive before engaging gear to put the boat alongside. It would be ideal to have steering where the ratio automatically changed according to the speed of the boat, such as in some high-value cars, but perhaps that is a complication too far.

Throttle location

We have seen how important the throttle is to controlling the performance of the RIB, but on most craft both the design of throttle levers and their location leaves much to be desired. With most RIBs you will probably be stuck with the control lever that came with the engine because the controls and the engine/drive are now

Race boats that operate at or close to the limits separate the throttle and gear levers, using the throttle at sea and the gears for manoeuvring in harbour. It is a system that works well and should be considered for any RIB that has to operate under pressure. You will only appreciate the joy of driving a RIB with separate throttle levers and their sensitive control when you have experienced it, but it is something well worth considering if you want to drive a RIB professionally. Because gearboxes tend to be operated electrically these days, the gear lever can even be replaced by a three-position switch that you click for ahead, neutral and astern.

The location of the throttle lever (or control box, if it is one of the common integrated units) needs to be carefully assessed. The critical part of the throttle operation is the section from full ahead to half ahead. This is the main range you will use when running the RIB in waves, so it should be given priority, with the throttle lever being mounted so that this section of the throttle range is more or less upright in relation to your horizontal arm that operates it. This will ensure you get maximum sensitivity on the throttle because

closely integrated. Most of these controls are designed for comfortable leisure use where the operations are not critical, but they are generally far from ideal for more extreme use. Because they combine the operation of the throttle and the gearbox into one lever, the throttle lever's range of operation in the ahead position is considerably limited, perhaps covering no more that 30°, and this can make it difficult to get the sensitive throttle control required for rough sea operations. It can take only a relatively small movement of the lever to make the change from full ahead to idle, when you may only want to reduce the rpm by a few hundred. This lack of sensitivity can be exacerbated by the involuntary arm movements that can occur due to the movement of the boat.

it requires more movement of the arm to make changes. However, when the throttle is part of an integrated unit, mounting the lever in this way could make the reverse section hard to operate.

On many RIBs, you see the control box mounted so that the driver has to reach over to operate the ahead section, meaning he has little sensitivity and very poor control when running in waves. It is for times like these that you should consider the actual location of the lever. So often it is simply bolted on to the side of the console because that is the only place it can fit. Hopefully, the top handle is reversible so that it can be accommodated alongside the console,

↑ On this RIB the gears are operated by electric switches leaving the levers to control the throttles only

↑ These throttle levers are not well located for sensitive ahead control

but if the handle is reversed, is the power trim switch easily accessible? Because of the strong possibility of making inadvertent throttle movements when running in waves, it helps to have some form of arm rest which would help to support the arm that operates the throttle. This is not easy to engineer on an open console, but it is well worth considering in an enclosed wheel-house RIB. An alternative is to have the throttle lever quite stiff so that it does not respond easily to involuntary movements.

When it comes to control units for the engines the manufacturers attempt to come up with a 'one size fits all' solution and so it rarely works well in a situation where you want maximum sensitive control. There are specialist manufacturers who make special control units that have separate throttle and gear levers, and these are worth considering, although they do tend to be quite expensive.

Dashboard

The layout of the dashboard has been included here because this is where you get information about navigation and monitoring when you are underway. It can be a tall order for one person to cope with driving the boat and monitoring navigation, communications and the machinery, and if you are going to drive the boat properly, your focus should lie with the controls and not the dashboard. In an ideal world there would be one member of the crew concentrating on the driving, while a second crewmember monitors everything else. Without that possibility, modern electronic screens are very good at providing the driver with navigation information at a glance, and when cruising or otherwise proceeding at less than maximum speed, it shouldn't be a problem to do both. It is only when the pressure's on that both driving and operating the controls require full concentration.

Dashboards are often cluttered with dials, screens and switches and much of this does not need to be in front of the driver. It can be distracting, making it difficult to focus on the essentials. So let's take a closer look at what the essential are.

The aim should be to simplify the dash as much as possible so that you get the information you really need, as quickly as possible, to drive and navigate the boat. The navigation screen should be the focus of the dashboard. The controls and dials concerned with the position of the flaps and power trim are also important and the dial should be close to the switch, although of course if the power trim switch is in the throttle lever this won't be possible. Rpm dials can be

↓ Surrounded by electronic displays this RIB driver is likely to be distracted from the job of driving the RIB

↓↓ Analogue engine displays are not really necessary on the dashboard

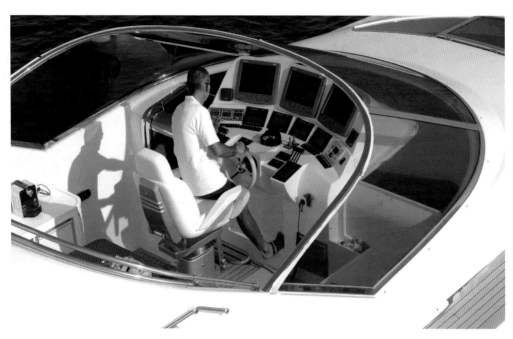

useful to let you know what the engines are doing, but they are not high priority, while the rest of the engine dials are not required in front of the driver. The chances are that you will not be looking at them if something does go wrong, and anyway there will almost certainly be a sound alarm that will go off if one of the parameters goes off the scale.

The VHF radio needs to be close at hand, but the chances of being able to use this and drive the boat at the same time are minimal and use of the radio at speed should be delegated to another crewmember. Then there are the switches for items such as the navigation lights, possibly the wipers on a wheel-house RIB and all the other lights – apart from the wipers, these do not need to be on the dashboard. Items such as depth sounders and speed read-outs are not generally high priority.

Everyone likes to see an impressive dashboard, with lots of dials and screens, and it can look great in harbour, but, as we have seen, it is not the most efficient layout for practical use at sea. Keep your dash clutter-free and you'll find the driving much easier.

SEA CONDITIONS

Before we look at driving a RIB it is important to understand the environment in which the RIB is operating. The surface of the sea is a complex area that is constantly changing and if you are going to drive a RIB intelligently, you need a detailed understanding of waves.

Waves

Waves are mainly generated by the wind, but can be influenced by other factors. The wave will start life as a ripple when the wind is just a zephyr and as the wind freshens, the wave grows in size. The Beaufort Scale gives a very good idea of the sort of sea conditions that are associated with different winds strengths, but remember that this relates to the open sea with a developed wind and the conditions in inshore waters could be very different. There, the wave conditions can also be affected by the topography of the land, as well as tides and currents.

If you sit on the shore and study the waves you will see that they are by no means regular. In any wave train (a series of waves spaced at regular intervals and travelling in the same direction) there will be high and low points that may be created by local wind effects, but more likely they are developed by smaller crossing wave trains. It is rare to find just one wave train in any sea area and there may be two or three criss-crossing the area. When two waves meet, the resulting wave will be the total of the two wave heights, which is why you get this variation in wave height along a wave crest. You need to be conscious of these different heights; because if you can run the RIB on the lower sections of the wave, you will get a smoother ride. Alternatively, you could find yourself going at a speed where the boat is happy in average wave height and then be faced with a considerably higher wave. There is no easy way to forecast when these larger-than-average waves will arise, but they are out there and you need to be ready for them.

◥ You need to understand the environment in which you are operating the RIB

RIB HANDLING

You can get waves double the average height at not infrequent intervals; much more rarely, there will be waves three times the average and, even more rarely, four times the average. You'll probably only experience these rogue waves in very strong wind conditions, which is unlikely to be normal RIB-operating weather. In 60 years at sea I have only come across three rogue waves that I know of, but 100-foot waves have been recorded in the open ocean.

We tend to focus on the high points of rogue waves, but there will also be associated deep troughs and these can be more dangerous because you will not see them until you pass the wave crest. The troughs can open up as deep holes in the waves and they are more likely to be found in the sea and created by tide races (*see* below) in inshore waters. The lesson, therefore, is to be prepared for the irregular nature of waves, especially those that demand close attention in any winds over Force 4.

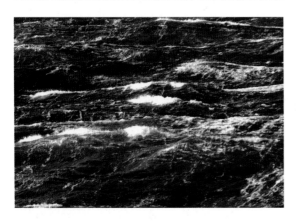

LANDS AND SHALLOWS Waves can be exaggerated around headlands and you can get reflected waves near to vertical breakwater walls. These areas can create crossing wave trains that form clapotis waves, a sort of 'pyramid wave' where the crossing wave trains create alternate peaks and troughs. Shallow water areas will slow down the wave train so that the waves catch up with each other, thus shortening the wave length. This leads to an increased wave gradient, making the wave more likely to break, which of course is what you see on a beach. You can often see breaking waves over a shallow spit that runs out to seaward from a headland and the shallows can combine with the tidal flow to create a series of standing waves – three or four lines of steep waves that appear to be standing still.

TIDE RACES In a tide race, the actual body of water is moving. When the wind and the tide are in the same direction, this movement of the water increases the wave length, thus reducing the chance of waves breaking. But

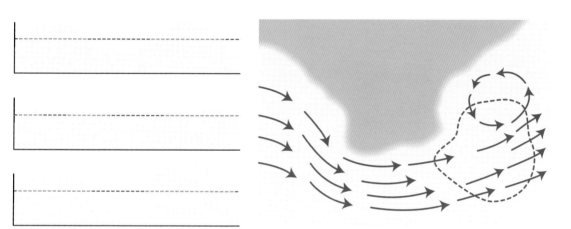

when wind and tide are in opposition, the wave length shortens, the gradient increases and the waves break much more readily. These tide races are more likely around headlands and in narrow channels where the tide strength is increased, and any shallow water off the headland is likely to increase the turmoil. The Portland Race (south of the Isle of Portland) is one of the more notorious tide races because the headland is so prominent, but here there is a narrow inshore channel where the seas may be less severe because of the reduced tide and you may be able to make a safe passage by keeping just a couple of hundred metres off the headland. Similar breaking sea conditions might be found in river and harbour entrances where the ebb tide is fighting a wind blowing onshore.

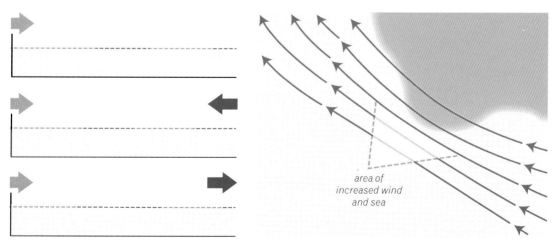

area of increased wind and sea

↑ The waves are normal when there is no tide (top) but can increase dramatically when wind and tide are in opposition (middle) and moderate when they are flowing in the same direction (bottom)

↑ Both wind and sea condition can increase round a pronounced headland due to the compression effect of the wind and tide

↓ Breaking seas off a headland caused by both shallow water and wind and tide in opposition

↓↓ Heavy erratic breaking waves in a tidal race

↓ Waves breaking as they encounter shallow water inshore

This is a brief analysis of some of the sea conditions that you might experience, but be aware that the sea and waves are a constantly changing scenario. The more you study the sea, the more you will understand its varying nature, and I would encourage you to spend time doing so. You will note that waves are not regular, that they have a steeper face or gradient on the side away from the wind (lee side) and that they constantly vary in shape and form. Understanding the environment in which you are operating is vital if you are to drive your RIB successfully.

RIB DRIVING

DRIVING IN CALM AND MODERATE CONDITIONS

This is RIB driving at its best, where the motions of the boat are minimal and you can take full advantage of the exhilarating performance. In these conditions it is largely a matter of opening the throttle and going as fast as you think fit. You will need to set the power trim for optimum performance once up on the plane, but there should be no need to adjust the flaps, unless there is wind on the beam when you might find the boat heeling into the wind, making correction necessary.

Fuel consumption

Your only concern in these conditions is likely to be the amount of fuel you are burning. Nowadays, it is socially unacceptable to burn huge amounts of fuel, and you can greatly reduce consumption by speeding along at close to the maximum

This is the figure that really shows how economic the operation is, but it is rare to see this depicted on any dashboard display. To calculate the figure, divide the litres per hour by the speed in knots, to find out how much fuel you are burning for every mile covered. However, there are other factors that could affect these readings, such as the loading of the boat and whether the wind is ahead or astern. If you want to operate your RIB economically – and most commercial operators and many leisure users do – it is worth taking the time to calculate this figure so that you have a clear idea of what is going on. When using GPS readings for the speed, be aware that the gauge may be 1 – 2 knots out because of the effect of the tidal stream.

rather than flat out. Fuel consumption will be highest if your outboard runs at its maximum of 5500rpm, but reduce it to 5000 or even 4500rpm and you will save perhaps a third, while speed will only drop a few knots from top speed. The leisure user may not get quite the same buzz, but he will certainly feel the benefit in his pocket. For the commercial user there can be considerable cost benefits to operating at reduced speeds and you might want to study the fuel consumption curve that is supplied with the engine while trialling a speed/rpm curve. This will enable you to establish optimum throttle setting for economy.

Many modern engines operating under electronic control have a readout on the dashboard display which shows fuel consumption. This will probably be depicted in litres per hour, which is useful information, but what you really want to know is the consumption in litres per mile.

Safety in calm conditions

It should be possible to find a comfortable speed and leave the throttle on that setting, allowing you to focus on steering the desired course, and certainly if you are running at around 30 knots you can relax to a degree. However, in any small RIB, you should always keep one hand on the throttle. You may come across a larger-than-normal wave in among the smaller ones or you might find the wash of a passing boat or ship suddenly produces larger waves ahead. If you are concentrating, you should be aware of any passing vessel and prepare for the wash accordingly.

This is part of the business of concentrating on the driving and the surroundings. When the sun is shining and the seas are calm it is so easy to let your mind drift and lose concentration, which can be dangerous. Remember that you are possibly travelling at half a mile per minute or more and things can change quickly at that speed. There may be debris in the water or that sudden wash, and you need to be ready for these. An open RIB does afford you a good view of the horizon so make use of it and be aware of what is happening, particularly astern where there could be someone approaching faster than you.

As skipper, you have a serious responsibility to all passengers. It is up to you to ensure that you give a safety briefing before you set out, indicating the safety equipment on board and what to do in case of an emergency. You should, of course, ensure that passengers are wearing lifejackets at all times, and that they tightly secure the straps – a crutch strap is a requirement if the lifejacket is to work effectively. If you are running at speed, even in moderate seas, inexperienced passengers can get injured if they do not hold on properly or if they land awkwardly after a wave bump, and you must be quick to respond. They may be screaming with delight at the bumpy ride or they could be in pain, and with the noise of the boat and the

sea, communication can be difficult. A visual aid should be agreed upon to ensure your passengers can communicate any distress. The standard signal is for them to raise their left arm, but even that is difficult if they are holding on tightly, so be sure as the driver to monitor all passengers carefully (tricky when they are usually behind you).

THE 'KILL CORD' The kill cord is there to stop the engine(s) if the driver moves away from the wheel either on purpose or

104

↘↘ Once the hull leaves the water
you lose quite a degree of control

↓ In slight seas the hull spans the wave crests
(top) but in moderate seas the wave length may
be longer than the hull (middle) while in rougher
seas the bow can be unsupported (bottom)

RIB HANDLING

involuntarily, so that if he does go overboard the boat will cut out. It has been known for a still-running boat to turn round and run people over, and it is not a pretty sight, so consider the kill cord an essential piece of equipment. In an open RIB the driver should wear the 'kill cord' (the exception is in general rescue boats, where the crew often have to move quickly about the boat and they do not want the engine to cut out at sensitive moments in a rescue). Be sure to keep a spare on board, since if the driver goes overboard and takes the first kill cord with him, the remaining passengers will need to be able to restart the engine.

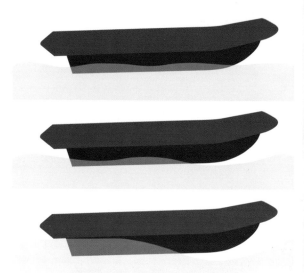

OPERATING IN HEAD SEAS

Head seas probably present the most challenging conditions for fast boat operations, because with the waves moving towards the boat, the speed of encounter with them is at its highest. The situation is compounded due to the boat encountering the steepest side of the wave (the lee side), meaning the driver has to adjust the attitude of the boat to account for the lift of the wave. Since the wave is travelling towards the boat, the time factor is compressed, so reactions have to be faster.

Because head seas represent such a challenge to fast-boat operations, most of the controls available to the driver are also geared to coping with these conditions. Both tabs and power trim are available to help keep the bow down and to prevent the boat flying off the crest of the wave as it climbs

over. Both these controls and the throttle can be used to improve the balance and attitude of the boat in head seas.

In calm and moderate conditions, you can simply set the throttle and go, but once the waves start to increase in size, you will need to make changes. For every set of wave pattern and each type of fast boat there is an optimum speed of operation, and while there are no hard and fast rules, the idea is to

↓ When turning like this the hull will be landing on the flat of the vee

match this speed to the prevailing conditions. What follow are general guidelines for operation of fast boats in head seas.

Full speed can be comfortable in slight or even moderate sea conditions depending on the size of the boat. Small, fast boats will obviously feel the impact of waves much sooner than larger boats and the best indicator that you are going too fast for the conditions comes when the boat starts to pitch, or it starts flying off the waves.

For full-speed operations, the wave length needs to be short enough to allow the hull of the boat to span the distance between the wave crests, so that both bow and stern are supported at the same time. The boat's momentum will help it to travel between crests with little or no change in attitude, so progress can be rapid.

Larger waves will have a greater distance between wave crests, i.e. a longer wave length, and they will also travel faster. This means that while the larger wave may be travelling faster towards the boat in a head sea, there is also a greater distance between the wave crests so that the actual speed of encounter may not differ greatly. Where the difference does become apparent is when the wave length becomes longer than that

Trim adjustments

Throttle opening *Bow up – quick response*

Throttle closing *Bow down – quick response*

Flaps down *Bow down – slow response*

Flaps up *Normal running trim – slow response*

Power trim out *Bow up – slow response*

Power trim in *Bow down – slow response*

Ballast tank empty *Normal running trim – slow response*

of the boat. Now there is a chance that the stern of the boat may still be supported by a passing wave before the bow encounters the next wave. In these conditions the bow of the boat can drop and you start to get the pitching motions familiar to fast-boat operators. When this happens, the attitude of the boat is not correct for negotiating the wave ahead and it is time to start doing something about it.

In these conditions, the boat will start to contour the wave, i.e. it will want to follow the surface shape of the wave rather than span the crests. Once that happens, the natural reaction is to slow down to give the boat more time to recover between each wave. However, operating at a slower speed in this situation is not always the best solution. At slower speeds the bow will tend to drop even further between waves as it

tries to contour them. Often, when slowing down like this, a comfortable ride will only be found once the boat is fully contouring the waves, which will mean that the boat is then operating quite slowly.

A higher speed will keep the bow up and the inertia also means that as the boat comes off the wave passing behind it, it will hopefully be in a better attitude to meet the next one ahead. The aim should be to meet the next wave with the bow slightly up so that the boat will ride over the wave in front rather than trying to plough through it. The boat should cut through the top of the wave so that it does not lift completely off. When you get it right, there should be a more or less level track for the boat through the waves. This is when you should start using the flaps and the power trim to give the boat the right attitude to the waves.

The speed of encounter with the waves in a head sea can be quite critical to the progress of a fast boat. Slowing the boat may seem to be the best solution to cope with deteriorating conditions, as this slows the speed of encounter and gives you more time to think. However, if you want to make rapid progress, it is worth experimenting with opening the throttle to lift the bow and to see if it is possible to get the boat to ride over the waves in a level attitude, using the flaps and the power trim to achieve the right balance for the conditions. When you get it right the ride is pure poetry, and it is hard to believe just how fast you can travel in quite adverse conditions. In a racing boat I have travelled across Lyme Bay at 104mph in a Force 4 head sea and the trim hardly changed at all.

It was a magic carpet ride, made possible by setting the flaps down a bit and keeping the trim adjusted by fine-tuning the throttle. Now perhaps you can see why that throttle lever position and movement is vital to delicate control of a RIB.

Using the throttle is the key to successful operation in head seas. We've learned how to use the throttle to trim the boat and this can be put to good use in head sea conditions. Opening the throttle will lift the bow and this is ideal for when the boat is approaching the wave so that the attitude

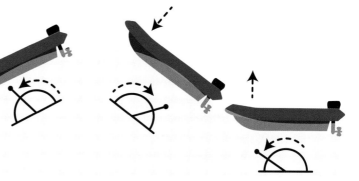

RIB HANDLING

of the boat is in alignment with the slope of the approaching wave. This change in trim can be achieved with little or no change in overall speed, as only a quick burst on the throttle is required.

If the power were kept on, the boat would accelerate up the face of the wave and would very likely 'fly' off the top. However, the quick burst of power is just enough to lift the bow. Then, by easing the throttle, the boat can be persuaded to cut through the crest rather than rise over it. Hopefully, the boat is now in a level attitude that will allow it to drop into the trough in a comfortable way before the throttle is opened again for the next encounter. The boat should pass through the crest with a degree of momentum so that it remains level. Without momentum, the bow will drop into the trough. Closing the throttle as the bow comes through the wave crest will encourage the bow to drop into the trough, which is the last thing you want to happen because the boat will not have time to recover before the next wave comes along. To get the sort of sensitive throttle control necessary you need the wide range of throttle lever operation and comfortable access.

Bearing in mind that wave encounters can occur every one or two seconds at high speed, this technique requires constant assessment and constant use of the throttle. This can only be achieved with a high level of concentration and this may be difficult to maintain for any length of time.

Rather than this constant use of the throttle to try to make rapid progress, a driver may use this ability to change the trim of the boat as a sort of reserve, for use when he sees a larger-than-normal wave approaching. By using the flaps and the power trim it is possible to find a comfortable balance for the boat to match the prevailing conditions. The flaps will be the main weapon in counteracting the upward lift of the bow in head seas.

If there is any doubt about what action to take in any particular situation in head sea conditions, open the throttle for a short burst of power to lift the bow. This is not an instinctive reaction but you certainly do not want to close the throttle if a larger-than-normal wave is approaching. Closing the throttle will dip the bow just when you want it to lift, but it is not easy to convince yourself that this is the right course of action.

If you find there is a need to slow down when approaching a wave, the boat is

probably going too fast for the prevailing conditions. Even then, you should only slow by a small amount and you should still open the throttle with a quick burst to lift the bow for oncoming waves. These quick bursts of throttle, which will immediately lift the bow without creating any increase in the forward speed, are the key to driving a fast boat in head seas. Their effect is more akin to trim control than speed control. Of course, you can only use this technique if you have a light and responsive boat, but then most RIBs come into this category, which is why they are so good in rough seas.

In head sea operations, the design of the boat also has to be taken into account. A boat with a fine, or narrow, bow section will generate much less lift when it encounters a wave in head seas, and therefore should be able to achieve a more level ride because the hull will be less sensitive to the passing waves. This is why high-performance boats are typically long and narrow. A RIB with full bow sections will be much more responsive to the shape of passing waves and thus will need to be driven more carefully in these conditions. You cannot change the hull shape once you are out there on the ocean, but anticipating the reaction of a particular boat design can help with finding the best operating solution.

OPERATING IN BEAM SEAS

With the wind and waves on the beam, the ride for a fast boat will be a lot easier than when trying to cope with head seas. In beam seas there will be fewer sudden changes in wave gradient than face the head sea driver. The ride should be a lot smoother, but the driver still has to be aware of the sudden changes in wave conditions that can occur in any wave train. Breaking wave crests can be a danger in beam seas and these can rear up suddenly alongside the boat. Also, with the wind on the beam, there is the increased risk that the boat will land on the flat of one side of the hull rather than centrally on the vee. There is a need for driving techniques to minimise this risk of impact.

In slight and moderate sea conditions, there should be no problem operating at full throttle in beam seas and the size of the boat will be less critical because the ride comfort will not be dependent on the wave length as it is with head seas. In beam seas you will become more aware of the irregular nature of waves and just when you think you're running comfortably along in

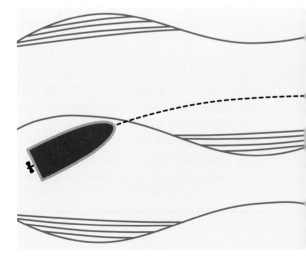

↑ Try to find a course to avoid the breaking crests when in beam seas

a trough, you will find a wave crest coming right at you. It is easy to forget that the waves themselves are moving downwind so to maintain a course that is parallel to the waves means that the crests will go past you, making it feel like you are going slightly upwind all the time.

In beam seas there is less requirement for matching the speed of the boat to the waves, but still the demand is there to find a comfortable speed at which the boat can operate without risk of serious wave impact or dangerous changes in the attitude of the boat in relation to the waves. The risk here comes mainly from the possibility of there being an underlying wave train coming from a different direction from that of the main pattern of the waves. You are less likely to notice this in head seas, but in beam seas it becomes more apparent.

These secondary wave trains can generate pyramid waves that can rear up without warning. In moderate seas they may not be big, but they can be a disconcerting change in what is an otherwise regular pattern of waves. There is also the possibility that the boat may have to cross over one dominant wave train and into the trough between the next two waves in order to maintain the approximate required course. In doing so, conditions may at times appear very similar to those found when operating in head seas or nearly head seas.

Unless you are in a great hurry, it is best to operate in beam seas with a degree of speed reserve in hand. Keeping this reserve will not only give the boat a chance to cope with some of the more difficult conditions but it also gives the driver the possibility

of accelerating his way out of a problem, whether it's avoiding the breaking crest of an oncoming wave up to windward that is bearing down on the boat, or simply avoiding a pyramid wave that has appeared close by. In beam seas you will find yourself using the steering much more than you would in head seas as you try to manoeuvre your way out of trouble, but of course you can also accelerate or slow down to avoid breaking wave crests, or steer away from them.

Ideally the speed in beam seas should be in the mid section of the planing range, i.e. if the boat has a top speed of 40 knots, a 35-knot speed would be appropriate. This allows the driver the flexibility to drop down to around 25 knots if a difficult wave is approaching and wait for it to pass, or to accelerate up to top speed in order to drive his way out of trouble around a wave, the latter often being the preferred course of action.

Beam seas will not normally call for constant operation of the throttle in order to adjust the trim of the boat. In most beam

↓ At least this small RIB is remaining upright as it leaves the water so the re-entry should be cushioned

sea conditions the boat can be allowed to operate at a constant speed and it should ride the waves comfortably, although a hand should still be kept on the throttle lever. If a challenging wave appears up to windward you have two options to avoid it. The first is to steer upwind across a lower section of the crest before the steep section arrives. The second, and probably a better option, is to steer away from the problem wave section by heading downwind. Steering away and opening the throttle at the same time will take the boat safely out of the potential danger area, and once past the crest the boat can be bought back on course and normal speed resumed.

In rougher seas, where the controls have to be used to make safe progress, good concentration is needed, as always. In the case of beam seas, concentration

levels need to be even higher, as a greater degree of anticipation is required in order to take avoiding action, because you need to start this action at an earlier stage. Most attention will be focused on the waves coming from the weather side, but you also need to keep an eye on what is going on ahead. There may not be the demand for the immediate response to the controls that there is in head sea operations, but the ability to power away from trouble is still important.

The course and action adopted in these conditions will depend, to a degree, on the course that you are trying to make good on, and while constant turning away downwind is often the easy option, it could take the boat some way off the required course.

When running in beam seas remember that a fast boat will tend to lean into the

wind and, under the steering control of turning the boat into the wave crest, the steering may also cause the boat to lean over further. There could arise a moment when the boat picks up a considerable angle of heel as it goes through a wave crest in beam seas and this could generate an uncomfortable landing on the other side. The transition through the wave crest should be done more by negotiation than by brute force.

In beam seas, a RIB driver will need to make a quick decision as to which of the alternative routes to take in order to avoid possibly dangerous breaking crests. Even if you do not notice the breaking crest until it is almost on top of you, there is still hope – provided that you have a responsive boat. Switch on the power and turn away downwind from the crest and there is every chance that you will outrun the breaking crest. One of the joys of RIB driving in rough seas is the way it will respond to your every command.

OPERATING IN FOLLOWING SEAS

Operating in following seas appears to be an easy route for fast boats because the boat is running with the waves rather than fighting against them. In slight or even moderate sea conditions, it is certainly easier because you will have less wind effect and the rate of encounter with the waves will be much slower than with head seas. In most conditions, you should be able to choose the speed at which you want to run. Only when

the bow starts to drop between waves do you need to start taking control and work the throttle.

Once the waves start to build, following seas can provide a real challenge for fast boats. They make it much more difficult to control the attitude of the boat. It is important to remember that the design of most boats is usually optimised for head sea operations and the controls, such as flaps and power trim, don't help a lot in following seas. Therefore, your main weapon in these conditions is the throttle and even this needs to be used with skill and care when the waves grow in size.

Running with the waves certainly reduces the chance of severe wave impact on the boat because, obviously, the speed of encounter with the waves is much slower. However, it is this slow speed of encounter with the waves that tends to make life more difficult. The slower progress in relation to the speed of the waves means that the boat

is much more liable to contour the waves, which can result in considerable changes of attitude of the boat and make it more difficult to control effectively.

The fact that the boat tends to contour the waves rather than leap from wave top to wave top means that it can end up pointing downwards on the lee slope of the wave. This lee slope will be steeper than the ride to the crest on the weather side and there can be a sudden drop and change in boat attitude as you come over the crest. This can be just at the point when the bow should be starting to rise to meet the next wave. No amount of throttle opening here is likely to produce the required change of trim to get the boat angling upwards for the next wave. The result is that the bow will tend to bury itself into the wave in front and, while it will eventually lift thanks to the buoyancy of the bow, it will only do so after generating a huge amount of spray and possibly solid water over the bow. Easing back on the throttle may reduce this impact, but doing so will make the

bow drop and possibly enter even deeper into the wave.

The way that a fast RIB behaves in following seas will depend on several factors. The speed of the boat is one, and when a boat has a speed that is more than twice the speed of the waves, there is a possibility that it can treat the approaching waves in much the same way it would in

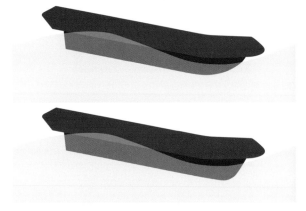

↑ A cutaway bow (top) will work better in a following sea than a deep bow (bottom) which will tend to act as a fulcrum and affect the steering

a head sea. With these higher speeds it is possible to maintain the attitude of the boat as it leaps from wave crest to wave crest, and rapid progress can be made. While 40 knots would probably be minimum speed for this approach, it is only really effective at speeds in the 50–60 knot range and above. As always, much depends on the relative size of the boat and the waves, and the relative speed between both. The higher the relative speeds the more chance there is that this tactic can be viable, as long as the wave length is fairly short. However, it can result in a rough ride because of the wave impact.

The various types of following seas will also have a significant influence on the way a boat behaves in them. Long, low waves are relatively easy to cope with and the effect of following sea waves will not have a significant influence until they reach a certain height, probably around the 1–1.5 metre mark in relation to, say, a 10-metre RIB. At this wave size, the boat should be able to come cleanly through the waves at their crests and maintain full speed, because the wave crests are relatively close together and the ends of the boat are not left unsupported which, otherwise, would allow the bow to drop towards, and into, the wave trough.

Short, steep waves with a short wave length are the worst following sea conditions for a RIB. This is particularly true when the waves are high enough to prevent full speed, and where the bow can start to drop into the trough before it has to lift to the next wave. These conditions can be very trying and operating in them may require the tactics described below.

OPERATING IN SHORT, STEEP WAVES WITH A SHORT WAVELENGTH

The speed at which a boat can travel in following sea conditions will not usually be affected when the waves are just a metre high, when full speed can be maintained in anything but a small RIB. A lower speed could allow the bow to drop as it comes over the crest of one wave before it encounters the next one, particularly as the lee side of the wave is steeper than the weather side. Once a boat starts this contouring between wave crests, the attitude of the boat is more difficult to control and the boat is likely to plough into the wave in front, rather than ride over it.

As conditions deteriorate and the waves become higher, the boat operator is faced with two alternatives. One is to maintain a speed considerably faster than that of the waves and attempt to lift the bow up over the waves with only a minimum amount of contouring. In this situation, keeping the flaps up and the power trim out will help to keep the bow up. If there is a chance to move weight in the boat this should be as far aft as possible to maintain bow buoyancy. In this way it should be possible to maintain speed as conditions deteriorate, but eventually you will be forced to slow down as the bow starts to bury into the wave in front. Here, the second option becomes viable.

This second option is for the boat to travel at or just above the speed of the waves. In this way it is possible to hold the boat on the back of a wave and to drive it over the wave in front only when you find this wave having a lower crest. This will allow the boat to cross over the lowered crest without fear of encountering a deep trough on the other side, since the lowered crest will often mean that the wave has just broken, with the water from the crest running forward to fill up the trough in front. This type of driving requires considerable concentration because it is very easy to go too slowly and allow the wave behind to catch up. If this happens and the wave crest behind is breaking, the boat could get into a broaching situation. Wave crests have a nasty habit of appearing and disappearing without warning and one challenge in following seas is to monitor the waves both ahead and astern.

If there are any doubts about what is happening behind, the best solution is always to open the throttle and drive out of trouble. A boat will accelerate naturally when it is on the lee side of a wave in a following sea. This downward slope of the wave causes the boat to accelerate under the force of gravity, so opening the throttle to lift the bow in this situation will only have a limited effect. A short burst of throttle might work to lift the bow but there is a risk of driving the boat into the back of the wave in front without enough lift to rise over it. Some high-performance designs are fitted with 'anti-stuff planes' at the bow to generate extra lift for this situation, and the buoyancy of the RIB tube should help as well, although this can put a very heavy stress on the tube fastenings at the bow and it has been known for the tube to peel off.

Finding a speed at which to operate in following seas requires careful judgement and becomes harder as the conditions deteriorate. When it gets to the point where control of the boat and its behaviour in a following sea is difficult, it could be time to revise tactics.

Controlling speed sensitively in following sea conditions is important and delicate throttle control is vital for making good progress downwind, but the technique of using the throttle in short bursts to lift the bow may not always work here. Coming over the crest of a wave in a following sea could easily mean that the propeller is not operating in solid water, and so the response to opening the throttle may not always produce the desired results.

Steering control can be used effectively in following seas but care needs to be taken when doing this. Ideally the boat should never be more than 45 degrees from the line of the wave crests in case a wave behind starts to rear up and break. At a 45-degree angle to the wave line there should be ample time to correct the course and still more to open the throttle and drive out of any potentially dangerous situation. However, concentration is vital.

Steering can be used to drive around larger wave crests, but here both throttles and steering need to be used in conjunction to give full effective control. Riding at an angle across the waves in a following sea will stretch out the distance between the wave crests, but because the waves are affecting first one side of the boat and then the other, the ride is likely to be uncomfortable. It may not always be easy to maintain effective control because of the way the boat is both pitching and rolling. It can be a wild and exciting ride in these conditions but it can be dangerous as well.

Reducing speed also opens up the risk of being overtaken by the wave behind, which in turn could lead to a broaching situation. In trying to achieve a comfortable rate of progress the best solution is probably to travel a little faster than or at the speed of the waves. A lot will depend on the particular wave length, the size of boat involved, even the design of the boat, and the wave gradients. You can experiment to a certain extent with altering course in relation to the wave crests, perhaps anywhere between 10 and 40 degrees, which might improve the ride somewhat. Experimenting with different speeds will also help you to find the best compromise to suit the prevailing conditions.

Broaching and avoiding breaking crests

Broaching occurs when a breaking wave overtakes the boat, lifting the stern. With the bow digging into the wave in front and acting as a fulcrum, the moving water in the breaking wave forces the stern to go to one side or the other and unless corrective action can be quickly taken, the boat will turn broadside to the wave with the risk of it being rolled over. It is a scenario that can happen very quickly and once put into motion there is very little that the driver can do, except become intent on survival.

However, there is a lot a driver can do to avoid getting into a situation where broaching can occur. The best course of action is to always be running at a speed at or above that of the waves. At these speeds there is no chance of a wave behind catching up with the boat and causing a broaching

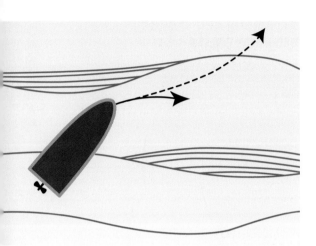

more prone to broaching because they have relatively little grip on the water to give them directional stability and the weight of the engines at the stern will encourage the stern to swing if the bow becomes a pivot point.

The golden rule when operating in following seas where there are breaking wave crests is always to travel faster than the waves. However, this is where difficulties can occur, because the lee face of a wave is steeper than the weather side so as the boat comes over the crest the bow can be quite suddenly unsupported and start to drop into the trough. You can't see into this trough until you come over the crest so the time to take action can be very limited. The resulting downward angle of the boat will cause it to accelerate down the wave front. In coming through the crest, the boat can also have the effect of making the wave crest unstable, with the wash of the boat dragging the crest of the wave forward and encouraging it to break.

Looking at RIBs that have capsized

situation. However, maintaining these speeds is not always simple in a following sea because even individual waves can move at different speeds. Just when it appears that the boat is safely on the back of a wave with the crest running just ahead of it, this wave in front can disappear and suddenly there can be a breaking wave curling up astern. Even in this position, escape is still possible simply by opening the throttles and driving the boat forward away from the breaking crest. In order to do this it is first necessary to be aware of the breaking crest behind and in these sorts of conditions it can be a wise precaution to have one crewmember watching the seas astern.

A broaching situation only becomes really dangerous when the stern is lifted and the bow is down, immersed to the point where opening the throttles will only drive the boat deeper into the wave in front rather than away from the breaking crest. Up to this point there is still a chance to power the boat away from the breaking crest. Fast RIBs operating at slower speeds are

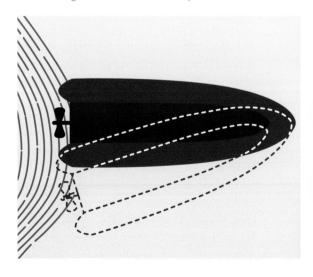

at sea, this usually seems to occur when the RIB is going slowly in following seas. Capsizes have occurred when a boat is coming alongside a mother ship and has slowed and then got caught in the wash from the mother ship. Another high risk area for capsize is in surf or tide races and again, the capsize will usually occur if the boat is going too slowly, perhaps even off the plane, so maintaining speed and concentration are the two keys to successful following sea operations in rough conditions. With rescue boats, they may have to go slowly when recovering a casualty and the risk of broaching or capsize can be high at this point, so it is best to undertake recovery heading into waves.

If you have a long run in following seas and you have found a speed where the boat is operating relatively comfortably, it can be good practice to occasionally turn around to see just what the wave conditions are like. When running in following seas, waves will generally appear much more moderate than they really are because the waves are breaking away from you. By turning around you will be exposed to the reality of the conditions. This can help you to decide whether it is safe to continue operating in the prevailing following sea conditions, or whether it would be better to consider an alternative course.

Operating in rough following seas requires considerable skill and judgement, and the penalty for getting things wrong can be quite severe. A driver should be just as interested in what the waves are doing behind him as he is in the waves in front of him.

NIGHT AND FOG OPERATION

Night

Operating a RIB in darkness adds a whole new dimension. The biggest challenge here is, of course, that you cannot see and read the waves and so quite naturally you will adopt a more cautious approach. In reality the best you can do at night is to find a speed and course where the RIB is operating relatively comfortably, which will allow a margin of safety for when larger-than-normal waves appear. The more cautious approach may work if you are just on passage, but for rescue work and for some military operations speed at night may be essential and you may have to push the margins harder than you might like and risk the consequences of encountering larger breaking waves. Modern RIBs will certainly take the punishment in these more extreme conditions and it tends to be the crew who are the weak point. If the ride does get very hard and there is a reluctance to slow down because of the urgency of the situation, one tactic that might work is to try heading off the desired course by a few degrees which may ease the ride with very little difference in the distance travelled.

Fog

In fog, the situation is very different and much will depend on the type of fog. If it is a radiation fog – the fog that is usually found early in the morning in still air – you can be reasonably comfortable that it will clear as the sun starts to warm things up,

RIB HANDLING

and also when you get away from the land. The challenge comes with advection fog, which is formed when warm, moist air meets colder water. This fog can last for days and can also occur in a fresh breeze, so there is the challenge of rougher seas. The visibility should be adequate to enable you to read the waves and to make rapid progress, but the challenge is in safe navigation. The electronic chart will give you the position and course quite adequately in fog, but

collision avoidance is a different story. If you have one, you'll need to concentrate on the radar display to 'see' other vessels when the boat is bouncing in waves so that you can take avoiding action. Small targets may not show up clearly and so it requires a combination of a good lookout and an ability to read the waves.

Fog is a challenging environment for RIB operations and the logical solution is to slow down so that you have more time to make decisions. For those who have to maintain speed in fog, such as rescue crew, the level of concentration needs to be very high and navigating and driving the boat should be very much a two-man job.

TACTICS TO IMPROVE THE RIDE

In most regular sea conditions it is possible to find a speed at which reasonable progress can be made in head seas, and this progress can often be improved by optimising the settings of tabs and power trim, and fine-tuning the ride through throttle control. However there will be conditions, such as when the wind is running against the tide or current, when the waves can become very short and steep, where the size of the waves means that the boat cannot ride over them in a reasonably true and level attitude.

Changing course
These conditions may be local in extent and it may be possible to navigate around them. If it is necessary to pass through them, a change in course can often bring about a

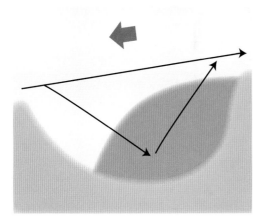

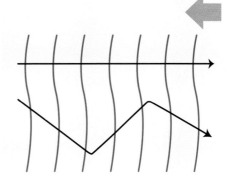

dramatic improvement in the ride conditions. It may be possible to make much better progress going upwind by 'tacking', like a sailboat, so that the waves are approaching from 45 degrees on the bow rather than directly ahead. This 'tacking' effectively increases the wave length because the speed of encounter of the waves is reduced, and the boat and the driver have more time to adapt to each wave as it comes along. This change in course will certainly produce

a more comfortable ride and reduce the stresses on both boat and crew, even though the rate of progress to windward may not be greatly improved. With fast boats, the fastest route is not always the shortest route.

This is certainly a tactic worth trying when head seas become difficult and even a course alteration of 10 or 20 degrees can have a significant impact on the rate of progress in difficult head sea conditions.

It would normally only be necessary to adopt this tactic when it is difficult to find the right balance and speed combination to cope when heading directly into the waves. However, it is always something worth trying if you are just looking for a more comfortable ride on a long trip. Anything that can reduce the stresses on the boat and crew is worthwhile.

When driving into head seas, breaking wave crests are something to avoid. A breaking wave will have a more vertical face and this makes it very difficult for the boat to lift over unless it has sufficient momentum. Because there is an actual body of moving water in a breaking wave crest, the moving water meeting a moving boat head-on can create a considerable impact and could cause damage to the boat and injury to the crew.

Dealing with breaking waves

Waves rarely break the whole way along their front except when they are in shallow water on a beach, and breaking wave crests tend to be found in irregular, isolated patches. These isolated breaking waves will have a steep wave front that a fast boat will find difficult to negotiate. The best solution in these conditions is to try to steer around them.

It should be possible to anticipate a breaking wave approaching one or two wave lengths away and this should give adequate time to turn the wheel to avoid the worst of the breaking wave. The alteration in course should be no more than 45 degrees because you do not want the boat to end up beam on or broadside to the breaking crest, because of the risk of capsize. A smaller angle of alteration should be adequate to avoid the crest in order to let it pass harmlessly down the side of the boat. If the crest cannot be avoided, as stated before, it is better to open the throttle in a quick burst to lift the bow rather than close the throttle and risk ploughing into the wave wall ahead.

In severe conditions, when breaking wave crests are increasing, it may not be practical to avoid all of them by steering around them. When breaking waves start to present a danger to the boat and crew, it may be necessary to look at the overall situation and decide whether trying to make progress to windward is the right objective. Tactics will depend on what you are trying to achieve by being out at sea in these conditions, but survival should take priority and it may be time to head for shelter if it is available.

We have already covered the idea of heading upwind or downwind in beam seas to dodge any breaking waves crests that may threaten the boat, but you might want to consider the idea of an alteration in course, a form of tacking to improve the ride. We tend to focus on throttle control to give boat and crew a more comfortable ride, but in beam seas even a 5 or 10 degree alteration in course might offer a better ride. It costs nothing to experiment and the results can sometimes be surprising. The same tactic can apply in following seas, although you need a bit more care about how big you make the alteration to make sure that you do not get caught by a wave on the quarter.

These are generally short-term tactics but in the longer term you might want to alter the route to take advantage of possible shelter from the land. A case in point here is when making a passage between two headlands, where the obvious route is the direct course although that may take you directly into the wind. However, by diverting into the bay you will not only put the seas onto the bow and effectively increase the wave length, but eventually you will enter an area of more sheltered water under the lee of the headland ahead where you can gain respite and make better progress. This tactic will not enable you to escape the exposed area around the headland but it could allow you to make better progress overall.

RUNNING AN INLET

Coming in from seaward into some harbours or river entrances when the wind is blowing onshore can be one of the more exciting times when driving a RIB. There should be no problem when the wind is off the land, because you will be entering sheltered waters as you approach the land, but even then the flow of water coming out of the entrance on an ebb tide or outgoing current can produce areas of breaking

waves generated by the shoals or narrow channels in the entrance. The real challenge when entering this type of harbour comes when the wind is blowing in from seaward, because not only can there be a wind-against-current situation, but there is also the added complication of narrow channels and shoals. At night the situation is much worse, since you cannot get a clear view of what is happening.

You may want to run the inlet to get safely back into harbour and this can be

↓↓ The mechanics of a spin out where the heavier weight of the engines at the stern causes the boat to over-react when making a turn

124

RIB HANDLING

a challenging task. Rather than rushing straight in, take time to stop and think things through. You may not have any option if you are running short on fuel, but if you are not happy with the conditions in the entrance, look to see what alternatives are available. Is it worth trying to raise someone on the VHF in the harbour who can offer an opinion about the local conditions? Are conditions likely to improve if you wait a while, perhaps for the tide flow to change or the wind to ease? Are you familiar with the harbour and marks so that navigation will be straightforward? It's worth considering all these aspects before deciding what to do. One of the problems in coming in from seaward is that you cannot always clearly see what the conditions are like because the waves are breaking away from you. You cannot judge the wave length of the breaking seas and it may not be fully clear where the channel lies, so time spent thinking about the situation is time well-spent.

You should do the actual run-in without hesitating. The breaking waves over the shallow water of the entrance or the wind against current are no place to stop if you are indecisive. So plan your navigation before you enter, and make sure that everything in the boat is secure and that the engines are all in order. The last thing you want is a breakdown. After that it is largely a case of using the driving technique shown on page 116 for operating in breaking following seas, riding in on the back of a wave and letting it break before you ride over it. This is one case where you really do need to watch out astern because the waves will be unpredictable, with the possibility of

large standing waves. It could be a wild ride and you need your wits about you and full concentration on the job in hand.

SPIN OUTS

A spin out on a RIB is only likely to occur when the boat is racing and you are under pressure to make the craft go as fast as the conditions will allow. The spin out can occur at a turning mark when the RIB has to be turned through a considerable angle, and the standard mantra is either 'wide in and close out or close in and wide out'. In other words, do not attempt to make the turn too sharply.

One type of spin out can occur when you start the turn and then close the throttle as the boat enters the turn. Closing the

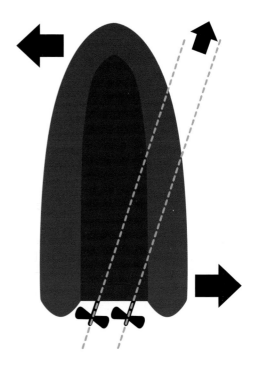

throttle will make the bow drop which
can then become a fulcrum, and with the
engine weight concentrated at the stern,
the momentum will cause the stern to want
to catch up with the bow and the spin out
occurs with the boat turning end for end.
There should be no harm done except to
your pride in most racing RIBs because the
tubes will help to keep the boat stable, but
the risk occurs when others boats are in the
vicinity and there is increased potential for
a collision.

The risk of a spin out will be increased on
a RIB with a stepped hull where the boat will
be riding on two or more points under the
hull. This means that the forward step could

act as a pivot point for a spin, particularly
when more weight is transferred to this
forward step when the engine thrust is cut
and the bow drops.

Another type of spin out can occur when
the RIB has dynamic steering, i.e. when the
propeller thrust is used for steering, as with
outboards, stern drives, water jets and some
surface drives. When the boat leaves the
water and then 'flies' off the top of a wave
and the propeller comes out of the water,
the steering effect is temporarily lost. When
the boat re-enters the water, the first part
to re-enter will be the propeller and if the
propeller thrust is angled to one side or the
other, there could be a short period when the

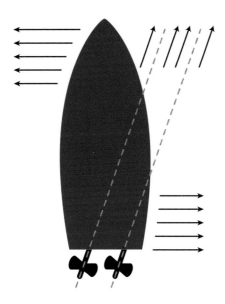

steering thrust has nothing to act against because the hull is still out of the water. This could put the boat into a dangerous situation of instability and this is thought to be one of the primary causes of a spin out in rough seas. In theory, the same situation could occur with rudder steering, but because the steering effect is considerably less with a rudder, the chances of this happening are much reduced. The solution here is quite simple. First of all, drive the RIB within its capabilities so that it does not leave the water. When the propeller comes out of the water it might look dramatic but you are going nowhere fast when the propeller is out because there is no effective thrust. Secondly, do not touch the steering if the RIB does get into this situation. It can be tempting to turn wheel because you might feel that the boat is swinging off course but wait until the boat is firmly back in the water before you do this.

ENGINE RESPONSE

In all this talk about using the throttle both for short-term changes of trim and for driving out of trouble, the engine response to throttle commands is important. With outboards and most lightweight petrol engines the response is good and almost immediate so that you can be confident your throttle commands will be obeyed more or less instantly. With heavier diesel engines the response may not be quite so quick, although today most modern high-speed diesels are very responsive. It is only likely to be in larger RIBs, where the boat itself can be heavy and the engines on the heavier side, that you may find a slow response to the throttle. This will reduce the number of options open to you when driving the boat in rough seas. You may also find that some modern diesels that have electronic control may not offer the quick response you want because the engine designers have introduced a slower response through the engine software in order to reduce the stresses on the engine that can be generated by quick opening of the throttle.

SUMMARY

There are no specific qualifications available for RIB driving. There are standard qualifications for powerboats, however, and these are taken as the yardstick for RIB operations. Courses are operated by the RYA in Britain, some with authority from the Marine and Coastguard Agency, and can cover all aspects of RIB operation from a personal qualification right up to the use of

RIBs for commercial operations. Powerboat Level 1 and Level 2 are the base courses and then you can graduate up to Day Skipper and Coastal Skipper before moving on to the gold standard Yachtmaster Ocean. For commercial operation of RIBs there are endorsements for these qualifications that can include fire-fighting courses, and most qualifications require you to hold a VHF Operators Licence and a First Aid qualification. More information can be found on the RYA website – www.rya.org.uk.

Remember that courses and qualifications are only the starting point. Experience is the most important part of learning to drive a RIB and with small, fast boats operating in waves it always seems that the more you experience and learn,

the more there is to learn. The sea is never predictable.

I see some RIB drivers who look on operating a RIB in rough seas as a direct challenge – they see the sea as the enemy and want to prove that they can conquer it. This is the brutal way to drive a RIB, which is not kind to the boat or its crew and both may arrive at the destination in no fit state to perform any task. RIB driving should work in harmony with the seas by negotiating and finding a course that minimises the stress upon boat and crew while still making good progress. It may not look quite so dramatic but it will get the job done and it is what really matters. That is the real skill of RIB driving and that is what a good helmsman should aim for.

WHEN THE RIB WAS BORN it was a utility boat: a tender or perhaps a beach boat (in addition to its early rescue function), and today many leisure RIB owners still use their boats over short distances, to ride to the nearest beach or for a high-speed blast out at sea. Divers were some of the first leisure-sector RIB users to take the craft seriously, opening up an entirely new world of RIB cruising.

The French inflatable builder Zodiac had introduced cruising in inflatables many years before RIBs were developed via Camping la Nautique, which saw a fleet of inflatables cruising in company in the warm waters of the Mediterranean during the day and camping on beaches at night. This was the catalyst that opened up RIB cruising to much more adventurous prospects (including the pioneering RIB cruise myself and others undertook in the 1970s – see page 22).

By their very nature RIBs can often reach places other boats can't, making them ideal for exploration (just imagine cruising among the rocks out near the Bishop Rock

↑ Fine weather and light seas are ideal conditions for RIB cruising

↓ Cruising in company can bring an added measure of safety

↓ A Mediterranean resort where refreshments are close at hand when cruising

↓ Some modern RIBs have cockpit fridges to provide refreshments

Lighthouse on the Isles of Scilly and going overboard to swim with the seals!). They are generally sound, seaworthy boats and are safe when handled correctly, yet they combine these features with the ability to travel at high speed in close contact with the water, setting the scene for adventure and fun. The fact that they are used by a wide variety of expeditions in remote parts of the world demonstrates their capabilities and for the leisure user; when used intelligently, RIBs can open the door to a variety of adventurous possibilities.

LONG-DISTANCE CRUISING

Many people view RIBs as ideal boats for short trips, but they also offer the prospect for long-distance cruising. Furthermore, unlike cruising sail and powerboats, the

RIB's shallow draft makes it possible to operate close to rocks and the coastline, enabling the user to see previously inaccessible coastal areas, land on remote beaches and gain access to rarely-seen wildlife.

Planning a cruise

Planning is not only the key to success for many long-distance cruises, but for many it is half the fun of making the voyage. There are risks involved in any type of long-distance cruise, and while enjoyment is an important factor, you must take certain precautions to ensure that safety remains paramount.

Ideally, boats should be twin engined so that any engine failure isn't a serious problem. An equally safe approach is to cruise in company so that there are other boats ready to help if one gets into difficulty. However, it is no good thinking that cruising

in company solves every problem: sure, the functioning boat can tow the disabled boat to safety, but this greatly increases fuel consumption – what if there isn't enough fuel to finish the voyage under tow? By increasing your awareness of the problems that could arise, you will be best prepared to plan your trip accordingly and establish alternative provisions should things start to go wrong. This is even more important if you are planning a cruise through a long open-water passage. While RIBs have the advantage of being able to access virtually every harbour, and if necessary, almost any beach in the event of an emergency, engine failure in open water presents a very different problem, and you should always keep fuel in reserve on these journeys. Fundamentally, careful planning and trials are necessary to establish the right level of safety for your trip. See the box opposite for an example departure checklist, which you can use before embarking on your next adventure.

↑ You need to do some route planning before heading out to sea

↑ A very crowded RIB can be uncomfortable for cruising any distance

← You will want good seating and well placed controls if you are going to cruise for several hours as standing can be tiring

↘↘ There can be enormous pleasure in solo cruising but you do need to plan carefully

↓ The world is your oyster when RIB cruising

131

Departure checklist

✔ *Enough fuel for the voyage plus a reserve*
✔ *Engine and gearbox oil levels*
✔ *Engine water levels*
✔ *Steering working*
✔ *Radar on and set up*
✔ *Electronic chart on and waypoints entered*
✔ *VHF radio on and working*
✔ *Portholes and hatches shut (cabin RIBs)*
✔ *Loose equipment stowed*
✔ *Crew safety briefing*
✔ *Life vests on if required*
✔ *All ropes and fenders stowed after departure*

ADEQUATE FUEL Carrying adequate fuel can be a problem on these long voyages. When calculating fuel requirements, you have to bear in mind that a twin engined boat operating on just one engine may burn considerably more fuel per mile than a boat that is up and running at speed on twin engines. Running out of fuel at sea is one of the biggest embarrassments you can endure, and careful calculations backed up by trial runs will help to calculate how much fuel you need on board to cope with every eventuality. Today's RIBs almost universally carry their fuel in built-in tanks – only the smaller RIBs still have portable tanks – so fuel tank types and stowages are no longer the concern they were many years ago.

Navigation and weather

Careful planning is the key to safe navigation on any voyage and it is an area that has changed dramatically over the years due to the introduction of electronic navigation. Fully waterproof instruments can be a great boon on a long-distance cruise and give you a sense of confidence on your trip. However,

132

↓ Check the tides before
landing on a beach

↓↓ Lifejackets should be worn
at all times when RIB cruising

↓ A cabin RIB can open up a lot
more options when cruising

conditions you could encounter and be prepared for sudden changes.

Weather is the one major uncertainty you run up against when planning a cruise. Some weather forecasts extend for several days ahead, but their accuracy is limited and you can only really plan for the weather a day or two ahead. RIBs are seaworthy crafts, but making a passage in rough seas or running into fog could put a whole new twist on your navigation requirements, and you need to ensure you know how and when you are going to make landfall if visibility is poor.

Such points on the voyage will force you to make the decision of whether to continue or divert from the intended route. Ensure

the systems are not foolproof and it makes sense to back up the fixed electronic chart display with a battery operated handheld unit so you still have position fixing and electronic charts should there be a power failure. Furthermore, I recommend that you still carry paper charts, which should be fitted into waterproof cases if they are going to survive in the damp environment of the rigid inflatable. Carefully mark all charts with the proposed course, as well as all possible options which may come into play during an emergency. Be sure to take into account the wide variety of weather

Organised cruises

When we started out long-distance RIB cruising we formed the Rigid Inflatable Exploration Club (RIBEX), which specialised in planning and executing long distance cruises to otherwise inaccessible islands or over long open stretches of water (including to the island of St Kilda in the Atlantic Ocean and up to the Faroe Islands, as well as less demanding trips to the Fastnet Rock and across the English Channel). RIBEX has to be stringent with safety procedures; these

voyages may be a tough test for both boat and crew, but they also provide a good testing ground for electronic navigation equipment in the harsh RIB environment, and the success of these voyages does demonstrate the possibilities of long-distance cruising with a RIB. Today there are RIB clubs in many countries in Europe and in the warm waters of the Mediterranean many of these clubs organise 'Raids' where there can be a whole flotilla of RIBs cruising in company.

these decision points are clearly marked on your charts and that a conscious decision is made should the need arise. If you are facing days of inclement weather, there is always the option to switch to calm-water cruising and explore rivers and estuaries in sheltered waters.

CLOTHING Apart from the safety of the boats for long-distance cruising and ensuring you have a multitude of options should the weather suddenly change, it is also vital to take the right type of clothing. An open RIB exposes you to harsh elements and during the period of several hours when you may be at sea over open water, good personal protection is essential. The risk of exposure in these conditions is very real, and you also have to be prepared for changes in the weather conditions en route which may prolong the voyage (we look at clothing and safety equipment in more detail in Chapter 11, page 210). If being

exposed to the elements is a turn-off, why not invest in a cabin RIB?

OVERNIGHT CRUISING

If you are cruising in an open RIB, you will need to find somewhere to stay for the night, whether that be at a campsite along the shore or in the luxury of a hotel or bed and breakfast. Cruising in RIBs does not have to be all heroics and hardship, and it can be carried out in a much more leisurely fashion, where cruising along a coastline with the option of landing on remote beaches or visiting bustling harbours can make for a very pleasant and interesting trip.

Camping, hotels and B&Bs
The idea of camping on remote beaches and being completely self-sufficient is one of the attractions of this type of cruising. Certainly camping on remote beaches has its attractions – cooking over a fire made

from driftwood, perhaps catching your own fish or launching the boat to go and buy a fresh catch from a passing fishing boat out at sea, enjoying the peace and quiet and remoteness of the surroundings. There is no real reason why you can't do this type of cruising with just a single boat, but again there is increased safety in numbers and additional manpower when handling boats

on beaches. A RIB can be a quite a handful when trying to pull it up a beach, so some form of wheel attachment could be a useful addition (when landing on a beach, if you are unsure of what lies ahead, you can always tilt the engine and paddle or row the boat into the shore). The Camping la Nautique style of cruising is a great way to undertake this kind of travel in company (*see* page 128).

If camping starts to get tiresome or the weather turns, you can can intersperse nights on remote beaches with going into harbour and staying in a hotel, where you can enjoy the luxury of a bath and somebody else cooking the food.

Cabin RIBs

Another option is to invest in a cabin RIB, meaning you carry your accommodation with you. Cabin RIBs first appeared in the 1990s when Scorpion pioneered their design. There are many types on the market today, but most start at around 10 metres in length. The accommodation might be a bit basic – perhaps a double berth in the bow plus a small galley and bathroom – but it can be enough for cruising in the short term and it does allow for the possibility of interspersing sleeping on board with the occasional night ashore. The real beauty of a cabin RIB is that you have the option of anchoring in secluded bays.

Anchoring

Finding an anchorage, whether it is just for a few hours or for an overnight stop, is a skill that can truly enhance RIB cruising. If you want a peaceful night you'll need to anchor in a cove or bay free of waves or an intruding swell. This is not as easy as it sounds.

The first step towards successful anchorage is to observe the weather and wind over the previous 24 hours. What is

THE COMPLETE RIB MANUAL

a sheltered cove in the evening could be very uncomfortable by morning if the wind has swung round to leave you exposed. Moreover, if the wind is freshening it can generate a swell, as well as more lively seas. When a swell rounds a headland it tends to be refracted around it and directed into the bay behind. Therefore, a bay that is sheltered from the west wind may still have a swell coming in from the south or south-west. A cove may look sheltered on the chart, but upon arrival you may find it untenable for anchorage, with a rolling swell coming in that would make for a very choppy night. A good pilot guide will often indicate problems of this nature, so be sure to read up on the places you plan to visit and carefully assess what the wind and tides are likely to be doing.

As well as observing the weather and wind before anchoring, it is important to

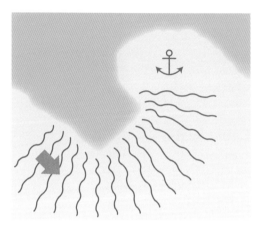

know what the seabed consists of before you drop the hook. Sand and shingle make a good holding ground, while mud can be more tenuous. A rocky bottom is bad news since it doesn't provide much in the way of a grip for the anchor and if and when the anchor does lodge under a rock, it may prove very difficult to free it (using an anchor buoy attached to

the crown can help to free an anchor that is lodged in this way).

The paper chart generally shows you what the seabed consists of, but this is not always the case with electronic versions. The pilot book may give some indication; otherwise, you may have to look for clues on the shoreline. If you see a sandy beach the chances are this will extend out into the bay, although some sandy beaches turn to rock as the water gets deeper. Rocks on the shore may extend out into the bay, but equally they can give way to a sandy bottom. Mud is usually found are the bottom of rivers and estuaries and hard clay might exist where there is a strong scouring by the current. Of course, in clear water you simply have to look overboard to see what the bed consists of.

Beyond bed make-up, other hazards to watch out for include submarine cables (which are shown on the chart) and mooring buoys, where the actual moorings can extend some way out from the buoy itself. Finally, there may be lobster pots in your nice secluded bay, and their presence may indicate the sort of rocky bottom that lobsters and crabs like.

When you are satisfied with your chosen anchorage, mark the spot on the

electronic chart before setting to work finding it. You can use the GPS to ensure your route avoids any off-lying rocks or shoals, but if you do this, be sure to back it up with checks on the echo sounder. Rather than aiming for a particular spot, it can often be better to work your way slowly in with the echo sounder running, and to wait until the sounder shows a particular chosen depth (bearing in mind the rise and fall of the tide) before anchoring. This way you can get as close to the shore as is comfortable and perhaps achieve more shelter under a headland than if you were simply choosing your spot based on visual observations.

ANCHOR LINES The anchor is not a high priority on a RIB and is often stowed away in the locker. However, if you plan to anchor as part of your cruising itinerary, you need to consider your anchor and its fittings in more detail. Assuming that you have an adequate-sized anchor for the size of boat, your focus should be on the anchor line.

On RIBs where saving weight is important, consider adding a rope line if you intend to make only temporary anchorage, for example over lunch. However, something more serious is required for overnight anchoring. Not only does the extra weight of a chain line make the anchor hold better, but it is resistant to chafing from stones, rocks or even gravel on the seabed where a rope line is not. (There is also the risk of chafe at the point where a rope leaves the boat, but RIBs usually have a grooved rubber fairlead over the bow tube to prevent this. However, you do need some form of catch or rope to hold the anchor line in the groove or channel.)

The usual solution for a RIB anchor line is a combination of both rope and chain, whereby a few metres of chain is attached to the end of the rope line, which adds enough weight for overnight anchorage and prevents chafe on the seabed.

When anchoring, always put out a minimum anchor line of four times the depth of the water and allow for a rise in tide when you do the sums. As for the size of the anchor, it should weigh in kilos about the same as the length of the boat in metres, with a bit extra. Do make sure that the inboard end of the anchor line is made fast to a secure point in the boat. There is nothing

more embarrassing than letting go of the anchor and seeing the tail end disappear overboard because you forgot to secure it.

RIB LEISURE USE

Diving

If you are a keen diver, a RIB is the ideal boat for the job. Indeed, today it is virtually mandatory to use one for diving. As well as providing a stable platform when stopped at sea, it provides fast delivery to and from dive sites.

Scuba diving also tends to require a lot of heavy equipment and with the limited space inside a RIB, you need to get organised. Probably the biggest problem you face is the safe stowage of diving bottles or tanks, since they don't take kindly to bouncing around the bottom of a boat! For that reason,

a form of rack, which is placed forward of the console or seating and on which the bottles are stowed vertically, is an essential piece of dive-boat kit. The rest of the diving equipment is best kept in stowage bags that can be secured inside the boat, preventing loose items drifting around the boat and getting damaged.

The stable platform provided by a RIB does make it relatively easy to put on equipment out at sea. The best method is to sit on the air tube and work from there (these same rounded air tubes also make it relatively easy to get into the water). Do remember that some diving equipment can have sharp points or edges and should be kept away from the inflatable tubes (spear guns can be a particular liability in this respect).

For the agile diver getting back into a RIB after a dive shouldn't be difficult. Remove the air bottle and the weight belt and pass these into the boat, but keep your fins on. Then, gripping the handholds on the air tube, give a kick with your finned feet and you should lift up enough to get a firmer grip inside the boat. One further kick and you should find yourself back in the boat, rolling in over the air tube. You can fix a boarding ladder over the air tube, but if it is going to be useful this needs to be a rigid ladder; a flexible rope ladder simply swings under the boat and it is very hard to get the required leverage to climb on board. Alternatively, you can use the engine as a form of ladder to climb back into the boat, which is a practical solution on a single engine, but is more difficult when twin engines are fitted, due to lack of space.

On a dive boat you do need an effective anchor to hold the boat securely in what may be quite an exposed anchorage position. If you are going to leave the boat unattended while the crew go diving, do check the anchor line carefully for potential chafe before you go into the water, and also go down to the anchor to ensure that it is firmly embedded and that the rope is not chafing on rocks below. While at anchor or when drifting and divers are down, a mast with a large diving flag is essential, both to warn other boats that might be in the vicinity, but also to help the divers relocate the boat when they come to the surface. Ideally in any diving operation one crew member should be left on board to cope in an emergency. A radio should be considered an essential part of kit, so that help can be summoned quickly in the event of a serious problem.

Water-skiing with a RIB

There is a tendency to think that water-skiing should be confined to the gloss and glamour

of gleaming sports boats. However, RIBs can be a very practical and effective solution to the water-ski tow boat requirement. A 3- or 4-metre-long boat can even be used, provided that there is adequate engine power, and while the skiing may not be especially exciting with this type of boat, it can provide a very cheap and viable means of having fun on the water. An engine of 20 or 30hp may be all that is necessary to get a skier up behind a small inflatable, but for more serious skiers an engine in the 50–70hp range would be better.

When towing a skier, a RIB behaves to all intents and purposes just like an ordinary sports boat. In fact, a RIB with a deep vee on the rigid hull will have a better grip on the water when a skier is being towed behind. You can fit a proper towing post perhaps a third of the way forward from the transom, which will provide you with better steering control, thus making the ride better for the skier (although do ensure that a hoop is fitted over the engine(s) so that the tow rope has a clear lead).

As with diving, RIBs make recovery of a skier from the water a simple and easy operation. The low freeboard helps a great deal and the soft air tube reduces the risk of injury when coming alongside. By the time you recover the skier from the water you should have the tow line well and truly recovered inside the boat. Since the person being recovered from the water is active, the approach to the casualty should normally be from downwind coming up into the wind, so that you keep them as far away from the propellers as possible. Stop the engines immediately upon making contact.

Stowing skis

Stowing water-skis inside the boat can be a problem, and the best solution is to place rubber shock cords alongside the air tubes or on the deck. This prevents the skis drifting around inside the boat when running to and from harbour, reducing damage to both the boat and the skis themselves.

RIB racing

Racing with RIBs has become a specialised sport and has led to the development of specialised RIBs, designed to maximise speed and excitement. The success of

Psychedelic Surfer in the first Round Britain race in 1969 was to be a turning point in RIB development and today there are two types of races that involve RIBs: 'round the buoys' and long-distance races, such as the Round Britain and Round Scotland Races, where RIBs come up against conventional craft. These marathons are in fact held over a number of days and involve a series of races around the coastline, providing a great testing ground for the craft. It is one of the remaining types of offshore racing that still attracts manufacturers who want to demonstrate their products' capabilities.

The safety rules in distance racing are very strict and they relate largely to commonsense equipment and capabilities that could extend to a cruising RIB. This type of racing remains one of the very few arenas where racing production boats is still practical and clubs such as BIBOA are heavily involved with bodies like the RYA to set the safety standards and rules. Some very extreme racing RIBs are now capable of speeds of over 100mph, but there are still classes for the everyday boats.

ZAPCAT RACING

This is a form of extreme RIB racing that involves small two-man catamaran-style

boats racing from open beaches, and combines a tough ride with a requirement for considerable driving skills. It is a relatively cheap form of RIB racing and offers a lot of excitement for the smaller boats.

In Zapcat racing a propeller guard is mandatory to protect anyone that may be in the water, and prop guards are becoming more common in general RIB use. There will be some loss of performance with a prop guard, but these losses are being reduced to the point where well-designed guards are viable. They could also become mandatory for diving and water-ski boats and may even prove to be a pertinent addition to sailing club rescue RIBs, which operate in areas where there are often people in the water.

River running

Rivers and inland waterways can provide an equally fascinating cruising ground for RIBs and you can tackle these at any competence level. The RIB is an ideal boat for cruising on rivers and waterways due to its ability to go alongside or land virtually anywhere.

However, at a more extreme level, RIBs are now used for river running, or white water rafting (although the pure inflatable is more suited to this sport). River running is characterised by travel down untamed rivers and negotiating rapids in a wild and seemingly uncontrolled ride, although the skill is in trying to read the river ahead to find the safest route, before attempting to steer the boat on to the desired course. Experience and development has shown that seemingly impossible river conditions can be negotiated by boats in this way and water-jet drive is more or less mandatory.

↓ A T-top can offer sun protection
in tropical waters

Of course, this sport involves certain risks and all participants need to be carefully briefed and equipped for falling overboard into the white water.

margins between success and failure can be quite small. But then, so often it is these very risks and your ability to cope with them that makes RIB operation exciting.

SUMMARY

In this chapter we have seen that the RIB's ability to cope with a wide variety of difficult or even extreme conditions has opened up a growing range of possibilities for exploration and watersports. However, when embarking on any adventure on the water you need to bear in mind that even the best boats can let you down at times, and safety should always be paramount. Planning and preparation are essential to understanding the risks involved and it is clear that in operating RIBs the

Insurance

It is important that you are covered by the right insurance, even for small RIBs. You may not be so concerned about damage to the boat itself, but once on the water you are responsible for your crew and if any of them are injured, there is always a possibility they may claim against you as the skipper or owner. Personal injury claims can mount rapidly, so always ensure you are properly covered.

YACHT TENDERS have grown in stature and importance over the years to the point where a tender is now a vital piece of equipment on yachts, both power and sail. There are some yachts that simply sail from marina to marina and tie up alongside so there is no need for a tender, but it is now recognised that a tender not only provides a means to get ashore when anchored or moored, but it can also extend the use of the yacht. For example, the kids can use it to learn boating, it can provide access to beaches or rivers and creeks and, in larger sizes of yacht, it can be a watersports vehicle. The tender's importance can be judged by the fact that most yacht designers, both sail and power, now incorporate a tender garage on new designs where the size of the yacht allows.

Forty years ago the Avon and Zodiac inflatable dinghies dominated the yacht tender market. They could be deflated and rolled up to make stowage on board easy and you could clip a small outboard on the back to save the effort of rowing. Some hardy sailors still use these tenders but they offer a sometimes wet and exposed ride ashore. The RIB has now taken over

↑↑ The simplest of yacht tender RIBs with no seats and a portable fuel tank

↑ A tender used from a larger vessel – note the green lifting slings for the crane hoist

↓ A simple modern yacht tender with an outboard with tiller steering

the yacht tender market to a large extent, and the convenience of easy stowage of the inflatable has been replaced by the more dignified ride and versatility offered by the RIB. It does not take a lot of power to get even a small RIB onto the plane and stowage on board, even on small power cruisers, can mean that towing the tender is no longer required. Smaller sailboats do not have the possibilities for easy RIB stowage and so

they are more inclined to tow the tender, but even this perceived handicap is deemed to be worthwhile when the advantages of the RIB are compared to the inflatable.

YACHT TENDER TYPES

The smallest RIB tenders are no more than 2 metres long and are simple in the extreme, mainly to keep costs down. On these tiny tenders the rigid section may not have the double bottom found on larger RIBs and may be just a single shaped moulding in GRP or even a piece of aluminium that is pressed into a boat-like shape. Glue this onto a simple tube shape and add a transom and you have a viable lightweight tender that can be powered by a small outboard. On such a simple tender any water in the bottom of the boat that might accumulate after rain or spray will not drain out and there may be a simple wooden or inflatable thwart

so passengers can sit up in the dry. The emphasis is on simplicity and light weight combined with low cost. These RIBs can be rowed as well as motor-powered and in addition to being used as tenders to carry or tow on board there are many yachtsmen who keep their yachts on moorings and their tender ashore to use as transport out to the yacht.

Moving up from this very basic tender, another metre on the length can make a huge difference to its capabilities. At 3 metres you will probably have a tender where the rigid section is a double moulding so that there is a deck inside the cockpit. This may or may not be above the outside waterline and be self-draining at rest but it should drain when you get the boat moving and the trapped water flows aft to the transom. A RIB of this size should be capable of handling a 20–30hp outboard and this will get the boat up onto the plane so you have the combined tender and mini-sports boat that can extend the craft's use. The basic layout is still likely to be the same, with some basic seating and tiller steering on the outboard,

but at this size you can also get the more sophisticated interiors that are a feature of modern yacht tenders.

Over the last few years small yacht tender design has taken off with the addition of style. This has been achieved by the use of a double moulding where the bottom of the boat is married to a top moulding that incorporates seating and a steering console.

This puts all the works of the boat such as the engine inside the two mouldings so that outside you have a clean, practical style, and importantly for tenders that have to fit into garages, there is a low profile. Much of the impetus for this new design style has come from the demand for small tenders to match the style of their mother yachts and to fit into garages. Today most of the major yacht tender builders such as Avon, Zodiac and Williams offer this sort of style.

For many designs, outboards are still the power units of choice because of their simple installation and the fact that they do not place heavy demands on the internal space of the boat. However, the availability of small powerful inboard engines coupled to water jets that were developed for jet skis has opened up the market for inboard engines so that the look of the tender can be more sophisticated. Indeed, Williams

Tenders now offers a 2.85-metre RIB tender with a 98hp engine and their own design of water jet to give exciting performance up to 40 knots, which shows just how far tender design has progressed. Williams is a tender builder who focuses just on this sector of the RIB market and it has refined the design of small yacht tenders considerably, looking at such issues of spray reduction, safety and comfort.

Most of these small tenders are still using petrol engines because of their good power/weight ratio and availability. However, there is a demand for diesel-powered tenders because many owners and their insurance companies are not keen on having petrol on board. Using petrol also complicates refuelling and in many harbours it may not be readily available. Petrol has to be stowed in well-ventilated compartments or on deck and it represents a complication that the cruising yachtsman can do without.

Research has shown that there are diesel tenders on the market as small as 3 metres in length but at present this is on the limit of practicality and of course a diesel tender will be heavier than its petrol counterpart and the performance is likely to be less than exciting. However, the compatibility of fuel with the mother yacht can be an overriding

↓↓ A high performance tender with a foam tube that can offer a superyacht owner transport ashore and high speed watersports

→ A customised superyacht tender with a double tube at the bow to reduce spray

consideration and the small diesel tender is likely to be an expanding market.

As we move up in size, yacht tenders get more and more sophisticated. There are still the conventional open RIB tenders in the 4 – 5 metre range but the trend is towards the double moulding style of tender where there can be seating for five or six people and you can go ashore in considerable style. Petrol engines may still be used, although but the trend is towards diesel power, but much depends on what the owner wants to use the tender for in addition to ferrying people to and from the shore. If the tender is used for watersports, petrol engines may still be the preferred choice but, again, the small powerful diesel is slowly moving into this market sector. This change may be being slowed down because many of these 'tenders' are also sold as stand-alone sports boats and in this sector of the market, it tends to be performance that counts and petrol as a fuel is far less of a problem. So

we may see a divergence in the market, with it separating into the dedicated yacht tender and the dedicated sports boat RIB but with both sectors based on the same RIB designs.

Above this size the roles of tenders and sports boats tend to merge, with the same designs meeting the requirements of both. Here we enter the realms of the cruising RIB where diesel power can be an attractive proposition for economy, while the sports RIB could use petrol as a fuel through either outboards or stern drives. Tenders in these larger sizes are likely to be diesel-powered but some of the larger RIB tenders have powerful outboards, when the yacht owner wants a tender that offers exciting performance as well as transport to the shore. There is a role here for what is often known as the crew tender on superyachts, a tender that the crew use when bringing stores from the shore or other utility tasks such as cleaning the hull. This size of RIB tender

↓ The foam tube on this RIB allows the designer more freedom for style

also encompasses the rescue-boat tenders that are required on superyachts. These may be to LSA 1 requirements on smaller yachts and to full SOLAS specification on the big superyachts and there are now many RIB builders out there producing tenders specifically for this market.

This brings us to the superyacht tenders where there are virtually no limits in size, style and capability. A 13-metre RIB such as the FB Design 42 can make a great tender for a superyacht, for use when the owner or his guests want some exciting yet safe high-speed boating at 60 knots, or when the owner wants to escape from the formality of the yacht for a while and go off cruising with basic accommodation for an overnight stop in a distant marina. There are now several RIB designs on the market that can meet this requirement and several of the large Italian RIBs that can be offered as superyacht tenders have quite amazing styling plus a level of luxury that was unheard of in RIBs a few years ago. Diesel power is the norm for these large tenders and water-jet propulsion is common because it keeps the overall height down for garage stowages.

There is a buoyant market in custom-designed superyacht tenders based on RIBs. Builders like Custom Tenders, Pascoe International and Scorpion offer the facility for fully customised versions, mainly of their standard RIB designs and the supply to this market has become a speciality of several of these British builders. Customising can be incorporated not only in the overall styling and colour scheme to match the mother yacht, but in many details such as easy access for disabled guests. Toilet facilities and covered seating areas with

air-conditioning allow guests to go ashore with dignity and style. This is the top end of the RIB market as far as design is concerned and the sky is the limit. This superyacht sector also features some very large RIBs for what is called the 'chase boat' role, a tender that follows behind the mother ship with one or more of the crew driving it rather than lifting it on board. Chase boats may also be towed rather than driven separately depending on the prevailing weather conditions. Some of these chase boats are large enough to carry their own tenders so here you have the tender for the tender.

A relatively new type of tender sometimes found on larger yachts is the landing craft RIB. This has side tubes, but the bow of the RIB has been squared off to allow it to accommodate a bow ramp that can be lowered to give guests direct access to a beach without having to clamber over the tube. This type of landing craft RIB has also been used for rescue work

where the ramp can provide a means of recovering casualties from the water in the recommended horizontal position well away from the propellers. There are even large versions of these landing craft RIBs that can accommodate a car, allowing an owner to have his own car on board which can be taken ashore by the tender. An alternative to having a bow ramp is to have a fold out ladder at the bow, which can allow dignified access on a beach landing or can be used as a swimming ladder.

STOWING

We will look at the launch and recovery of RIBs in the next chapter and this applies to tenders as well, but the use of garages for yacht tenders emphasises the importance of the tender on so many modern yachts. The fact that space inside the hull is dedicated to carrying the tenders demonstrates the value that owners put on them and these days you

can find garages on motor cruisers as small
as 11 metres in length. Of course the space
is compact, which is one of the reasons that
the small but capable 2.7/2.8-metre long
tenders have been developed. Today some
garages are designed around a specific
tender so that the space can be optimised.
Garages can also be found on sailboats, but
you have to look at a yacht that is 13 or 14
metres before a garage becomes a viable
proposition. This is because the transom
on a sailboat is narrower than on a motor
cruiser and the tender has to fit in end on
rather than across the beam as is often the
case on motor cruisers. The normal garage
is located above the engine compartment,
which of course restricts space there, but
everything on yacht design is a compromise.

On larger yachts the garage stowage
may be at the transom, with another garage
on the foredeck when two or more tenders
are carried. With superyachts the trend is
towards side garages with hinged up doors
on both sides to reveal a garage space that
is the width of the yacht. This arrangement
leaves the valuable space at the stern free
as a watersports centre. An alternative
used on many cruising yachts is to have the
tender stowed in the open on the flybridge
with a crane used for launch and recovery.
You might think that tender space could
be saved by deflating the tubes to allow a
larger tender to be carried but this is rarely
the case because owners and crew want
instant access. Headroom in garages is
often limited and RIB tender designers
show considerable ingenuity is creating
RIBs with a low profile. Steering consoles
can be made to fold down along with their
windscreens and they can even rise and

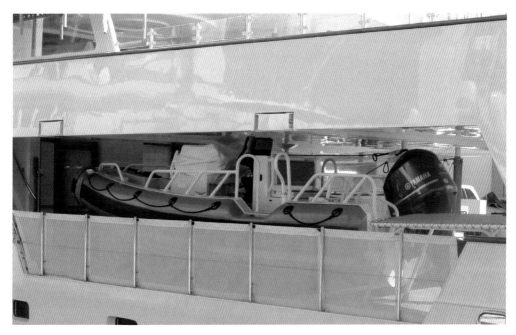

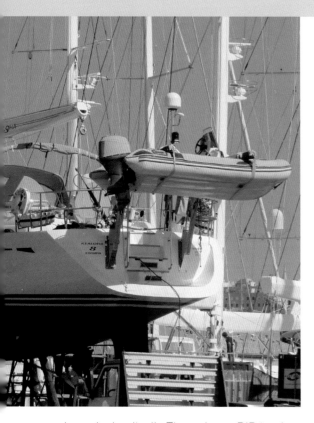

the tube. Finally, the type of ratchet strap that might be used could be one used on tucks, and corrosion of the metal fittings could be an issue in the marine environment. So the obvious solution is not going to work too well here, and it is necessary to attach any securing straps to the rigid parts of the hull, usually at the bow and the stern.

This means securing the tender fore and aft from fittings on the transom and at the bow. This can make sense because if the chocks that support the tender are well designed, they will secure the tender against any sideways movement so the fore and aft tie downs will complete the picture. The only problem here is that access to the securing points might not always be easy, particularly within the confines of a garage.

With garage stowages the securing is normally achieved simply by hauling tight on the winch line; the slope of the slipway on which the tender sits does the rest. In lively sea conditions you might want to add a stern securing point in order to help prevent any movement and to hold it down tightly in its chocks. It is so easy with a garage stowage to just haul the boat up into the garage and close the door, thinking that everything is secure in a sort of 'out of sight out of mind' attitude, but tenders probably need more attention in their stowages than when in use. The tube of a RIB can be sensitive to any hard objects rubbing against it so think about this before just throwing any fittings and equipment into the boat when on passage.

If the tender is stowed on the swim platform, you need extra care when securing it because in adverse conditions it could be

lower hydraulically. These days a RIB tender can be tailored quite precisely to the yacht it is carried on, both in size and style.

Securing a RIB tender on board can be something of a challenge. The logical solution is to put a strap around the tender and ratchet it tight down to the deck securing points. The first problem you come up against here is that the strap is passing over the inflatable tube and as the pressure in the tube can change with temperature, there is every chance that the strap will become slack when the pressure in the tube changes. Then you need to consider that there will always be some slight movement in the tender in its stowage and this constant movement could lead to chafe on

struck by waves, imposing a heavy strain on the fastenings and on the tender itself. Good, well-designed chocks and strong securing points are the best option, and being aware of what might be happening back aft when you are at sea is the best advice.

TOWING

Stowing a tender on board is the best solution when on a passage, since it removes any worry about the tender when you are at sea. However, this is not practical on many smaller yachts. Sailboats in particular can be a challenge because you need the deck space to work the yacht and there may be no space for a garage. Towing then becomes the main option. The tow line should always be attached to the eye fitted into the bow low down, and not over the tube into the boat. The low eye attachment will help to lift the bow when under tow and this should give the tender better directional stability as well as reducing the chance of the bow burying into a wave. Taking the tow line over the tube and into the boat introduces the risk of chafe on the tube where the tow line passes over it and there may not always be a suitable strong point inside the boat to which to attach the line.

Then there is the question of how much tow line to put out and there are several schools of thought here. You see many sailboats with the tender pulled hard up against the transom, almost lifted out of the water at the bow, and this can work for a small tender provided that the outboard is removed. Towing like this does reduce drag and you will be very aware of what the tender is doing and be able to detect any undue

movement. As an alternative you can do the towing with the tender just a metre or two from the transom, and for this to work it is best to take the yacht end of the towline as high as is reasonable, perhaps up to cockpit level on a motor cruiser, so that the bow of the tender is lifted, which will reduce any tendency to sheer about. With this sort of very short tow line there is less chance of getting it caught around the propeller if you are under motor and you forget that you have the tender there when you slow down. This is a very real possibility with a longer tow line on a motor cruiser where there may only be a limited view astern, and you are particularly vulnerable when coming to an anchorage or when slowing down to enter harbour.

A longer tow line does reduce the stress in waves and you need to try varying lengths of tow to find one where the tender follows a reasonably straight line behind the yacht

and does not sheer about. My experience is that somewhere around 4 or 5 tender lengths astern is about right, but much will depend on the underwater shape of the tender and the wind and sea conditions.

Apart from superyachts, towing is only likely to be done with smaller tenders, and here it is a good idea to remove the outboard before towing. It is not unknown for a tender to flip when being towed and that experience would not do the outboard any good. For outboards that are clamped onto the transom rather than bolted on, it makes sense to check the clamps at frequent intervals anyway and also to attach the outboard to the transom with a chain so that if it does come adrift it will not be lost. Add a padlock into the chain link and you have a measure of security for the outboard when you leave the tender at a pontoon or quay in harbour.

Davits fitted to the transom are one solution for tender stowage found on some sailboats. A couple of tackles are connected inside the tender and this can allow the boat to be hoisted manually. Try to balance out the weight between the two davits because on an outboard tender much of the weight is concentrated at one end and if the tender is tilted to drain any water from the inside of the boat, this could overload one of the davits. Failures of this kind are not unknown.

BOARDING

One of the attractions of using a RIB as a tender is that you have the tube as a built-in fender. The topsides of a yacht will normally gleam in the sun and present a smooth contour that you do not want to damage with the sharp edges of a tender alongside. Select a tender on which there are no hard bits to touch the yacht, except perhaps the outboard, which should be well protected anyway by the tube extensions at the stern.

↑ Fold out bow steps that allow easy access to a beach

↓ Similar fold out steps but with a swim ladder to provide water access

The tender will look great if you pump up the tubes to a high pressure and iron out all the wrinkles, but if you do this you might find that you struggle to get it alongside the yacht or a pontoon or jetty in the harbour. As we have said before, if the tube is too hard it bounces and it can be quite fun watching a tender trying to come alongside when the tubes are over-inflated. Every time it touches it immediately bounces off, usually just before anyone can get hold of the yacht or jetty. A soft tube will allow you to ease alongside and it will all look a lot more professional.

On motor cruisers and larger yachts you will usually be boarding the RIB tender from the swim platform aft. This is usually placed 30 – 40cm above the water on small cruisers and so there is no fear of the tender ducking underneath it. On larger yachts this can be a problem when the platform is higher, and you do need to take care, particularly if there

is any sea running when the tender could easily get trapped under the platform. Some yachts have a portable fendering system that extends below the water to prevent this, and of course the lift and lowering swim platform often used as a launch platform for the tender removes this problem.

Getting in and out of the tender onto the swim platform leaves you a bit vulnerable because there is nothing to hold onto in the immediate vicinity. Some yachts may have a portable rail to help here but it can be nerve-racking if the mother yacht is moving about in a seaway and you cannot balance yourself securely. Therefore make sure everybody using the swim platform and the tender is wearing a lifejacket – although if it is that bad maybe you should not be using the tender.

On a sailboat, boarding is usually done at the side of the yacht with the shrouds offering a good handhold for getting in and out. Some sailboats have a relatively narrow swim platform that can be lowered down from the transom which looks like a good tender boarding point but, again, these are often high and there is the risk of the tender going under.

SUMMARY

The RIB really is the perfect yacht tender in many respects. It offers a stable platform when getting in and out of the tender, it has built in fendering and it looks smart and practical. Today the yacht tender sector is a huge part of the modern RIB market with virtually all yachts sold having a RIB tender of some sort. The pure inflatable still has its place, particularly among sailboat owners where the tender may have to be stowed

on deck on a longer passage, but they are becoming the exception. There is probably no superyacht sailing these days that does not have a RIB tender and these tenders have been the catalyst for much of the advanced styling seen on RIBs today.

8 LAUNCH, RECOVERY AND TRANSPORTATION

THIS CHAPTER DIVIDES into two main sections. The first covers how the boat is carried on board a mother ship, such as a yacht, an offshore oil vessel, a patrol boat or a naval vessel, and the second concerns launch and recovery by road trailer and transport. In many cases is it the ability to launch and recover a RIB that dictates how and when it can be used and its effectiveness. Launch and recovery from a mother ship/boat can pose particular problems, and while it can be relatively easy to launch a RIB in adverse conditions, it is the recovery that is usually the limiting factor. It is a key consideration in RIB design, and in all areas of launch and recovery there is considerable scope for further development to reduce risks and increase effectiveness.

LAUNCH AND RECOVERY FROM A MOTHER SHIP

Small yacht tenders

The techniques for launch and recovery from a yacht vary considerably depending on whether the boat can easily be handled by manpower or whether you need mechanical power. In its simplest form the yacht tender can be launched over the rail by one person, and recovered in the same way. It is just a question of picking the boat up and launching it, and the operation is certainly made easier if the rails of the yacht can be removed. These small boats are generally light enough for one person to handle quite easily. Two people, one each side of the boat, make the job even easier, but in either case it is a sensible precaution to make the painter line fast before you put the boat overboard. It is so easy to forget this when launching, and before you know it the boat is drifting away from the mother ship.

It's preferable to keep the inside of the boat as dry as possible, so try to prevent water slopping over the transom as the boat goes into the water. There is generally plenty of buoyancy to keep the water out, but in lively sea conditions you may want to choose your launching position on the lee side or at least where the water is less active.

Large yacht tenders

When dealing with larger yacht tenders, which are too heavy to be easily manhandled, some form of mechanical help is necessary and this will depend on where the tender is stowed. One of the traditional means of stowage is on davits across the transom. A couple of small tackles are connected between the tender and the davits, and hand power is usually enough to lift the tender. This means that lifting points for the tackle attachment are required in the boat, and on a RIB these are fitted into the rigid section of the hull, usually two at the transom and one forward. Two or three lifting points are generally adequate (three giving the boat a bit more stability when launching), and you simply hook on and hoist the boat out of the water or use

A RIB tender stowed on davits makes for easy launch and recovery but increases the overall length of the yacht

the reverse procedure when launching. The davits, which extend out over the transom, and the boat carried in them, can be vulnerable when you are manoeuvring in a marina and, of course, the extra length will add to your marina charges, but the system works fine for the yachtsman who uses moorings or anchoring. Be aware that the main weight of the tender tends to be at the stern so the davit at that end must be adequate for the unbalanced load.

DAVITS Another version of this davit system is one in which the inboard edge of the tender is hooked onto attachments on the transom or outer edge of the swim platform, creating a hinge that allows the other side of the RIB to be pulled up. The hinge acts as a fulcrum and the boat is stowed flat against the transom. It makes for a secure, tight stowage and provides quite a practical and space-saving solution. This is mainly a sailboat fixture, with the topping lift being used to provide the power to bring the tender inboard where it can be secured. There are several ingenious systems along these lines that reduce the need for a tender to be towed.

You still see such davit systems on sailboats, but they are now rare on motor cruisers, where there tend to be garage or swim platform stowage and a slipway or lowering swim platform launch. In a garage stowage there is usually a ramp with rollers fitted, perhaps with the garage door folding out to create the launching ramp into the water. Alternatively there may be a fold-out ramp extension to span the gap over the swim platform so that the RIB is simply lowered down the ramp into the water with a powered winch controlling the launch and the lift for recovery. It is a compact and simple solution that allows for one-person launch and recovery and, again, there have been quite a few ingenious designs to match the system to the available space and facilities.

Having a garage for tender stowage

RIB HANDLING

does complicate things because there has to be hydraulics to open and close the garage door, and of course the garage space can take up a lot of room inside the hull. However, it is a clean, tidy and safe arrangement. Do bear in mind that if you have an outboard-powered tender or one with an inboard petrol engine you are stowing a potentially dangerous fuel inside a closed compartment, which requires ventilation.

GARAGE AND SWIM PLATFORM SYSTEMS The lowering swim platform is a more recent development that can be used in conjunction with a garage stowage

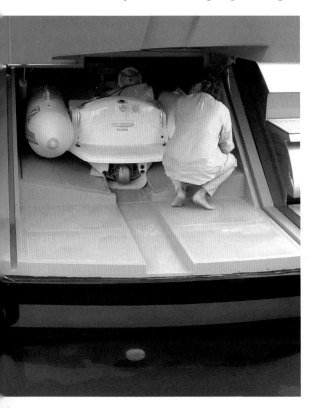

where the tender is stowed athwartships. It is mainly used, however, where the tender is stowed on the swim platform itself. The swim platform is mounted on a series of levers and hydraulic cylinders that allow it to be raised and lowered, while the platform itself remains horizontal. When you push the control button, the platform simply lowers the tender into the water. Recovery is in the reverse and the tender is floated onto the submerged platform and held in place while the platform is raised. Things can get a bit complicated because you don't want to be standing on the platform when it is going up and down, so space for operating the system may be limited. Furthermore, stowage of the tender on the platform usually means that it has to be launched before the platform can be used for its swimming function.

Garage and swim platform systems are also used on larger yachts and here, with the tenders becoming larger and heavier, the launch and recovery systems get more sophisticated. When you have a tender that weighs a tonne or more, you need to control its movement (particularly during recovery) to reduce the chance of damage. The garage stowage and slipway system offers one of the best options. The tender might have a permanent short line attached to the bow eye ring and taken over the bow, making it much easier to connect and disconnect the winch line, which saves crewmembers having to delve under the boat when it is approaching and leaving the 'slipway'. Garage launch systems work well in fine conditions but if there is any sort of sea running, as could be the case at

an open anchorage, the movement of the tender as it comes into the slipway needs careful control and the crew needs to be agile to make the winch connection.

Side garages are used on some of the largest superyachts and the launch and recovery is usually by means of a twin powered hoist from booms that extend out from the side when the garage door is opened. These are tenders that may weigh several tonnes, so the whole operation becomes more critical. A boat rope rigged along the side of the yacht can help to hold the tender in place during the connecting and disconnecting of the hoists, and with the pristine paint job on the side of the yacht's hull, good fendering is essential. Launch and recovery with side systems could be limited in a seaway, partly due to the often limited headroom under the booms and also because of the difficulty of hooking on the hoists as the tender is rising and falling.

CRANE SYSTEMS The alternative to garage stowage is stowage on the open flybridge deck or in a covered stowage on the foredeck with launch and recovery by means of a crane. Special electric or hydraulic cranes that match the contours of the yacht are often used but there is usually just a single hoist point which can create several problems. The single hoist may be attached to the tender by means of a three- or four-point sling with a ring attaching it to the hoist hook. This is fine when launch and recovery are in calm seas, but in more lively seas, connecting that ring to the hook can be risky. It takes two hands to do the job, one to lift the ring and one to hold the hook, which means that the person doing the job is not holding on. Then there is the risk that, once hooked on, the slings can snap tight and the crew need to be well clear of them when this happens. You can meet similar difficulties when launching if the hoist hook is swinging about, or has become slack.

⬇⬇ A RIB being launched using a
four point sling which can be a risky
operation when there is a sea running

⬇ A quick-release hook
on a RIB

Yachts usually launch and recover their tenders in fine conditions where there should be no problems with movement of the mother yacht and the tender. When the mother yacht is moving, just trying to control the tender when it is hoisted poses problems. It could be swinging and possibly spinning, and it may take several crewmembers to control even a smaller tender under these conditions. Lines attached to bow and stern can help, but you also want a bow line on the tender when it enters the water, particularly if there is any current running that could take the craft away before it can be unhooked. On-load release hooks disconnect the hoist wire even when it is under load, but of course the danger is that the hoist can be disconnected before the boat is in the water, with dire consequences for the crew on board. In an ideal world a tender should

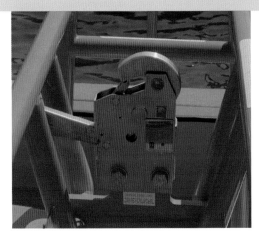

be launched without anyone on board, but this is rare in practice because someone usually has to be there to disconnect the hoist, start the engine and control the boat. Never underestimate the risks that can be associated with launching and recovering tenders when the mother yacht has some movement, however slight, or in lively sea conditions.

Military and commercial boats

The commercial industries and military are using RIBs more and more as very capable tenders. Indeed, there is a growing trend for military mother ships to carry and deliver the tender to the activity site, and then for the tender to actually do the job of interception or boarding. In the offshore oil arena, standby ships and other support vessels carry rescue RIBs, and it is mainly these boats that will do the rescue job. Therefore, launch and recovery is critical to the success of any operation and the more capable the system, the more effective will be the whole operation. Launching is usually more effective, and it is usually during the recovery part of the operation when accidents are likely to happen. This places considerable pressure on the captain, who has to evaluate a safe recovery. It can be a tough call because in most cases you do not know until you try, but there are ways in which the operation of the mother ship can aid the process of tender recovery.

Like the yacht sector, there are two main methods of launch and recovery used commercially and in the military: the crane/davit launch and the slipway launch. The former tends to be used in the commercial sector because it requires little or no modification to the mother ship. The military, however, are moving towards slipway launch and recovery as new ships enter service and today even quite small patrol craft have a slipway launch system built into the stern.

SLIPWAY LAUNCH SYSTEMS The primary advantages to a slipway launch and recovery are that they can be done when

the ship is underway and they are generally quicker and more effective. The problem is that the slipway can take up a lot of valuable space within the hull or on the deck on smaller vessels. Compared with yachts, the designers are less concerned with the aesthetics and more with the effectiveness of the system.

On smaller vessels, the boat is usually carried on board in an angled recess in the deck where it sits snugly, usually just below deck level. The angled stowage is fitted with rollers on the slipway and a transom gate, which closes off the stowage area when the boat is not in use, providing protection, particularly in following seas. This gate is operated hydraulically, and it may hinge down to form an extension of the slipway, which allows the boat to slide directly into the water and clear of the mother ship.

During recovery the boat is driven directly onto the slipway at a fair speed so that it ends up half clear of the water. The

engines are kept running ahead until the winch line is attached and tightened. This is the most critical part of the operation, and you can use a temporary line to get the boat clear of the water, which allows time for the permanent line to be attached. When launching, simply let go of the hoist line and the boat slides stern first down the ramp into the water – with the ship moving ahead, it is immediately clear.

The advantages of this ramp system are that launch and recovery can be carried out successfully in quite difficult conditions because by steaming ahead, the mother ship creates an effective lee at the stern and tends to smooth out the water in this area. It does require skill to aim the boat at the slipway on recovery and the consequences of a miss could be quite serious, depending on the layout at the stern, and if the ship is pitching, there is always the risk of the end of the slipway coming clear of the water at a critical moment during the boat approach.

While launching is mostly straightforward, teamwork and skill is required to effect a recovery in adverse conditions. Various systems have been developed to help smooth the recovery and avoid the need to attach the hoist wire until the boat is clear of the water and more secure. The large German lifeboats that have slipways for small rescue boats have an endless chain system that rotates and can engage automatically with a connection hook on the keel of the boat, to bring the boat at least partially up the slipway on recovery. Alternatively, a system that temporarily holds the boat in place on the slipway while the winch wire is attached is a possible solution, and there is considerable scope for innovation here if the recovery is to be safer and more effective.

Another advantage of a slipway launch and recovery is that the crew is on board throughout the operation, meaning the engine can be running as the boat is launched so that it is immediately ready to go. Starting the RIB engine out of the water requires specialist facilities to maintain

→ A tender bowsed into the ship's side prior to launch

engine cooling. It is also essential that any water-lubricated bearings in the propulsion system are replaced with more suitable bearings that can run when out of the water. Water-jet propulsion is also used almost exclusively on these slipway launched RIBs so that there are no protrusions below the bottom of the boat that could be damaged by the slipway. To run an engine out of the water, the water pumps need to be capable of running dry, so specialist pumps need to be fitted to replace the conventional pumps which have rubber impellers.

It is essential that the slipway stowage recess is made self-draining to reduce the likelihood of retaining large quantities of water, which could affect the stability of the mother ship. Simple large drains in the transom are the answer, usually closed off by outside flap valves.

On larger ships the slipway may be below decks and provision needs to be made for the recovery crew who let go of the boat and pass the lines on recovery. As in all launch and recovery procedures, teamwork is necessary for a slipway system to be effective.

CRANE AND DAVIT LAUNCH SYSTEMS

Cranes or davits are the alternative professional launch and recovery system. There are two schools of thought regarding davit or crane launches, the first suggesting that it is best to have the RIB tender alongside the ship and lower or hoist from there, and the second to have it away from the ship's side during the operation. In the first situation, having the RIB against the side of the ship stabilises it. Furthermore,

it cannot rotate on a single hoist and the amount it can swing as the ship rolls is reduced. However, if the boat does swing away from the ship's side, it can impact when it returns.

Launching and hooking on away from the ship's side does reduce this risk of side impact, but it can make the release of the hook more difficult and the coxswain requires greater skill to hold the boat in position. The boat can also spin under the hoist, so it will have to be stabilised before it can be stowed.

On balance the first method probably has the least risk because the boat is more controlled and the swinging in and out as the ship rolls can be reduced by using a tricing line around the hoist.

The RIB rescue boats that are required to be carried on board most passenger

168

↓↓ A man-overboard RIB
on a passenger ship

↓↓ A sophisticated
wave-compensating davit

→ A complex davit system for
launching a large RIB tender
on a Coast Guard vessel

RIB HANDLING

ships today can pose a particular problem for launch and recovery. They are usually davit-launched and the problem stems from the height at which the launch has to take place. Stowage can be as much as 15 metres above the waterline and once the launching operation starts there is nothing to control the movement of the boat hanging from the davit wire as it descends, increasing the risk of damage to both craft. It may be possible to get some level of control by attaching a painter to the RIB, which will at least stop it swinging, but combine this difficulty with a crew who are not practised in the operation and who are probably not familiar with small-boat operations, and it can be a high-risk scenario.

I developed one of the first systems in which the davit arm carrying the weight of the RIB was supplemented by a secondary arm that controlled the movement of the boat as it came inboard or was swung

out. Any tender on a single point hoist will swing about and twist due to the rolling and pitching of the ship, and it can require considerable crew numbers to provide the manpower to control this with ropes. The critical part of this control is during the transition from the stowage to the water in the davit when the boat is lowered down the ship's side, which will help to stabilise the RIB tender.

There are now several further davit systems on the market that have secondary arms to control the movement of the tender during launch and recovery, and these reduce the chance of damage to the RIB. Another type of davit system has the lifting frame on the tender lock into the davit head so that it cannot move or swing as the mother ship rolls.

It is normal when launching the boat to have the mother ship with headway on so that the dynamic stability of the ship is

improved and the rolling reduced. When the RIB hits the water it will then be carried aft. However, unless there is a quick on-load release for the hoist wire, it can become impossible to release the hook as the boat is carried aft due to the weight staying on the hoist. The solution is to have a boat rope led forward, which will hold the RIB in place while the hoist is released. If the boat rope is made fast right in the bow of the RIB, as is often the case, it will tend to bind the bow into the ship and make it harder to get the craft away from the ship's side when it is released. It is much better to make the boat

rope fast to a point off the centre line on the turn of the bow, which will not only allow the boat to lie much better alongside, but it will be easier to sheer the boat away when leaving. Small techniques such as these can make the job of launching much easier.

The same technique is used when recovering the tender with a davit hoist, but now the crew is faced with attaching the hook by hand rather than just pulling a lever to let it go, as in launching. More and more RIB tenders are now fitted with a central single point lift where the hoist hook connects directly into a dedicated

→ Showing how a boat rope can be rigged for a tender with the ring rope for bringing it inboard once the tender is clear

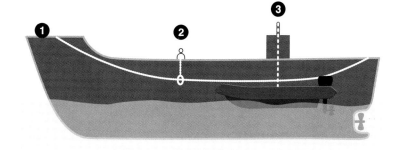

rigid fitting on board. Indeed, there may be just a ring on the hoist wire and the actual 'hook' is included in the on-board fitting. A ring or hook that is fitted with handles can help the person doing the hooking on to keep his fingers out of danger, but it is never easy on a RIB that is bouncing around alongside the ship. It becomes even harder when the attachment to the RIB is by means of webbing slings attached to fixed points in the hull. In that case, you'll need both hands – one to lift the ring and one to guide the hook – and the risks are multiplied as you could get caught when the slings snap tight. Therefore, a fixed hoisting point is always safer, but this is still a high-risk operation. Due to these risks, I developed a hook-on system that is semi-automatic, allowing the crew to keep well clear when the connection is made.

The alternative to a davit launch system is a crane. This gives the ship more flexibility in that the crane can be used for other purposes and is not dedicated to boat launch (which is the case with a davit launch). Crane launch systems may use a hydraulic knuckle or extending boom crane. The problem, however, is that once the boat is hoisted out of its stowage on the single point lift of the crane, it can swing in all directions and ropes from the boat are required to try and reduce this swinging and the risk of damage to both craft. Lightweight RIBs can be controlled by using ropes, but this does require increased manpower for the launch and recovery operation, something not always available with the limited crew on board some of these vessels.

With the heavier rigid inflatable, control by manpower becomes more difficult and the only satisfactory solution is a fully integrated launch and recovery system that keeps the movement of the boat firmly under control, whatever antics the mother ship is going through. One such system has a metal frame attached to the head of the crane, and once the boat is lifted from its stowage, it engages to this frame, thus preventing all except controlled movement until the boat is swung out over the side, lowered out of the frame and into the water. Once over, the boat can be kept close into the ship's side to control its movement to a considerable degree. The lowering of the boat should be as rapid as possible to reduce the time it is freely suspended in the air. Similarly, on recovery, the hoist wire is hooked on and the boat hoisted clear of the water, where it engages with the frame on the crane and is then under full control while it is transferred from the ship's side into its stowage. The frame can be rotated under hydraulic power so that the heading of the boat can be varied to match up with the stowage. Such a system provides a very practical solution to the problems of launch and recovery and makes the whole operation controllable by one crane driver.

SLING SYSTEMS With the recognised dangers associated with flexible slings, there is a move towards the use of what might be termed 'rigid slings', which are metal tubular frames constructed in the boat with the lifting point at their apex. A rigid sling is usually fitted with a quick-release connector, which is controlled from inside the boat, allowing the coxswain to release the lifting wire when he sees fit (reducing the likelihood of any lifting apparatus falling on his head, as could be the case with flexible slings). For recovery, the crewman first gets hold of the lifting wire and its hook with one hand as the boat comes alongside, leaving him with the other hand free to hold on to the lifting frame. In this way he is more fully in control of the situation and can clip the hook in quickly to allow hoisting to begin.

The less time the RIB tender spends alongside the mother ship once it has been launched or is being recovered the better, because it is always vulnerable in this position. The mother ship will normally have headway on when the launch and recovery operation is taking place, helping to reduce the motion and increasing control when the RIB is coming alongside for the recovery operation.

LAUNCH, RECOVERY AND TRANSPORTATION

⇓⇓ Large military RIBs being launched by trailer

During recovery, it is probably adequate for the helmsman to hold the boat alongside using engine power while the crewman hooks in the recovery wire, but such a system may not always work for launching. Here, as soon as the boat is launched it will tend to drift astern because of the headway of the mother ship, and unless the lifting wire is released quickly the boat can turn broad side on and be pulled along sideways by the lifting wire, creating a situation which can rapidly worsen unless prompt action is taken. Ideally – for the launching operation at least – a painter should be run out from the bow to a point well forward of the launching point, which will serve to hold the boat in position alongside while the hoist wire is being disconnected. Such a system is essential if a quick-release hook is not used, but even with the hook it is a good safety precaution to use a painter in this way. In fact, it is essential if the engine of the boat cannot be started until it is in the water, as is often the case with outboards. The painter can be taken back on board the mother ship when it is released rather than stowed in the boat itself, which does mean that you need one more crewmember to handle it, but this is a sound and seamanlike way of boat launching anyway. Again, launching with a sling requires teamwork and an understanding of procedures if the whole operation is to run smoothly.

Other launch systems

A further launch and recovery system uses a cradle into which the RIB is driven as it comes alongside. The cradle is then simply hoisted. This removes the need to connect the falls onto the RIB, although it does require careful driving of the craft into the cradle, with an increased risk of damage to the boat.

One of the promising lines of development is to have cradle launch and recovery at the stern, somewhat like a portable slipway that can be lowered and raised. Several systems that follow this concept have been developed, although its use is yet to be expanded. However, this could be an alternative to using a slipway with a considerable saving in space on board.

I have worked extensively on the development of launch and recovery systems and one of the more interesting concepts is a system where the attachment and release of the hoist can be achieved largely automatically. Not only could it reduce considerably the risk of getting fingers or hands caught, but an automatic attachment system could be of great benefit to the expanding market for unmanned RIBs.

There is a trend for operators to buy the boat and the hoisting equipment separately and then try to marry the two together. If the whole system is to work efficiently, however, these two items need to be fully integrated. The whole system needs to be carefully planned and engineered if it is to work successfully in difficult conditions.

Launching large RIBs

The launch and recovery of tenders is one of the more risky operations carried out at sea and it needs both a well-trained crew and effective equipment if it is going to work successfully. This can become even more critical when launching large RIBs from a mother ship. The Jigsaw project in the North Sea saw the launch of 18-metre RIB rescue craft which used a twin fall davit system. Twin falls is the traditional ship's lifeboat system, but lifeboats are only designed for a one-way trip, i.e. launching. If a twin fall system is going to work, it needs a disconnecting system that releases both falls at the same time and slick work by the crew to connect the hoists on recovery, with the forward fall always connected first. Twin fall systems see frequent use in the launch of large tenders from superyachts, but here the operations are normally less critical because of the generally fine sea conditions for launch and recovery.

HANDLING THE MOTHER SHIP

We have mentioned that it can be difficult for the captain of a mother ship to decide when to launch a tender, because the critical part of the operation is in its recovery. However, the handling of the mother ship can do a lot to improve the conditions alongside during the recovery operation when the sea is rough. First you want to head into the wind at slow or moderate speed as the RIB approaches, and then slowly turn away from the wind towards the side on which the RIB is being recovered. This slow turn should be timed so that the RIB is alongside and being recovered when the ship is about 45 degrees to the wind, still with headway on. This turning of the ship will create a temporary patch of

RIB HANDLING

smoother water alongside, and it will remain there long enough to enable the recovery of the tender. It is a technique that assumes adequate sea room for the operation, and the recovery needs to be completed before the ship starts to roll with the change of wave direction, but there should be five minutes of reduced motion and improved lee.

Recovery is normally done with the ship having headway on. This reduces its tendency to roll because of dynamic stability, although the ship does create a wash. On a displacement ship, this comes away from the bow and the stern, so avoid these waves on approach, since they can cause higher disturbed waves just at the moment the RIB is slowing to come alongside. There have been several cases of RIBs capsizing when they pass through these wash waves at low speed during approach. On faster craft, such as patrol boats, the wash pattern changes at different speeds, so it pays to study the patterns before planning a recovery operation.

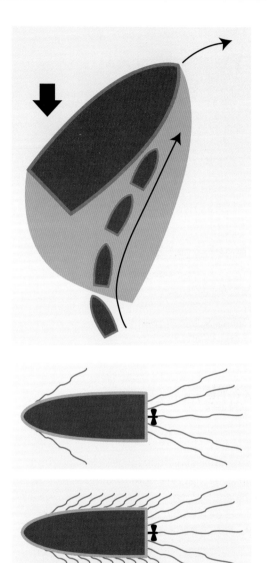

TRANSPORTATION

By car

The simplest method for transporting RIBs of up to 3 metres in length by wheel is to stow the craft on the roof of a car or truck. However, it will be the weight rather than the size of the RIB that will dictate the feasibility of this type of transportation. You can put the boat upside down directly on top of the roof, which reduces wind resistance (in fact, wind passing over the boat tends to press it down on to the roof of the car rather than lift it up). Moreover, if carried the right way up there is always the risk of the boat starting to fill with water if it rains, which will add extra weight and stress to both the boat and the car (if you use this

method of transportation, ensure the drain plug, if there is one, is left out). Stowing upside down is not a foolproof method, however, and there will inevitably be a degree of movement, which can lead to paint scratching, particularly if there are any protruding items on the inflatable tube. Therefore, a specialist roof rack is the best solution, and this also provides you with some means of attachment for the boat. Ropes leading from the boat to the front and back of the car are also a good back-up when driving at high speed. You may also wish to take the engine off when stowing the boat on a car roof.

When you transport any type of boat in this way it is sensible to stop every hour or so to check the security of the boat and its lashings.

↓ A typical sports RIB
on its trailer

By trailer

Trailers are both an effective and popular means of transporting RIBs, and indeed for the larger sizes a trailer is the only effective means of road transport. It is easy to dismiss the road trailer as an auxiliary piece of boating equipment, but if you are to trail the boat reliably and safely, you must be prepared for quite a high investment. Costs can be as high as 20–25 per cent the overall cost of the boat, and you need to bear this mind when planning your budget.

Towing a trailer also subjects you to a considerable number of rules and regulations regarding size, weight and speed, and you need to be aware of these restrictions when on the highway. Your insurance company (whether it is your boat or car insurer) will also want to know that you are transporting the boat by road, and there will probably be additional premiums to pay on one or both of the insurances. Third-party insurance for car and trailer is mandatory.

SECURING THE BOAT TO THE TRAILER

First, you will need to modify your car with a towing hitch and a plug-in electrical system for the trailer. Second, it goes without saying that whatever type of boat you are carrying, you need to firmly secure it to the trailer. All trailer attachments should connect to the rigid part of the RIB hull. At the bow, the winch wire normally doubles up to secure the boat when towing, pulling the boat tight up into the vee notch. Use webbing straps in preference to ropes if they have to pass over the tubes so that there is less possibility of chafe, but try to avoid this altogether if you can. Take all loose gear out of the boat when you are trailing it on the road because there is always the risk that it will fly or bounce out. If you have to leave anything in the boat, ensure it is firmly lashed in place and can't rattle around. A cover helps to secure loose items and also prevents any dirt flying off the road getting on to your RIB.

Take care to ensure the RIB is balanced correctly on the trailer to avoid too much downward force on the towing hitch; too great a force and the handling of the car will be affected, particularly when going downhill. While the trailer should be front-heavy, you ought to be able to lift it quite easily when the boat is on board, meaning there is a weight of around 13kg on the hitch. If there's any more than this, the RIB needs to be moved aft on the trailer; less and it will have to be moved forward. If the required change in balance is not too great, it can often be achieved by moving fuel tanks or other items of equipment to a different stowage place inside the boat. Any change in the position of the boat on the

RIB security

*Theft of RIBs is on the increase and it
becomes even more likely when the boat is
out of the water and on its trailer. You may
think that locking the trailer so it can't be
moved is enough, but some enterprising
thieves move the boat from the trailer and
to their own. Therefore, ensure the boat is
fully secured to your trailer when it is not
in use.*

trailer will almost certainly mean changing
the adjustment of the supports. Where
rubber rollers on the trailer support the rigid
part of the hull, it should not be possible to
turn any of them with the RIB in position;
however, they should all turn when the boat
is moved on the trailer.

When you have determined the final
position of the RIB on the trailer, make
sure than it is well-supported and that the
supports are properly adjusted, since the
boat probably suffers more stress and strain
when being towed by road than it ever will
out at sea.

DURING TOWING When you are towing,
think about doing everything at about half the
speed that you would during normal driving.
Allow more time for braking and turning, and
if you are on the motorway, remember that
your vehicle is now more than twice as long
than without the tow. Regulations limit speed
when towing and in Britain the limit is 50mph
on single carriageways with an additional
10mph on dual carriageways. You do not have

access to the outside lane of motorways
when towing.

Check the allowable towing weight in
your vehicle handbook: if the trailer has
brakes the weight will be around 85 per cent
of the weight of the vehicle; without trailer
brakes you are limited to 50 per cent. Your
driving licence will also need to encompass
towing, particularly if towing a larger trailer.

Larger RIBs should be towed with the
outboard(s) fitted in place and where they
extend beyond the limits of the back of the
boat, you need to cover them with a plastic
bucket or bag to reduce the chances of
injury in a rear-end collision. Finally, you
should afix a number plate and light board,
which must be identical to and synchronised
with the vehicle's lights.

If the boat is well balanced on the
trailer as described above, it should tow
comfortably without any snaking about.
If snaking is still a problem you can fit a
stabiliser connection between the trailer and

the vehicle, which increases the friction and the resistance to turning, hopefully reducing the chance of unplanned movements. Check that the electric light cable does not drag on the ground and the braking system, cables and hinges are all lubricated to ensure free movement. Unless they are sealed, the wheel bearings should also be greased, particularly after a long winter of inaction

and each time the trailer has been in the water.

This all makes trailing a boat seem like an arduous operation, but once you get into the routine it is quite straightforward, plus it opens up access to a wide variety of new cruising areas. Allow plenty of time when trailing your boat around the country and if you plan to take the boat abroad, make sure you meet your destination's national regulations (beyond towing, this also applies to temporary importation of the boat and its operation in foreign waters). In general, towing rules in other countries are much the same as in Britain; however, clubs and organisations such as the RYA can assist with the particular and often changing requirements of international destinations. There is often a width restriction for towing boats, which is a shade under 3 metres, and with a large RIB you may be able to overcome this by letting down the air tubes and folding them in. It is not a happy or tidy solution, so you could always resort to wide vehicle status, which in some countries can restrict the times at which you can travel.

LAUNCHING FROM A TRAILER
Towing a boat by road is one thing, launching it off a slipway is another, and the trailers required for these two operations are rarely compatible. Corrosion, particularly in the wheel bearings and the electrical system, is a major problem. Modern trailers are well-sealed against the attacks of seawater and can safely be used to launch the boat down a slipway as well as on the road. On a shallow gradient slipway you may have to go a long way into the water to get an adequate

depth for the boat to float off; one option is to use a break-back trailer that has a double chassis. By removing a pin, the rear section of the trailer hinges down to form a steeper ramp for launching and recovering the boat. On a slipway with a reasonable angle, this type of trailer also allows for the boat to be launched without the trailer wheels entering the water. It can also make recovery easier, although you do need to factor in the extra weight of such trailers.

The usual galvanised trailer chassis will resist corrosion pretty well and shouldn't cause any trouble. It is the wheel bearings that can suffer most from immersion in water, particularly salt water, and this corrosion can start in a very short space of time, which could lead to bearing failure on the road. The ideal is to launch the boat without putting the wheels in the water,

but in most cases this is not a practical solution. Water ingress shouldn't be a problem with modern, fully sealed bearings, but seals often get old and worn through neglect or when using the trailer on a sandy beach. Apart from regular checking of the seal if you can see it, bearings only need to be stripped and packed with fresh grease once a year. If the wheel bearings are fitted with grease nipples, use these to pump fresh grease into the bearings every time the trailer is immersed, in order to force out any water.

Road trailers seldom operate effectively over open beaches, even if you leave your car behind and manhandle the trailer over the beach. For beach work, whether it is over sand or gravel, you need wider tyres with lower pressure than you would for road use, but even then trying to manhandle a boat

over soft sand or gravel can be a difficult operation, and it only really becomes practical if the boat is relatively small and light. In that case, you might consider it easier to carry the boat rather than to

wheel it across, and the success of such an operation will depend on how firm the conditions are on the beach and how many people you have available. Obviously if you are towing your vehicle with a four-wheel drive and it is permitted, you may have more flexibility in taking the vehicle on to the beach. If so, consider fitting a towing hitch on the front of the vehicle as well as the rear. You will find launching using a front towing hitch a much easier proposition than trying to peer over your shoulder at what is happening behind you.

A variety of specialised launching trailers have been developed for professional use, with rescue boats in particular making use of them. Professionals using road transport to get their boat close to the scene of an incident require trailers that provide a simple, smooth launching operation, and the tilting trailer that allows one to adjust the angle provides a useful solution.

For beach launch and recovery of larger

RIBs in adverse conditions the RNLI has developed a series of self-propelled trailers that use hydrostatic propulsion in each wheel. Capable of operating over both rough and soft terrain, these trailers are simply driven into the water to a depth where the engine of the boat can be started. The trailer holds the boat securely in place with its bow pointing seaward, while the engine is started and the crew is on board. The engine is then simply put into gear and the boat driven out of the trailer. The trailer has a Y-shaped chassis so that the propeller(s) are kept clear during the launching process. For recovery, a catching net is rigged in the trailer and the boat is simply driven at speed into the trailer, where the net brings it to a halt. The trailer is then driven out of the water and the boat is ready for launching again. This is a specialised type of launch and recovery system, but it does give some indication of what can be done when the circumstances demand it.

By container or air

An extreme method of RIB transportation, a standard 40ft container, is confined mainly to military and commercial use. This method can offer a safe and secure transportation system over long distances and is much cheaper than shipping an open boat. Those RIB builders having their boats built a long distance from their markets might consider container transportation, although the beam on larger RIBs is often too wide to fit the confines of a container, even with the tubes deflated.

The final challenge for transporting military RIBs is to move them by air. Here,

size and weight limitations are critical and there are now military RIBs designed specifically for air transportation, to enable them to be mobilised quickly and routed to remote areas of conflict.

SUMMARY

In all circumstances, launch and recovery is an area of RIB operation that is often too easily dismissed. The operation often tests the skills of both professional and leisure users more than handling the boat at sea, and teamwork is vital to success. There is something of a no man's land between the boat and its launching system, and often little attempt is made to harmonise the two, to the detriment of the launch and recovery operation. Therefore, time and money spent on developing the right system for the job will be well repaid in the increased efficiency and the reduced damage and wear to your craft.

9 COMMERCIAL AND MILITARY RIBS

AN IMPORTANT PART of the RIB market is that dedicated to what might be termed the serious user: the professionals who use their RIBs for a wide variety of commercial, para-military and military operations. There has been an amazing transformation of design in the application of RIBs to these challenging operations, where the RIB is now the vessel of choice rather than the exception, and it has now expanded to shore-based craft, such as pilot and patrol boats and harbour and survey craft. It is the versatility of the RIB and its stable platform when going slowly that has been responsible for this change in attitude. Para-military applications, such as police and customs boats, have been an obvious RIB application because they are required to go alongside other craft at frequent intervals. For the military, the RIB has replaced the traditional

sea boat carried on board naval ships and RIBs are now widely used by Special Forces as their interception boat of choice.

It is these commercial and military applications for RIBs that has led to the development of very sophisticated designs and to the improvements in RIB reliability that has been seen over the past 20 years, and in turn these improvements have filtered down into the leisure sector where cost can be a more critical factor. We are now seeing RIBs in larger sizes in many commercial applications, with full-size wheel houses and the ability to install a wide range of operational equipment. On the military front, the emphasis may be more on seagoing capability, but patrol RIBs are getting larger in size and because the crews have to operate on patrol for long periods, these RIBs need to be equipped with a range of crew comfort facilities.

COMMERCIAL RIBS

Pilot boats

Perhaps the ultimate accolade for the RIB is found in their use as pilot boats. This has tended to be a very conservative sector of the market because pilot boats can have a very tough operating scenario, going alongside ships in the open sea and having to provide a reliable service, often in adverse conditions. You might think that the RIB is tailor-made for this type of operation but it has taken time for the larger designs of RIBs to prove themselves capable for this role. One worry has been the risk of puncturing the tube against the rough side of ships and the fact that the tube can increase the gap that the pilot has to step across when boarding. Against this is balanced the increased safety you get with an inflatable tube, which offers a measure of security should the pilot fall during the boarding operation, by providing a very temporary safe haven between ship and boat. However, there is a trend for RIB pilot boats to use foam tubes rather than inflatable ones and this can remove some of this potential benefit.

This comparison between foam and inflatable tubes for commercial RIBs is one that will continue, and there is no easy answer for which is best. The foam tube offers the perceived benefit of greater durability in arduous use, and because the vessel can still operate even when the tube is damaged, there could be less downtime. Commercial RIBs do not want any downtime due to the unavailability

of the boat so this could be the deciding factor. If an inflatable tube is punctured, downtime is inevitable, but then how often is a tube punctured? One solution found on some pilot boats is a hybrid tube, which offers a combination of foam tubes on the section where the RIB goes alongside and an inflatable tube around the bow where it can help improve the sea-keeping. The double tube concept of a layer of foam surrounding the inflatable tube can be another compromise and indeed it is now possible to tailor commercial RIB design to give the boat the required characteristics for the particular operation it has to carry out.

One of the largest RIB pilot boats so far has been built in Australia. This 16.8-metre RIB was built by Woody Marine. Its tube is made from foam with a rubber insert that acts as the fender contact and which takes the hard wear and tear of going alongside. This RIB is based on an aluminium hull with a unique multi-chine hull shape.

Charter RIBs

RIB charter is another aspect of the commercial market, and fleets of these RIBs are often made available at major sailing and marine-related events such as the America's Cup. It is better for the organisers to charter from the fleet of RIBs that are needed for patrolling the course and for press and VIP access, rather than buy a fleet that then has to be disposed of after the event. This requirement can be fertile ground for RIB builders, but when a fleet of RIBs is required, the price has to be very competitive. The requirements range from small open RIBs up to sizeable open or wheel-house RIBs.

← A series of identical RIBs designed for patrol duties at a marine event

Passenger-carrying RIBs

RIBs are also used for carrying passengers, offering so-called 'thrill rides', or for coastal tours that embrace wildlife or offer whale watching. A RIB with inflatable tubes offers a cushioned environment for a small passenger boat and the very appearance of the boat can give confidence. The authorities tend to like RIBs as passenger boats, because of the added reserve buoyancy and stability offered by the tube, but for thrill-ride applications the seating is the critical part of the design. On a thrill ride, passengers are looking for a bit of excitement – having the boat career around at high speed is something akin to a fairground ride. However, they can only enjoy this if they are securely seated and have adequate handholds, and this has been a weakness in the design in many small passenger RIBs where operators have used

more or less standard leisure RIBs for the job. Seating needs to be well cushioned and supportive and good handholds are vital. At the same time any hard objects such as rigid hand rails or other fittings need to be removed from or protected in the passenger areas because passengers may not always remain secure in their seats in sharp manoeuvres or when the boat hits a larger-than-normal wave.

Passenger-carrying RIBs are a challenging design environment and in the future we are likely to see a move towards more dedicated designs rather than adaptations of leisure RIBs. The question of securing passengers in their seats is a thorny one and seatbelts can only be used if the seat itself is one that offers good support. One possible solution might be the type of securing found on funfair rides, where a securing arm descends once the

edges where the crew can impact if they are not secure in their seats and seating may be located close to the side windows where heads can be banged in a sideways motion of the boat (some lifeboat RIBs have adopted a form of saddle seating inside the wheel house because of this).

Handholds are still essential inside the wheel house, and present another area where improvements could be made. In most operations the crew will remains seated when underway, but in larger RIBs there can be a need to move about. Handholds should be placed so that there is at least one available in all situations when moving about the boat and these handholds do need to be strong because a crewman can put his whole weight on them if the boat takes a lurch. Handholds can also be essential on deck if the work of the boat means that the crew has to work out there at times. Indeed, the entire arrangement of a wheel-house RIB should be treated more like an open-decked RIB in many respects.

people are seated. This would need to be well-padded, since on a RIB the passengers will be going up and down and possibly sideways, and anything hard that rubs on the body could cause chafe or injury.

Wheel-house RIBs

Traditionally RIBs have been open boats but as they have got larger and been adapted to operations that demand long hours at sea, they have acquired wheel shelters and full wheel houses. The design of these has been transferred from traditional workboats but the ability of the RIB to perform better in adverse conditions has led to many designs falling short of the requirements for RIB wheel houses (I know of one RIB builder who lined his wheel-house RIBs with the sort of neoprene foam used for wetsuits to reduce the risk of hard contact). You still see sharp

You will never have the same level of visibility inside a wheel-house RIB, but designers could do a lot to improve things here. The mullions on wheel house windows have to be strong to resist the pressures of possible wave impact, but this does not mean that they have to be wide. On patrol or when operating pilot boats or lifeboats, good visibility is essential for making contact with the outside world and in many cases this is sadly lacking. In adverse conditions, such as on a lifeboat, good visibility is an essential requirement for safe operation in challenging conditions. There has to be a balance between the protection offered by a wheel house and the demands of navigation, and it is not easy to find this balance.

For many operations the wheel house is essential, particularly when long hours on patrol are required. The warmth and protection offered by the wheel house (or perhaps the air-conditioning in hot climates) will keep the crew operational for longer, but this has to be balanced by the isolation of the crew from the world outside.

↓↓ A large wheel-house RIB designed for survey and personnel transfer

↘↘ Stylish sprung saddle seating that offers very little lateral support

→ High speed RIBs designed for offshore patrol duties

SHOCK MITIGATION

Whatever the RIB application, but particularly when operating with crew, the employer has a 'duty of care' towards his employees. This duty of care means providing adequate protection for the crew to reduce the risk of injury, but with RIBs it is hard to say where that risk exists. The safest RIB is probably one that does not go to sea, but the operating environment of most RIBs is a challenging one in which one must find the balance between crew safety and getting the job done efficiently. One area where there is now a focus in RIB design is in shock mitigation, reducing the chance of injury through impact loadings as the boat operates in waves. EC legislation regarding the duty of care of boat operators towards their boat crews is focusing attention on improved seating for RIBs, but this is only a partial solution.

Seating has always been the focus of shock mitigation methods and there are a number of specialised RIB seats on the market that offer a varying degree of support and springing. There is no doubt about the effectiveness of many of these seats, and objective and subjective measurements have shown this to be the case, but installing sprung seating is only part of the story. This is a solution to a problem that has been created by both the design of the RIB and the way the boat is being operated, so why not look first of all at trying to remove or at least reduce the problem as far as possible by lessening the impacts on the hull so that they are not there to be transmitted to the crews?

What I am proposing is that a more holistic approach could offer a much better solution. If you reduce the chance of impacts occurring as the RIB makes fast progress in waves, there is less of a demand to introduce springing and other solutions to protect the crews.

The question of shock mitigation was less of a problem in the early days of RIBs because the crews had to drive their boats more gently to prevent them breaking apart. The boat was the weak part of the operation, but today that position has been reversed and the boats, engines and equipment will stand up to a great deal of rough treatment

to the point where it is the crew that has become the weak part of the operation. This may be a good safety factor in many ways but it can test crews to the limits when they are under pressure.

Hull design to reduce shock mitigation

The deep vee hull does a great job of reducing the shock loadings as a boat leaves the water and then re-enters, the vee angle of the hull providing the cushion of a more gradual re-entry. It is only when the deep vee heels over that the boat lands more on the flat of one side of the vee and loses part of its cushioning, leading to high impacts. So if you can prevent the boat heeling over or if you can prevent the boat from leaving the water when operating in waves, you will immediately reduce the shock loadings. Let's look first at the design of the hull with a view to keeping it upright.

With a deep vee hull operating at speed the lift will be focused more towards the stern when on the plane. When the hull heels over, the lower side becomes more

horizontal, generating more lift than the other side and thus helping to bring the hull back upright. However, for this extra lift to take effect and for the hull to start to right itself, it has to heel over quite a lot, perhaps 10 – 15°. The righting lift is then generated on the lower side of the hull, but this is at the expense of the cushioning of the hull that occurs when it is upright. The amount of this righting lift will reduce as the hull lifts in the water at speed, and as this extra righting lift only becomes really effective when the chine is in the water, the boat might have to heel

↓ A trio of FB Design high speed
patrol boats for the Italian customs

some way over before there is a significant
increase in righting lift. This change of angle
at the chine can develop considerable lift
as the water flow is deflected downwards.
So if we could introduce a secondary chine
or a wide, perhaps angled, spray rail closer
to the apex of the vee, this would be more
immediately effective as the hull starts to
heel and exert its lifting effect earlier. It
would reduce the chance of the boat heeling
over towards the point where what should
be the angled vee of the hull is now close to
becoming a flat surface in relation to the
water.

Another aspect of hull design that
can cause impacts is a wide chine. This
flat surface can impact the water with
considerable force, even when the boat is
upright, so that rather than having a single
wide chine, perhaps a two-stage chine
might reduce the impact loadings. As we
discussed in Chapter 3 (see page 44), there
can also be an element of bounce with RIBs
that have their tubes inflated too hard, which

can make the ride harsher. This can result
in impacts in waves when the boat heels
over and the tube bounces, causing quite
violent lateral movements. This can be
easily solved by reducing the air pressure
in the tube, but the cause first needs to be
identified.

Having a fine entry at the bow would
enable the hull to slice through waves
rather than riding over them, and this could
help to reduce the pitching motions of the
hull. It would also reduce the chance of the
hull 'fling' off the top of a wave, which can
create heavy impact loadings when landing.
There are some wave-piercing designs
being tested and maybe these will help to
smooth the path of fast RIBs, but a narrow
hull will tend to heel over more readily than
a wider hull. The use of the latest generation
of shock mitigating sprung seating may help
to reduce the impacts, but the extra weight
of these seats, which can be mounted quite
high up in the boat, will make the boat less
stable and more sensitive to heeling.

Driving to reduce shock mitigation

While modifications to the hull design could be used to reduce the chances of the boat heeling over in a seaway or otherwise reduce the chance of wave impact, the way the boat is driven is also an important factor. There is particular pressure for rescue RIBs to move fast under pressure, so how do you they do this while reducing wave impact?

This is where you need to use the two main controls, the wheel and the throttle, in a sensitive way (*see* Chapters 4 and 5 for further information). It needs a very

delicate hand on the throttle, plus the ability to read the waves to achieve this level of harmony, and this is a skill that generally only experienced coxswains acquire. The gung-ho driver who bangs and crashes his way through the waves trying to impress should have no place in serious commercial or military operations, while the considerate driver will probably make just as fast progress and still have a crew who are ready and capable of performing when they reach the destination.

COMMERCIAL AND MILITARY RIBS

Seating to reduce shock mitigation

Even the best driver is not going to be able to maintain the concentration needed to avoid all wave impact, and the more this can be minimised the better shape the crew will be in to carry out their tasks. Dr Johan Ullman was one of the first people to explore the problem of shock mitigation in a scientific way, and he came up with sprung seating, a design that was at least a start down the road of improvement. Today, there are three main types of seating to be considered for shock mitigation:

1 saddle seating, that may be strung or unsprung;

2 the more conventional type of sprung seat;

3 the supportive seat that may have a sprung squab.

Before looking at these different types, we should consider the merits of using mechanical springing systems or foam as the means of allowing the occupant some form of shock absorption.

MECHANICAL SPRINGING SYSTEMS

Despite Ullman promoting this system, I have tried a lot of types of mechanical spring seats and I am not a fan. This is because, unless the damping system is carefully tuned, you can find yourself going up when you should be coming down because the springing is not in tune with the varying movement of the boat. Having said that, some of the modern sprung saddle seating is much better and the designers are starting to realise that it is not so much the softer impacts that need absorbing but the really hard bangs. Therefore, you feel the seat 'give' when there is a hard bang but then they can 'bottom out' once the limit of the springing is reached. The springing itself does not seem to be progressive, and it should ultimately be stiff enough to avoid terminal bang.

Damping out RIB impact is never going to be easy because of the huge variation in the direction and strength of such impact, and in addition, with mechanical springing there will always be the question of wear and tear as the equipment gets older. This is why I propose that it is best to stop the impacts before they occur, or at least minimise them with improved hull design and driving techniques.

FOAM SYSTEMS

The alternative to mechanical springing is foam, and this has been the cushioning of choice for many builders because it is relatively cheap. However, foam has had a poor reputation, mainly, I think, because of a poor choice of the foam used. There are so many different types of foam available these days that it is

↓ Good lateral support on these fixed seats.
Note the lowering squab that allows sitting or
standing driving positions

↓ Sprung deck covering that offers a degree
of shock mitigation when standing

193

COMMERCIAL AND MILITARY RIBS

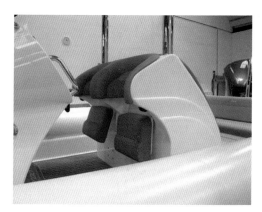

now possible to pick the right foam for the job. Obviously, the foam has to be closed cell so that it does not absorb water and what I propose for RIB seating is a form of progressive foam with maybe three layers, each having different characteristics. The top layer – that in contact with the body – would be a relatively soft foam about 2cm thick, which would deform under normal bodyweight. Its main function would be to keep the person in the seat comfortable. The middle layer would be much stiffer, perhaps starting to deform under loadings of around five Gs, which is somewhere near the point at which the impact starts to hurt the body. This would be a thicker layer and this would absorb most of the normal RIB impacts. The final bottom layer would be very stiff, perhaps starting to deform at around eight to ten Gs, and this would provide the final impact absorption to protect the body from the worst of the impacts. In theory, with such a seat there would be no bottoming out and the body would be protected progressively from even the worst of the impacts.

Then we come to the types of seating available. Having seen what a difference

saddle seating made in the early days of RIBs, this is still a viable solution, but it only offers limited support against the lateral movement of the boat. As the vee of the hulls of fast boats has got deeper, so there is a greater tendency for the boat to heel over further, and this has generated much more lateral movement, which can cause as much discomfort and possible whiplash injury as the vertical impacts. The saddle seat helps to secure the bottom half of the body, but most of the bodyweight is concentrated in the upper half of the body, which remains unsupported (see pages 90-91, for more information). You can protect against this to a certain extent by having widely-spaced handholds that can help with lateral support, although you rarely see these on RIBs, so a seat with good side support might be a more effective solution.

On smaller RIBs there may not be space for side support seating and the saddle seat remains the best option, but on the larger RIBs now being used for many rescue and military operations side-supportive seating is viable. In its simplest form this seating provides support around the hips, but in a

← This Dutch lifeboat RIB has the tube extending around the stern to give extra buoyancy in following seas

Side support seating is now being offered by many seat manufacturers, which is perhaps a recognition of the problem of lateral movement, but it does add to seat weight. A sprung seat can weigh as much as 15 – 20kg, with much of it mounted quite high in the boat. Add in the weight of the crew, who are also mounted quite high, and you have a considerable weight high in the boat, which can accentuate the lateral movements, increase the shock loadings and possibly make the boat more prone to capsize in adverse conditions.

more developed form there is support around the shoulders as well. Some seats of this type have a squab that is sprung, which can be raised or lowered under electric control so that there is the option of standing or sitting, or a bit of both.

Finally, there is the sprung seating that is a bit like the seating offered to truck drivers. This is probably where much of this type of seating originated, and while they are often adjustable in terms of rake and height, they

↑ Supportive seating with sprung squabs that can be lowered when a standing position is required

→ A wider span of handholds can give the required lateral support with saddle seating

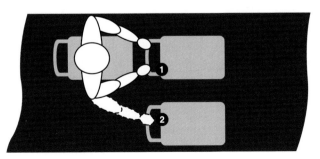

⬇⬇ A Dutch all-weather
RIB lifeboat

⬇⬇ A RIB boarding boat stowed
on board a Spanish patrol boat

⬇ Sprung saddle seating that
only offers a very limited amount
of lateral support

195

rarely offer adequate side support and the springing may not be suitable to absorb RIB impacts. Such seating is often installed as passenger seating in pilot boats and other RIBs that have to accommodate passengers, but here at least there can be the option of fitting a seatbelt. A full four-point seatbelt can be a great addition to a seat for passengers because it reduces the need to constantly hang on against the movement of the boat. Good padding is needed on the shoulder straps because of chafe when the boat is going up and down.

MILITARY RIBS

The RIB has opened up many new avenues in military thinking and it has become a military workhorse. When you see photos of military operations involving piracy, illegal immigration or smuggling, there is usually a RIB present. The military is moving towards larger RIBs, which is putting pressure on the launch and recovery systems, meaning some of the newer military systems are at the forefront of development.

RIBs for the military do not normally differ a lot from other rescue and commercial RIBs, except perhaps in the mountings for guns and, in some cases, ballistic protection built into the sides. There is the same demand for reliability and performance found in most modern RIBs and, of course, the colour tends to be grey or black. New to the military market, however, is the demand for higher and higher performance, which has two purposes. First, if you are going to catch your adversaries you need a boat that is faster than them and second, with a fast boat you have a greater chance of using the element of surprise when trying to stop them. Short of firing on them, trying to stop another boat at sea and board it when its occupants do not want you to is extremely difficult, and the element of surprise is the strongest weapon you have to achieve this, particularly if it is just a single boat trying to stop another boat.

The element of surprise

There are many techniques for achieving the element of surprise, and some of the techniques included below have come from training exercises I have carried out with the US Coast Guard and the Singapore Police Coast Guard. For security reasons I cannot give a lot away on interception techniques, but there are some instances that are based in common sense.

If you are trying to stop another boat, you will have a much better chance of getting close without them knowing if you come up astern. In any fast boat the driver and crew will be looking ahead for perhaps 90 per cent of the time because that is where the waves are approaching and that is where they are headed. By coming up astern the noise of their engine will hopefully drown out any noise from yours and you could be lost from view in any rooster tail or wake they are throwing up. You could be virtually alongside before they even become aware of you.

← Hoses can make life difficult for RIBs trying to intercept a ship

↓ Night vision can help on night time interceptions

A helicopter can assist the interception by hovering overhead, which creates a good diversion. When you come up astern and you want to stop them, one very bold method if they are outboard powered is to simply run up over them from astern!

Even if your adversaries see you coming up astern they will almost certainly start turning. In that case, you go for the side that they are turning into, with every chance that you can be alongside them before they can fully react. If they are aware of you early on, you will struggle to get alongside with just a single boat because they can always turn away from

you before you can come alongside.

At night it is much easier to employ stealth as you can approach with no lights on. If you power alongside, make sure you do it very positively and force your boat alongside the other boat to hold it there. Boarding at speed can be exciting and you really need to force the RIB alongside, or a gap can quickly open up, and it is safer for any boarding crew if the RIB is held firmly alongside. Switch on all the lights and sound the horn, which will help to disorientate your adversaries as the boarding is done.

There is every chance that any vessel being boarded will have a higher freeboard

→ A large RIB slung below a helicopter for rapid transit to an operation

↓↓ A RIB being launched from inside a military cargo plane

than the RIB, and this can add to the dangers and difficulties when boarding. There are various bits of equipment and techniques for getting up a ship's side from a boat, but it is never an easy operation and the element of surprise is usually long gone. Nearly every boarding situation will be different and the tactics depend on the speed of the other vessel and its willingness to stop. Having said that, there are a huge number of boarding operations done in the open sea without the pressure of having to make the other vessel stop. Operations such as fishery protection, customs and immigration boardings, pilots and even harbour patrols can all entail boarding at sea and this is where the RIB comes into its own. In fact, it can make the leisure side of RIBs seem quite tame by comparison. No wonder so many leisure RIBs try to emulate military RIBs in style and performance.

Disabling adversaries with an armed boat

If guns are involved in any stopping or boarding operation it may not be necessary to get so close, but trying to fire guns accurately from a rapidly moving boat is extremely difficult. You want to aim to disable the boat, which will mean either the engine if it is in sight or possibly the helm console. If two boats are being used for an armed boarding, it is vital that each boat has its own arc of fire that the other boat does not enter.

CODES AND STANDARDS

The military can make their own rules and set their own standards of RIB design, construction and equipment, but in the commercial sector there are codes that apply standards. Most commercial RIBs would come under the Brown Code of practice developed by the MCA, which is a merger of many earlier standards and covers workboats and passengers boats that carry not more than 12 passengers and are up to 24 metres in length. There are separate codes for open rescue boats up to 15 metres in length, for what are termed 'Small Passenger Craft High-Speed Experience Rides', which means 'thrill rides', and for pilot vessels. There are also variations in standards depending on how far offshore or from a safe haven the vessel operates. For RIBs, the construction standards are mainly those established by the various SOLAS standards developed by IMO, which are internationally recognised. These include a drop test of the completed boat, which is a pretty good way to check that the boat will stand up to hard use.

The requirements of these codes are very comprehensive but in general they leave enough flexibility to introduce new concepts and ideas. They cover everything from the stability of the vessel to its equipment, and there are specific requirements for RIBs in many areas. These standards could be a useful guide for many leisure RIB builders as well, and the fact that many builders use the same basic designs for both leisure and commercial use suggests that there are a lot of RIB builders out there that set high standards of safety and security. After all, it is in the interests of any RIB builder to set high standards so that there is no comeback if there is an accident. These days any marine accident involving personal injury or death is investigated, and while most accidents in the commercial sector can be attributed to operator error, the standards of design, construction and outfitting are coming under more scrutiny.

10 RESCUE RIBS

RIBS WERE ORIGINALLY developed for rescue work and today they are widely used in many aspects of rescue at sea. In its simplest form, a rescue RIB is used to monitor and patrol fleets of sailing dinghies where the risk of capsize can be quite high in a fresh breeze. The RNLI and many other rescue organisations have embraced the RIB concept for a generation of small, fast rescue boats and in the North Sea oil arena, RIBs are used as the primary rescue system on the stand-by vessels that have to patrol at every installation. SOLAS requires many classes of ships, including passenger ships, to have a fast rescue boat and other ships have what is affectionately known as the DOTY boat (Department of Trade rescue boat) as a means of escape (although these tend to be inflatables rather than RIBs).

In many of these applications for rescue, there is no mandatory requirement for the rescue boat to be a RIB and there are many hard-hulled craft out there that could do the job, particularly in the sailing club rescue boat role. In the larger sizes of rescue boat/ lifeboat, the RIB is widely used, although the foam tube is often specified in preference to an inflatable one, mainly because of the perceived reduced maintenance. The options, therefore, are numerous, but the RIB reigns supreme as the rescue boat of choice for those who take their rescue seriously.

It is easy to follow the philosophy that if you provide the rescue boat the job is done, but that is only the start. Rescue at sea is one of the most challenging scenarios you can encounter. On any leisure cruise, you head off to sea with your passage plan done, you know where you are heading and how to get there, you are aware of the weather and tides. With rescue work, however, there is no plan – you are heading into the unknown and you have no control over the weather conditions and very little

warning. This is where experience counts: you have to work out how to handle the situation in hand, you need to know the capabilities of your rescue RIB and you need a crew who know their job. It is a tough role, but most of the time it works.

Even that sailing club rescue boat needs experience. You may spend hours patrolling the dinghy fleet in relative calm, but along comes a sudden squall and half the fleet capsizes. The situation is made far more urgent when the water is cold and survival time in the water is reduced. Now you are one boat trying to cope in a treacherous situation. Most dinghy sailors practise self-righting of their dinghies, so if you are faced with this emergency, prioritise locating the sailors who have been separated from their boats, and the dinghies that remain upside down, since there may be crew trapped underneath. In shallow water the dinghy mast may be stuck on the bottom and the crew may need help to get the boat upright. There are so many eventualities, and you need to work hard to attend to them. A radio is a vital piece of rescue boat equipment, since you'll need back-up as fast as possible.

RESCUES FROM THE SHORE

Approaching a casualty in the water

In making the approach to a water-bound casualty you need to be conscious all the time about that turning propeller at the stern of your boat. If you have a choice, head upwind. Stop the engine when the casualty is close to the bow and then allow the bow to pay off towards the casualty. The problem with outboards and stern drives is that you lose steering when you take the engine out of gear, so you may need to keep the engine in gear up until the moment when the casualty is actually alongside and the crew has got hold of them. This calls for fine judgement,

↓ Rescue RIBs often operate in close cooperation with helicopters on rescue missions

particularly in rough seas when just keeping the casualty in sight can be a difficult. If you don't get alongside the casualty at the first attempt, turn tight round for the next go. Always turn the bow towards the casualty as this will take the propeller at the stern away from them. Again, fine judgement is required to avoid accidents. Keep as close to the casualty as you reasonably can because there is nothing worse for a casualty to see a rescue boat heading away from them, apparently into the blue. I have been on both sides of rescue operations and it is a nervous time for both the casualty and the rescuer.

There is a tendency for a casualty to assume he is rescued when he sees a rescue boat approaching but he is not safe until he is out of the water or, better still, on shore.

Pulling a casualty from the water

You might think that pulling a person out of the water would be easy, but this can be one of the most demanding jobs for a rescue boat, and it is one that needs practice. During a rescue, a RIB's stability is one of the factors in its favour because much of the weight will be on one side of the boat. While in other crafts this could cause instability, in a RIB that side of the boat lowers, making recovery easier. If the casualty is active, even better.

If there are two people in the rescue boat, grab the person under the arms and literally heave them on board. You can try ducking them first and the 'bounce' can help the first part of the lift, but casualties tend not to be too receptive to this approach. When the casualty is unconscious or unable to help themselves, the task becomes all the more challenging, since you now have a dead weight to lift. Medical advice is to recover the casualty in a horizontal position. The crew at the casualty's head have an almost impossible task of lifting, while at the leg end it is relatively easy. There are several proprietary systems that can be carried on board a rescue boat to help with this situation, most of them entailing passing a line or a lattice under the casualty and then pulling up on the outboard side to roll or parbuckle the casualty into the boat. This is where the soft, rounded tube of the RIB helps because it creates a relatively smooth path for getting the casualty on board.

Once on board, the temptation to rush the casualty to shore should be resisted, since the priority at this stage is to assess his condition. If he is conscious, find a comfortable place for him, preferably protected from the wind, perhaps wedging him into position with lifejackets. Check for any apparent injuries before heading, preferably at a gentle speed, for harbour. If the casualty is unconscious and not breathing, it is vital to administer first aid before anything else. However, it may be possible to drive the boat at slow speed towards the shore while carrying out the resuscitation procedure. The value of a radio in these conditions cannot be over-emphasised and contact with the Coastguard will usually produce a helicopter or lifeboat at short notice to assume responsibility of the casualty.

These procedures all sound so easy when you see them on paper but in real life they can be very challenging. On a small rescue RIB, such as one in use at a sailing club, deck space is limited, which can cause problems when attempting a resuscitation (you may need to hold the casualty on the tube, and it pays to take special care in rough seas when the boat may be rolling around). Bulky lifejackets and loose clothing can also make recovery more difficult, although they at least offer options for gripping the casualty (wetsuits present particular difficulties for rescuers). One way in which you can avoid pulling the casualty on to the boat is to use the landing craft RIB, which has a ramp that can be lowered at the bow. This allows the rescuer to slide the casualty up the lowered slipway and bring them aboard horizontally (they are also kept well away from the propellers).

Towing rescues

When towing with a RIB, the first challenge is to get a line across to the casualty. This is a relatively easy operation if you are trying to rescue a yacht with a broken down engine out in the open sea, as the RIB can usually

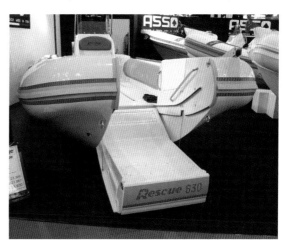

↓↓ The tow line and towing bitts on this rescue RIB

↓↓ The crew are protected by this net in case the tow line should part and spring back

↘ This amphibious Sealegs RIB can operate on land and water

go alongside or close by to pass the line. It becomes more of a challenge when the casualty is a vessel that has gone aground. Here you might want to get the entire crew off rather than simply attempt to rescue the casualty, but towing can achieve both aims so, again, this is where good judgement is called for. Getting close to a casualty in among rocks or in shallow breaking seas can put the rescue RIB at risk, so you might want to use an anchor to hold the RIB up into the waves and then back down by paying out the anchor line. This enables you to hold the RIB at any point in the operation and re-assess the situation before backing down further. It also gives you a means of securing the RIB while you are passing the tow line across and it increases the control gained from manoeuvring the RIB under engine alone, when you could end up joining the casualty on the rocks.

Other emergencies

On dedicated rescue RIBs, such as those used by many rescue services, the crews have to be prepared for a wide variety of rescue operations that might include casualty recovery from the water, towing, fire, medical emergencies and searching. On a small RIB it is not possible to carry equipment to deal effectively with every eventuality, so the rescue boat represents the first line of defence with the more specialised equipment to follow. There is a tendency for rescue RIBs to end up looking a bit like Christmas trees, carrying equipment for every conceivable emergency, but this has to be resisted if the RIB is going to be effective. However, in most cases the rescue boat will cope.

Perhaps the most challenging rescue situation is a search, whether it be for an overdue boat or a person who has fallen overboard. Here the main problem is likely to be the datum point from which to start the search, which is rarely accurate. A RIB rescue boat does not allow you the possibility of spreading out the charts to organise the search, although some electronic chart systems have search patterns built in, which can help with the planning. Any search, therefore, is likely to

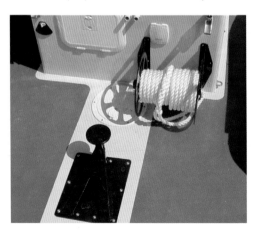

→ A large RIB lifeboat towing a cargo ship

be co-ordinated from the shore and usually involves more than one vessel, meaning the rescue RIB is more likely to be searching in a particularly tight search area. This suits the RIB, since its low vantage point reduces the possibility of seeing a survivor in the water more than 200m away.

One possible scenario that both dedicated rescue RIBs and leisure RIBs might have to deal with is a small boat that has blown ashore. The wind will be blowing into the shore line, and if you head in there to help, you are at risk of capsizing and even if you don't capsize in the surf, the boat may be touching the bottom. This is a potentially hazardous situation where you could easily end up in just as much trouble as the original boat. One solution here is to drop the anchor and then turn into the wind and sea, before dropping back to the vessel in distress on the anchor line. Your boat is then held up into the wind and sea while you edge alongside the vessel. You alone can judge whether this is a sensible course of action, so be sure to stop and think before you rush into any rescue.

OFFSHORE RESCUES

Stand-by rescue vessels

The rescue boats used in the offshore oil arena (which are launched from dedicated stand-by vessels) are similar in many respects to those used for rescue work from the shore, and indeed the specifications for these rescue boats were drawn up from experience with shore rescue. Here, however, the focus is on rescuing personnel from oil rigs or platforms. The distances involved are often minimal, but the crews of stand-by ships tend to be 'big ship people' rather than 'small boat people', so training and practice are a requirement. Dedicated rescue boat crews should undertake a training course in how to handle their boats and carry out rescue work, and from then on the boats should be launched and recovered frequently when the ship is on station to ensure the crew gains experience.

Although in most cases these rescue boats are called upon to save someone

who has fallen overboard from a rig, the possibility of having to cope with a major disaster is very real and working in among the debris of a rig that is on fire or collapsing creates an extremely challenging environment. The number of potential casualties that could be involved is high, although the rigs do also have their own lifeboats for evacuation.

Rescue RIBs on board ships

Stand-by vessel rescue boats face operational limitations depending on how they are launched and recovered, and the same applies to rescue RIBs carried on board ships. Their role is partly to cope with any man-overboard situation, but they must also control and muster the liferafts in the event of a major abandon ship. While these are sound motivations for having rescue boats on board ship, the reality is far less than effective. The sheer challenge of launching and recovering one of these RIBs from the height of a passenger ship stowage is daunting even for a trained crew, since there is little that can be done to control the swinging of the rescue boat as it is lowered down the side of the ship, risking damage. Worse still, a ship's crew will have had very

little practice of launching and handling a rescue RIB. While they are required to undertake a similar training course to that taken by the crew of offshore oil standby ships, there is very little, if any, chance for the regular practice needed to maintain effectiveness on the tight schedules of a passenger ship. It is easy to make rules for safety, but do they always provide the level of safety required?

VOLUNTEER RESCUE CREWS AND RESPONDING TO DISTRESS CALLS

One of the problems with volunteer rescue boat crews is that of experience. They may go out on training exercises but there is often a lack of basic seamanship experience and this is a trend that is growing, because experienced seamen often do not have the availability for rescue work. Then there is the high cost of have a dedicated rescue RIB standing by and not being used for maybe 95 per cent of its life. One solution here is to combine the duties of rescue boat with that of a routine harbour task, and in this way the

← An RNLI volunteer rescue RIB crew. Constant training is required

↓↓ A rescue hovercraft can operate successfully over both ice and water

207

RESCUE RIBS

crew get familiarity with operating the RIB and at the same time it is readily available for rescue work. In some cases the role of pilot boat has been combined with that of rescue boat and where I have seen this done it seems to work well, with the rescue work taking priority when required.

The world of search and rescue can provide a challenge for the dedicated rescue boats but when you are out at sea in your RIB, whether for leisure or commercial purposes, you are obliged to respond if you hear a distress call on the radio. You may even come across another vessel in distress and be obliged to go to their aid. The radio is a vital aid in any search and rescue situation so your first response should be either to respond to the distress message or, if you see a vessel in distress, to contact the shore stations, normally the Coastguard, and let them know the situation and your proposed actions. They can then send extra help to supplement your actions or they can include you in their rescue or search response. If you go to the aid of someone in distress you are

faced with much the same problem as the dedicated rescue services and you have to work out a course of action. The temptation is just to rush in and do something but take some time to think through what you are proposing and try to see an end game to the action. So much depends on the situation and the weather and sea conditions that it is hard to give fixed advice, which is all the more reason to work things out beforehand. For instance, there may be a medical emergency on board the other vessel and then there is the question of whether you transfer the patient and perhaps subject them to a lively ride taking them ashore or wait for a helicopter for the transfer when they can deliver the casualty direct to hospital. The authorities on shore can give guidance in this sort of situation, and if time allows it is usually best to let the professionals take over the situation, but if you come across something like a capsized dinghy out at sea, this is the time to move in and do the rescue yourself. With anyone in the water time can be critical so do not

hesitate too much. This particularly applies in cold weather when survival times can be measured in minutes.

While organisations such as the RNLI have developed their own training courses for rescue work, there are specific courses and certification you must take before qualifying for rescue work. For all those who work with yacht club safety boats, there are two-day courses to hone your skills and you must have at least an RYA Powerboat Level 2 Certificate, which covers general powerboat handling, operation and navigation. Many of these courses are carried out on RIBs, making this a great qualification for anyone taking up RIB driving. It is also a required qualification if you want to act as rescue boat crew in many organisations, including those in the offshore oil arena.

The RYA Safety Boat course teaches you the basic skills of boating safety and then offers the chance to hone those skills further with a syllabus that focuses on rescue.

The course includes preparation, boat handling, dinghy rescue, windsurfer rescue, kayak and canoe rescue, towing, end-of-day procedures, suitability of craft, local factors, communications and rescuing other water users. This provides you with a pretty comprehensive base from which to develop the necessary skills and from that point on you can fine-tune what you have learnt with practice and experience. When you first enter rescue work, you will likely start as an assistant before graduating to helmsman as your skills develop.

THE RIB AS RESCUE BOAT: MOVING FORWARD

The RIB has now graduated into the arena of full size, all-weather lifeboat and there are many advantages to its use. RIBs offer a more seaworthy solution than most conventional lifeboats, but perhaps their main advantage is that the tube offers fendering, reducing the risk of damage if the lifeboat has to go alongside another vessel

at sea. However, there are disadvantages to using RIBs in rescues. They can, in fact, make recovering casualties from the water more difficult, since the casualty may disappear from sight under the tube when he is brought alongside and the distance from the top of the tube to the water is considerable. Conventional lifeboats usually have a lowered section of deck for survivor recovery, but this is difficult to achieve on a RIB lifeboat.

The current trend in RIB lifeboat design is towards using foam tubes. These are a good compromise because they tend to be narrower than an inflatable tube and the shape is not dictated by inflation. While the foam tube may not have the resilience of an inflatable, it can be shaped to meet requirements and some lifeboat designs incorporate the foam tube in their hull designs for desired characteristics. Here the foam tube becomes an integral part of the hull and creates additional buoyancy in the bow area, which reduces the chance of

stuffing the bow in a following sea. Foam tubes also act as deck-level spray deflectors.

The Italian Coastguard (Guardia Costiera) use lifeboats that have a gap in the side tubing to aid survivor recovery, and this is one option that may prove useful in other designs. But what works in one rescue scenario may not necessarily work in another, so designers will need to find some sort of middle road as they continue to develop rescue RIBs.

11 SAFETY AND SURVIVAL

IT IS VERY EASY, in the enthusiasm that comes from driving a RIB, to forget about topics such as safety and survival. In many ways the RIB is such a forgiving boat, one that lets you get away with making all sorts of mistakes and still come up smiling, that you tend to get the feeling that it is impregnable. The larger sizes of inflatable and rigid inflatable are some of the most seaworthy boats ever produced and the problem is that they do tend to get driven near to, or at, their limits. This means that when something does go wrong it tends to happen quite quickly and suddenly, and there is almost a feeling of surprise that the boat has let you down when you thought it was infallible. You have to work quite hard to put a foot wrong with a RIB, but you need to remember that every boat has its limits and it is as well to recognise what the limits of a RIB are, so that you can operate well within them.

Safety comes from keeping within the operating parameters of a particular boat, and survival comes in being able to cope with the situation when you exceed these limits. There are two main approaches that you need to take. The first is the personal requirement, which includes ensuring you wear protective clothing, lifejackets and carry items that allow you to survive in the marine environment even when things go wrong. The second is what might be termed 'boat survival', which is the action you take and the equipment you carry in order to make sure that you can cope with most of the emergency situations which are likely to come your way. Like most things connected to safety, it is no good waiting

until a situation develops and then hoping you have the right equipment to cope with it. Anticipation is the name of the game, and you should go through the 'what if' scenarios, trying to picture the sort of things that could go wrong and how you are likely to cope with them. You probably won't anticipate every scenario – the sea is notorious for throwing up situations that you could never have dreamed would happen – but at least you will have thought about some of the possibilities and, consequently, you should be much better prepared to cope with an emergency when it does occur. In most emergencies it is the action that you take in the first few minutes that really counts and which dictates the outcome of the situation, and so the value of anticipation cannot be overestimated.

PERSONAL SAFETY

Protective clothing

It is important to appreciate that on an open RIB you are very exposed to the elements. You may be able to huddle behind a windscreen and get protection of a limited sort, or you may have the luxury of a small wheel house or dodger on larger craft, but on most RIBs you have to accept that you are very exposed. On a hot, sunny day when you go to sea for fun it may be difficult to visualise the need for any protective clothing. The spray can have a nice cooling effect and the wind provides a comfortable breeze. However, there are two things that can spoil this illusion. The first is that if you happen to leave it late in the evening before returning to base, you could find the temperature dropping rapidly, and so the need for protection becomes obvious. The second, potentially more serious situation is if something goes wrong – perhaps your engine breaks down and you are drifting at sea waiting for help – and it turns cold. Now there can be a serious risk of exposure. Therefore, the moral is always to take some sort of protective clothing to sea with you to guard against a change in the conditions. It can be stowed away on board (and clothing is one of the easier items to stow), and if you are lucky you will not have cause to use it, but if the conditions do change, having this protective clothing on board will be worth its weight in gold.

There are four different categories of protective clothing that can be used in RIBs.

1 The thin, lightweight, oilskin type with a single skin, which generally serves to keep you reasonably dry but – perhaps more importantly – it can provide a barrier against the wind. A minimum lightweight protective clothing of this type should be on board at all times during the boat's use.

2 The more comprehensive, what might be termed 'yachting

gear' suits, which generally have an inner lining and good seals at the ankles and wrists and perhaps even at the neck.

3 The wetsuit, much favoured by divers, which is made from foam neoprene rubber to provide an insulating barrier against the water.

4 The dry suit, which usually incorporates its own boots and has rubber seals at wrist and neck and a waterproof zip to allow entry and exit.

Each of these categories of clothing has a role to play in RIB boating and the selection is, to a certain degree, a personal choice, but it is also likely to be dictated by how you intend to use the boat, and by the length of time that you will spend on the water.

1. LIGHTWEIGHT CLOTHING The lightweight, oilskin type of protective clothing is fine when the conditions are warm or hot and you go out for perhaps a swim or to fish. You may need to wear it on top of normal clothing when the boat is going along at speed and the wind-chill factor starts to make its presence felt, but as soon as you stop you can take it off and relax in casual clothes. It will also prove useful if you get caught out by changing conditions.

If you use your boat more seriously, extending its use outside the hot summer's day when boating is a pleasure, you want something more than lightweight clothing. Once you move into the realms of operating in colder conditions or over extended periods, as could be the case of the professional user or when on a cruise, the wind-chill factor acting on rain or spray can produce very intense cooling. The lack of protection in the boat will accentuate this and without adequate clothing you can find yourself getting very cold, very quickly. In this case you have a choice between the three more serious types of protective clothing listed above, and each has its merits and its problems.

2. 'YACHTING GEAR' SUITS The oilskin type of suit which usually combines a jacket and trousers, but could equally be a single-piece suit, has the benefits that it is easy to put on, it is comfortable to wear and it can be worn over the top of normal clothing. Given the high-waisted trousers on a two piece suit, the water protection provided by the modern materials from which these suits are made is generally adequate, but the weak point is always around the neck where it is virtually impossible to get a positive seal and you have to rely on a towel to soak up the damp that collects in this area. If you plan to wear protective clothing for a long time, one of these suits is probably the most comfortable, and they are generally fitted with a hood which gives vital head

protection. A great deal of body heat can be lost through the head and good protection here is crucial in colder conditions. These suits can be worn ashore where they can even be fashionable but, except for the type of suit designed for the ocean sailor, they rarely provide the complete protection that is required when there is a lot of spray flying about, and at RIB speeds it may be difficult to keep the hood in place.

3. WETSUITS The wetsuit provides an insulating layer next to the body that remains effective no matter how wet you get. However, these suits are primarily designed for use when you enter the water, since the trapped layer of water in the foam is warmed by body heat. Out of the water they are fine while they remain dry, with the foam providing good insulation, but if they get wet through spray there will be evaporation of the water from the wetsuit, which can lead to a cooling effect. However, generally speaking, these suits are adequate for use in RIBs, and when wearing a wetsuit it really doesn't matter how wet you get.

Wetsuits come in a number of shapes and forms, but for serious RIB boating the only one which really counts is a full one-piece or two-piece suit that incorporates a hood and is used in conjunction with bootees to give maximum overall protection.

You do need to strip off all your clothes before getting into a wetsuit, and they do tend to have to be made to measure in order to give the necessary good fit. Therefore, a close-fitting wetsuit can become uncomfortable to wear over long periods and some people find that the material causes chafe around sensitive areas, particularly when you are seated. Furthermore, a wetsuit is not the most elegant wear when you go ashore so if you plan to step off your boat and head for a yacht club or a café, you might want something more appropriate. You could wear a wetsuit underneath a set of conventional waterproofs so that you get the best of both worlds.

For the diver the wetsuit is probably mandatory wear, since it works better when in the water than when out of it, but if full-weather protection is required, non-diving operators tend to prefer the dry suit.

4. THE DRY SUIT The dry suit is made from synthetic rubber-impregnated fabric rather similar to that used to make the inflatable tubes, although obviously of a lighter grade. The soft rubber-stretch seals at neck and wrists usually have to be trimmed to match the individual's size if the suit is to be worn comfortably (although, because it is sealed and there is no breathing through the fabric, it can become uncomfortable over long periods). The dry suit is a very practical garment to wear for RIB boating and you can keep bone dry inside, so they can be put on top of normal clothing, although sometimes the smell when the suit is taken off after a long period of wear tends to make other people want to move away from you! Furthermore, if you work off a beach or slipway and you need to enter and exit the water frequently, some dry suits incorporate heavy-duty boots which will keep your feet dry. However, if you try to swim, the trapped air inside the suit can cause buoyancy problems and you

might float feet upwards! The solution is to stand or float upright and squeeze the air out through a vent you create in the neck seal (on some suits there is a valve to release the trapped air).

HEAD AND HAND GEAR The dry suit doesn't have a hood built into it and the need for one, preferably of the lined type, cannot be over-emphasised, especially if you are operating a RIB in cold conditions. Some of the hoods found on normal protective clothing can cover both the mouth and the nose so that only the eyes are left exposed. A possible alternative favoured by rescue-boat crews is to wear a crash helmet. This provides both cold and impact protection, but the need for such gear is something each user should determine.

Helmets are becoming lighter in weight so that they are more comfortable to wear over long periods and they have become quite a fashion item among RIB crews. They are now pretty much standard on commercial, military and rescue RIBs, and there are helmets available with built-in headphones and a microphone so that you can have hands-free VHF communication, which avoids the need for shouting. Another option available is to fit a video camera into the helmet to record operations – a useful feature on police and rescue RIBs.

The helmet weight is important, since the often jerky movement of the RIB can put a strain on neck muscles. Try to get one that has some sort of approval certificate to its name so that you can be assured of it doing its job when it comes to the crunch.

Goggles, generally of the ski variety,

should be worn to give eye protection and can be valuable on any boat which is travelling at over 30 knots, since they save you having to constantly rub your eyes to maintain vision.

Hand protection can be just as vital, and here you have to find a compromise between the ability to use your fingers and handle things like switches and the controls of electronic systems, while getting adequate protection. Probably the best type of gloves for use in an inflatable boat are those made from thin neoprene foam, rather like a mini wetsuit. These allow adequate finger movement and while this foam doesn't give the same protection as the thicker wetsuit foam, it certainly insulates the hands from the wind and provides you with an acceptable level of protection for your hands.

Protective clothing in winter months

If you are using an inflatable or RIB during cold winter months, you must pay very careful attention to protective clothing if the crew is to have a chance of both surviving and carrying out useful duties. When assessing clothing requirements you should always bear in mind that the wearer may well end up being thrown or knocked overboard, and so your suit may have to double up to allow survival in cold water for a useful period of time. Below is a recommended list of clothing for RIB crewmembers operating on North Sea oil industry rescue boats.

- Thermal undergarments
- A one-piece fibre pile suit

- A dry suit with a front entry and incorporating wrist seals and boots with toe protection
- Neoprene fingered mitts for hand protection
- A wool balaclava hood and/or a crash helmet for head protection
- Ski goggles incorporating double lenses

It is the first two items that provide the thermal insulation and the dry suit that provides the seal to keep the water on the outside. The head protection could probably be improved by using a foam rubber balaclava-type helmet, such as divers wear, but what this list does show is the need for a fully effective set of clothing which, while providing adequate thermal protection even if the wearer is in the water, must not restrict movement to the point where the wearer might find it difficult to operate the boat.

SURVIVAL SUITS There are several types of survival suit on the market, which aim to give the wearer a much longer period of survival even in ice-cold waters, and for serious RIB operations in the winter these might be considered as an alternative. They are expensive and many users may prefer the multi-layer approach to protection, such as the list above, to enable the level of thermal protection to be adjusted to suit the ambient conditions. Furthermore, many survival suits do not give the wearer particularly good manoeuvrability, making them unsuitable for boat operators. However, there is a new generation of survival suit appearing on the market which combines good-weather protection for everyday wear and a lifejacket

that can be inflated when its benefits are required. The suit itself can also be inflated to create a thermal layer, which converts it almost instantly into a fully effective survival suit. Boots, hand mitts and head protection are also incorporated.

Lifejackets

There is also a choice in the type of lifejacket you use. At one end of the range there is the SOLAS type, which uses fully inherent buoyancy usually of a comparatively hard, closed-cell type of foam. These lifejackets are designed primarily for passenger ship use and have no real place in the world of inflatable boats, although some thrill-ride operators use them since they are approved for passengers, and with full foam buoyancy there is little or no maintenance required. However, they are very bulky and not very comfortable to wear so they would not be very useful within the confines of a RIB.

At the other end of the scale there is the compact inflatable lifejacket which is easily and unobtrusively worn over the top of protective clothing and can be inflated either manually through an oral inflation tube, or by simply by pulling on

a lanyard on a gas bottle (some versions have automatic gas bottle inflation that inflates the lifejacket when you enter the water). This automatic inflation type is probably the best solution for RIBs, but there is always a small risk that if the boat gets inundated with water the lifejacket may inflate inadvertently. Furthermore, if you partially inflate the lifejacket orally as a precautionary measure, firing the gas bottle could actually burst the lifejacket because the pressure will get too high.

A third type of lifejacket is a compromise between the two described above because it has partial inherent buoyancy and partial air inflation buoyancy, allowing you to select the level of protection you feel appropriate for your personal requirements. However, this requires you to be prepared to inflate your lifejacket once you have fallen overboard. If you see a potential risk up ahead, you can always put some air into the inflation chamber to provide some buoyancy, but with RIBs any emergency is likely to happen at very short notice and the chance of recognising a developing situation and inflating your lifejacket prior to that situation occurring is remote. Therefore, you have to decide whether the risk of going overboard unconscious can be balanced against the comfort of wearing a small, unobtrusive lifejacket (although most lifejackets of this type are still fairly bulky and tend to restrict movement, and there's no guarantee they will provide the full self-righting effect of a lifejacket that will keep your head face-up above water if you are unconscious, as is the case with a fully inflated lifejacket, or one with full inherent buoyancy).

In conclusion, therefore, there is no perfect solution to the question of lifejackets. You must make up your own mind about what you are prepared to spend, what the risks are and what level of protection you feel is appropriate. The risk of going overboard unconscious is comparatively small, particularly if you are wearing a helmet, so a fully inflatable lifejacket with gas bottle inflation is probably the best compromise solution, and is the one adopted by the RNLI after several years of research (although their lifejackets do incorporate automatic inflation). Lifeboat crews require the best, since if they are in trouble, there may be no one to come to their rescue. The lifejackets used by the RNLI crews in their RIBs, therefore, are becoming ever more sophisticated and they now have extra inflatable buoyancy and even a head and face cover to reduce the risk of exposure. When they are inflated these lifejackets are very bulky to the point where it could prove quite difficult to recover a person wearing a jacket of this type from the water.

Whatever type you choose it makes a great deal of sense to wear a lifejacket at all times when using the boat, and I would suggest that they be mandatory. The RIB's low freeboard, the often violent impacts and the unpredictability of the movement put you at almost constant risk of being thrown overboard, and if it does happen it will do so very quickly, with no period of anticipation, so you need to be ready.

Other items

SIGNALLING FOR HELP There are various items of personal equipment you can carry in your pockets to give you a further level of protection, or at least hasten your recovery from the water. It is possible to get pocket-sized packs of flares, with each flare being fired by a pistol-type apparatus to alert others nearby to your predicament. However, flares do have a very limited range of visibility and many countries require you to be in possession of a firearms certificate before you can purchase them.

Once they have been fired off, hand flares tend to spew out a lot of hot ash, which will rapidly burn through an inflatable tube. If you do have to contemplate using a hand flare in an inflatable boat, make sure you hold it well out to leeward so that the ash will blow off downwind and not out over the tube. With parachute flares, the problem is not so great because on firing the flare the exhaust from the rocket rapidly disappears away from the boat up into the air and the risk of anything burning is negligible.

Another possibility that can help when signalling for help is a pack of dye marker which, when released in the water, colours a considerable area around you, helping to make your location known from the air.

By far the best way to attract attention is to use a VHF radio because not only can you indicate what your problem is so that the right help can be sent out, but you will also know that your call has been heard and that help is on its way. This is a great morale booster and the radio is a great bonus if you have to deal with an injured crewmember or if you have had to deal with someone injured on another boat or have recovered a casualty from the water. The coverage for VHF radios at sea is generally very good, but there can be blind spots under cliffs and in remote bays. Even then, another boat vessel out at sea will usually hear your call and help with communications.

The VHF radio is is a fairly expensive solution that few inflatable boat users could probably contemplate. However, if you are operating the boat on your own, do think seriously about purchasing a radio of this type because it could represent your only means of calling for help if you do get thrown into the water and you cannot get back to the boat. Another option is an EPIRB (emergency position-indicating radio beacon), which sends out a distress signal. These can be quite compact, are fully waterproof and have a considerable range, but they only offer one-way communication and you have no knowledge of whether your signal has been picked up.

MAN-OVERBOARD DEVICES It may be hard to believe that anyone going overboard from a RIB will not be noticed by the rest of the crew, but it could happen to a crewmember sitting in the stern on his own with the rest of the crew looking forward. There is now a range of man-overboard devices that will automatically trigger a signal if you go into the water. Most of these are linked to an on-board unit that not only alerts the crew on board to your situation but also allows for quick location. There are no firm regulations when it comes to these units so once again it is up to you or the operator of the RIB to decide the level of safety required. On commercial craft in the larger sizes there could certainly be health and safety reasons for fitting these devices because the operator could certainly come in for criticism if he didn't.

A kill cord is another essential piece of RIB equipment. The standard kill cord connects the helmsman to the engine

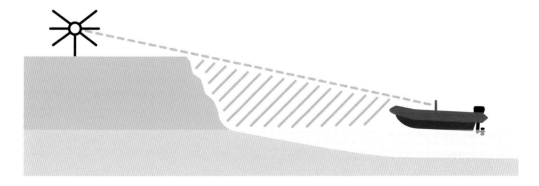

control box with a cord, which when pulled will automatically stop the engine. The idea is to stop the boat if the helmsman goes overboard rather than have it come round and run over the person in the water, which can cause horrific injuries. There is now also an electronic version that does much the same job and which will work for any of the crew, but it does mean that a person actually has to be in the water before the engine will cut out. This is because the system relies on the loss of a radio signal to trigger the engine stop. The same system will also work with distance, and if you place a sensor in a tender being towed it will sound an alarm if the distance increases, to alert you that the dinghy has broken adrift.

SURVIVAL SITUATIONS

Engine failure

There are a number of situations where RIBs could get into difficulty which can be anticipated, and engine failure is probably the most obvious one. Many RIBs with a large single engine as the main propulsion carry a smaller, perhaps 7 or 8hp outboard as an auxiliary get-you-home engine, and if both engines are outboards, there is compatibility in the fuel. However, if you are on a single engine boat and you can't fix it, the only solutions open to you are to attract the attention of passing boats or to call for help with the radio.

Without any propulsion you can put out a sea anchor to prevent the boat drifting too much, particularly if it is drifting in towards an inhospitable shore or on to rocks. A sea anchor will only reduce the drift – it won't prevent it altogether – and if you do find yourself getting close to the shore, it is time to get out the anchor ready for action. You want the anchor to hold at the first opportunity, so pay it out to virtually the full extent of the line over the side so that it will touch bottom as the water gets shallower. It may not hold for quite a while because initially the pull on the line is virtually straight up and down, but gradually, as the water gets shallower, the anchor will start to dig in, the pull on the line will become more horizontal and eventually – with luck – the anchor will hold before you drift on to the rocks or get

SAFETY AND SURVIVAL

into the heavy breaking surf on a beach. It is mainly for this emergency use that you want a good scope of line on the anchor line, and 30 metres of line should hold adequately in a water depth of 5 metres, even when the wind is blowing strongly on shore. This is a temporary solution until help arrives, but it could buy you very valuable time.

You could extend this technique a bit further if you want to allow the boat to drift ashore on to a beach where there is a heavy surf. With the motor out of action you would stand a strong risk of capsizing the boat in this situation unless you can keep it head on into the waves. The technique is to let the boat drift inshore and put out the anchor just before you enter the surf. It requires fine judgement to get the anchor out in the right place because if you put it down too soon, there won't be enough line to hold the boat as it passes through the lines of surf to reach the beach, and if you leave it too late the boat will be picked up by the surf and probably be capsized by the first wave. Always be on the lookout for that extra big wave which will break further out to sea than the general trend of the waves. Rather than wait until the last minute before throwing out the anchor in this situation, lower it so that it is just touching the seabed as you drift inshore. It won't hold in this situation, but it will soon get a bite as you slack out a bit more line, and this should help you to judge your timing much better. Even when the anchor might be dragging in this way it should still hold the bow of the RIB up into the waves, which is what you are trying to achieve. Because of the limited amount of anchor line you have available, this technique

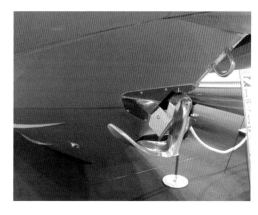

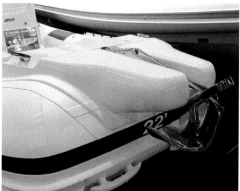

is only suitable for use when there are one or two lines of surf; otherwise, you will run out of line long before you get through the surf area, although the dragging technique could extend the range of possibilities.

An alternative is to use a sea anchor for this role, but because the boat will be surging heavily backwards in the surf, the sea anchor and its line need to be adequately strong to withstand it. The lightweight liferaft-type of sea anchor, with its quite fragile line, is unlikely to be strong enough for this job, but even something like a strong bucket tied to a line might do well in an emergency.

Capsizing

Probably the worst fear of any RIB operator is capsizing. This is most likely to happen when you are travelling slowly in a following sea and a wave coming up behind overtakes you and the boat broaches, i.e. the stern swings round and the boat becomes beam-on to the breaking wave crest. (In a faster RIB there should be no real risk of capsizing providing that you maintain concentration, reading the waves all the time and negotiating with them, rather than trying to do battle with them, and focusing on overtaking the waves rather than letting them overtake you.) Escape from this situation, provided that you recognise what is happening early enough, is simply a question of opening the throttle and running before the waves, but you have to be aware of the situation in order to do this, and it can happen so quickly. Even in a head sea there can a risk of capsize if you adopt the technique of zig-zagging through the waves, looking for the lower crests to get through the surf region, and here you could find yourself inadvertently getting round beam-on to the sea just at a time when a big curling wave face comes up on your windward side.

In my experience nearly all RIB capsizes have occurred to rescue boats of the open type, as they are the main type of RIB likely to have to operate slowly in surf conditions. When operating on inshore rescue operations, this risk of capsize is always present, particularly when you have to go in to rescue somebody in the surf area, and self-righting equipment was developed for RIBs to account for this situation. This comprises an air bag mounted on a roll bar with gas bottle inflation. This equipment won't stop the boat capsizing, but it does give you a means of righting the boat once it has capsized. It is not automatic but requires one of the crew to pull the gas bottle activating trigger to initiate the self-righting, and this should only be done once all the crew have escaped from underneath the boat and have swum clear. Once the inflation of the righting bag has been initiated, the righting moment is very quick and could certainly cause injury to any crew caught up with it. Once righted, the crew can climb back on board and hopefully with the sealed engines and the various cut-out systems it will be possible to restart the engines afterwards. The righting bags are usually fitted with a rapid deflation hatch, allowing the bag to be deflated after use, but these are one-shot bags, and once the air cylinder has been activated you cannot use the system again. I can understand the logic of having a self-righting system because it gives you a further chance of coping with a capsize, but if one capsize has occurred in the prevailing surf or breaking wave conditions there will always be the risk of a further one before you can sort yourself out and regain control. With this in mind, it could be sensible to leave the righting bag inflated until the boat is fully recovered and it has moved out of the surf region. In surf in shallow water, the inverted boat could make contact with the seabed and there is also a risk that the boat will end up ashore before the boat can be righted and brought under control again.

Any self-righting system adds

→ This hoop over the outboards
keeps the line clear when towing

complication and extra maintenance issues
to a RIB, so the vast majority of RIBs do
not have them. In these RIBs, a capsize
means that righting the boat has to be
done manually. With small RIBs this might
be possible to achieve and it means tying
a line on one side of the boat, leading this
over the upturned boat and then standing
on the tube away from where the line is
attached, leaning backwards and using your
bodyweight to pull the boat up and over. If
the side of the boat you are trying to lift is
kept upwind the task will be easier because
once the wind gets under the boat it will help
you to complete the righting task.

Trying to right a RIB which is anything
over 5 metres in length is probably an
impossible task, one which is made harder
if powerful engines are fitted. The chances
are that it will not be possible to restart the
engines again anyway, because they will not
be protected in the way that the engines on
self-righting boats are, and so you might
consider calling for assistance by any means
available rather than expend the effort
trying to right the boat. You can usually sit
quite comfortably on the upturned boat,
particularly if you rig a rope across the boat
to give you something to hold on with. One
reason to secure all the equipment inside
a RIB is so that you will not lose it in the
event of a capsize, but, of course, the best
solution is to avoid capsize in the first place
by means of careful and sensible driving.

Towing another boat

The average RIB is quite small and it may
not have a lot of grip on the water, making
towing another boat a difficult task, since

if the vessel is a larger boat, it can end up
steering the RIB rather than the other way
round. The vee bottom of a larger RIB is
certainly better for this task, but anything
larger than a dinghy will have to be towed at
very conservative speeds. One of the biggest
problems on a RIB is finding somewhere
strong enough to make fast a tow line. You
may have a water-ski tow point but these
are normally found on the transom, which is
not the best place to tow from. The best tow
point is about one-third of the length of the
boat from the transom and this will allow
you much better steering control, but towing
from a point here assumes that you have
a clear run for the tow line over the engine
and no arch mast or other fittings aft. Some
RIBs have a low arch that just clears the
outboards on the transom that can help to
keep a tow line clear.

If you can't find a suitable attachment
for a tow line, it may be possible to rig a rope
bridle which will spread the weight of the

tow line between two or three attachment points. You could use handholds or lifting points for attaching a tow line if there is no other towing point, but spread the load between them and at all costs keep the tow line clear of the propeller and of the engine and keep your speed right down because these attachments are only as strong as the glue that attaches them.

Using a tender as a liferaft

The authorities tend to frown on the use of RIBs as substitute liferafts and rarely sanction their use where there is a mandatory requirement for liferafts, but RIBs can provide a viable alternative in many situations, provided that you understand the limitations involved and the risks inherent in using an inflatable instead of a fully effective liferaft. However it should be borne in mind that no matter how well it is converted for this role, no inflatable can fully meet the survival requirements built into a liferaft. One of the major areas of difference is the fitting of stability pockets into the bottom of the liferaft, which helps to reduce the possibility of capsize. Liferafts also tend to have an inflatable floor, which provides good insulation between cold seawater and any occupants. On the other hand, a RIB could provide a viable means of escape in an emergency and it makes sense to have a grab bag handy with items such as flares, a sea anchor, a knife and other emergency equipment ready to take with you into the RIB.

Many RIBs used for commercial operations, particularly those carrying passengers over a certain number, also have to carry a liferaft. This might seem a superfluous requirement but the authorities tend not to differentiate between RIBs and other types of craft when writing the rules, so you have no choice. You should always consider liferafts as a last resort and your chances of survival will always be greater if you stay in the RIB itself, unless it is actually sinking or on fire.

Dealing with fires on board

Fire in RIBs seems a remote possibility because there is usually so much water around, but with a petrol RIB you are carrying a large amount of flammable liquid around with you and a leak in the engine compartment could generate a fire, or it could possibly start in the electrics. For that reason, a fire extinguisher is an essential piece of equipment on a RIB of almost any size and with larger RIBs with inboard engines a fire-smothering system in the engine compartment makes sense too.

ENGINE FIRES Your first indication of a fire in the engine compartment may be the engine faltering or stopping, and it could flare up if you open the hatch. The automatic systems can be fired off from a helm switch, but remember that fire needs oxygen and fuel to burn, so you need to prevent air from reaching the engine compartment. Don't be in any rush to open the hatch to see if the fire is out, because you only have one shot with the extinguishing system and if the fire flares up again when the hatch is opened, you're left with only the hand extinguisher to put it out. If you can turn off the fuel supply from outside the engine compartment, that will also help. You are surrounded by one of the best fire-fighting mediums available – water – and if you have a bucket available use this to quell the flames, but do remember you are filling the boat up with water when you do this.

One cause of fire on a RIB with inboard engines could be a failure in the engine seawater cooling system. This cooling water not only cools the engine but is also normally pumped into the exhaust line to cool the hot exhaust gases. Therefore, a failure in the cooling water could lead to these hot gases not being cooled and the rubber section of the exhaust pipe could catch fire. An added problem in this situation is that water could also be flooding into the boat from the failed pipe, so you could be on fire and sinking all because of a rubber pipe failure. Prevention is better than cure so checking and renewing these vital pipes at regular intervals is the best solution.

ELECTRICAL FIRES Electrical fires could be caused by wiring chafing or breaking due to the constant and lively motion of the boat. There could also be corrosion of the terminals, so a regular check should find the problem before it causes a failure and a fire. One problem with many RIBs is that the wiring is hidden away below the deck and you cannot reach it or even see it, so you have to rely on the RIB builder for high-quality work. You would not normally get high-voltage electrics in a RIB, except the larger wheel-house RIBs, but the batteries can also be a source of problems unless they are firmly secured. Any movement in the batteries or in their heavy-duty cables could lead to sparking and a possible fire.

There is so much that could go wrong, but RIB builders today generally build a safe, sensible boat with reliability in mind so the risk of fire should be small. Nonetheless when you are operating in lively seas with a fast RIB, do not take anything for granted.

SAFETY AND SURVIVAL

PART THREE

RIB MAI

NTENANCE

THE ENGINE is a vital component of the RIB, and it has been the development of advanced engines and propulsion that has progressed RIB design and capability. In the early days of RIB design, when weight was a critical factor, the outboard motor reigned supreme because of its lightweight and incorporated propulsion. Today, the outboard is still probably the most popular form of RIB engine, but the advent of lightweight diesel engines and water-jet drives has opened up new markets and has been responsible for some of the more advanced RIB concepts.

There are three main types of engine: outboard, which probably covers a high proportion of RIBs on the market today; inboard diesels driving through stern drives or water jets; and the comparatively new sector of small inboard petrol engines coupled directly to water jets. The military and commercial sectors, as well as the yacht tender markets, are focusing more on diesel/water-jet installations, but much of the leisure sector still relies on outboards.

OUTBOARD ENGINES

As far as RIB propulsion is concerned the outboard still has a lot to offer. It comes in power outputs ranging from 1hp to the massive 300hp+, meaning it can meet most RIB requirements in either single or twin, or in the case of some larger RIBs, triple and quadruple engine installations. Imagine a RIB with four 300hp outboards on the stern and you have a high-performance package with probably the best power/weight ratio available. Another major advantage is the amount of free space an outboard leaves inside the boat, with the engines behind the transom.

Outboards in larger sizes have a reputation for being very thirsty, but the early two-stroke engines have largely been replaced either by much more sophisticated two-stroke engines with electronic control and fuel injection, or by the slightly heavier, although much more economical, four-stroke engines. Modern outboards have seen off their bad reputation and are now highly reliable, quiet and

◂◂ Outboards that are capable
of running on alternative fuels
are becoming more available

▾ A twin diesel outboard installation
on a North Sea oil arena rescue boat.
Note also the propeller guards

227

economical power units, making them the
engine of choice for many RIB users. The
only limitation in using petrol outboards in
these larger sizes might be the access to
fuel supplies, and the problems that can
arise from storing that fuel on board
a mother ship.

Diesel outboards

There have been attempts to introduce
diesel outboards, and Yamaha offers a 35hp
diesel unit. Even in twin installations, two
of these outboards are barely enough to
get a reasonably-sized RIB onto the plane,
but there is a demand for larger diesel
outboards, mainly from the military because
they do not like highly flammable petrol
and they want fuel compatibility with their
other forms of transport. High-power diesel
outboards have been developed for military
requirements, which are a modification of
standard petrol units, but these are both
complex and expensive and they have not
found their way into the leisure or even
the commercial RIB sector. Barrus has
developed a 50hp multi-fuel outboard that
can offer flexibility in the fuels used, which
was created to meet military requirements,
with the engine capable of operating on all
NATO fuels.

Outboard installation

The outboard is easy to install, with
the smaller units simply clamped to the
transom and the larger units bolted on. For
the smaller units, up to about 40hp, tiller
steering makes the installation even simpler,
but above this size you normally need to
have a steering wheel and remote throttles.

The engines can be tilted so that when not
in use the propeller can be raised clear of
the water, which also facilitates changing
the propeller should it get damaged. Power
tilting is used on the larger outboards and
this is often part of the power trim system
that enables the outboard angle in relation to
the transom to be altered when under way.
This power trim can be used to improve the
performance and is a significant adjustment
for optimising performance. When multiple
outboards were installed on the transom it
used to be the case that the engines could
not be tilted individually because of the
steering system and tie bars linking the

RIB MAINTENANCE

engines. Now modern outboards in the large sizes have a 'fly by wire' steering system that does away with these hard links so engines can be tilted individually. This offers a lot more flexibility to a multiple outboard installation because the boat can be run in economical mode with just one or two engines operating, and the other tilted up to reduce drag. For high-performance RIBs such an engine installation can offer many more options in the way that the engines are operated, and when in harbour you might just want to use the two outboard engines on a four-engine installation to give maximum manoeuvrability.

While the installation of outboards is simple, there are two important factors in the way that they are set up. With a single-engine installation the trim tab found on the bottom end of the drive leg has to be set up to act as a balance for the propeller torque that introduces a pull on the steering if it is left in its central position. By angling the trim tab a few degrees there is compensation for the propeller torque, so that the steering remains light and comfortable. The right setting for the tab has to be found by trial and error and it will take half an hour out on the water to set this up, adjusting it a few degrees at a time. This setting can be particularly important with a single powerful outboard where, without the setting, you could find a pull of several kilos on the steering, making it hard to control and very tiring to use, quite apart from the fact that the boat could have a harsh ride because it will tend to land over on one side in waves.

You don't need to adjust this setting with a twin-outboard installation, but you should

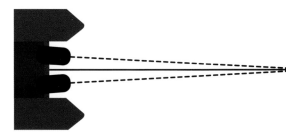

set up a bit of 'toe-in' on the engines, which will make them slightly more efficient. This setting adjusts the engines so that they are slightly angled in to each other rather than directly parallel (when you look at the wake, the engines will meet about a couple of boat lengths behind the propellers). Do this by adjusting the linkage between the two engines in calm water, where you can clearly see the engine wakes.

Transom height is also important and here you have a choice of standard or long shaft. Most RIBs will use long shaft outboards because of the vee in the hull that extends the depth of the hull but setting the correct transom height is important to engine efficiency and it is a bit of a compromise between having the propeller deep enough in the water to get good low-speed torque and yet to have it work effectively at high speeds. This is where power trim comes in to reduce the compromise, but on some high-performance RIBs the engine might be fitted slightly higher to focus on the high-speed end of the operations.

Propeller choice is another variable, and here it is best to take advice from the dealer. The diameter of the propeller is usually fixed, but the pitch can be varied in steps of about 1in, with each step varying the engine rpm by about 250 revs. The aim should be to get the engine operating at full rpm when the throttle is wide open, but of course the loadings will vary with the load of the boat, and there are other factors that make propeller selection a compromise.

Outboard developments

Exposed propellers on RIBs have always been a cause for the authorities' concern, particularly where RIBs are operating around and close to beaches. Therefore, some RIBs fit propeller guards to reduce the risk, should there be people in the water. For instance, the racing Zapcat RIBs have these guards and while they do reduce efficiency to a small degree, they offer a measure of protection. Court cases in the US have suggested that it may become mandatory for boats to have propeller guards in the future, but at present the debate is wide open.

Some outboard motors now have a water jet fitted to their bottom end rather than a propeller, and these offer the advantage of

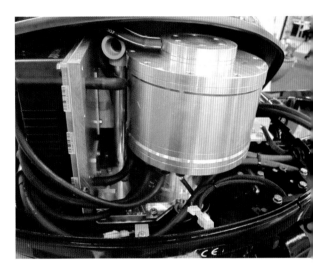

safer operation when there are swimmers in the water. Barrus offers one on a 30hp outboard with a pump jet replacing the propeller, and this is combined with an Avon inflatable to make up a rescue package.

Many RIB users are looking into ways to make their usage of their boats 'greener', and one development has been in electric outboard motors, with 140hp units now available. While the weight of the batteries needed to power the outboard and the limited range offered might be negative factors to most, electric outboards do meet the requirements of those users interested in operating their boats at low emissions. There is now a 50hp electric outboard on the market that offers two to three hours of cruising at moderate speeds, which could meet the requirements of some leisure users, perhaps divers who only want speed when travelling to and from the dive site. Moreover, the latest lithium-ion batteries are helping to bring the overall weight of these types of engines down, so that electric

power could work for some harbour patrol applications where the batteries can be recharged at intervals during the day.

On larger RIBs, hybrid systems could provide a viable solution and boats with this sort of electric power are already in operation. The main engines are a pair of electric motors with enough power to get the boat onto the plane. These electric motors are supplied with power from a bank of batteries, and there is a diesel generator that can either supply power direct to the electric motors or which can recharge the batteries, or do both. A sophisticated computer-controlled system manages all of the switching and control. Hybrid systems have the ability to operate silently and smoothly and with a reduced fuel consumption, since the generator is operating at a fixed speed designed for maximum efficiency.

Electric power in one form or another will become ever more prevalent and the viability of such systems will depend a great deal on how a RIB is operated. In many cases, a RIB is only operated at full power for a short time, making electric power a viable option for the times when the RIB is working at a reduced capacity. At present, there is a cost penalty in the use of electric or hybrid systems, because they tend to be developed individually and the batteries are expensive, but as the use of electric power widens the costs will reduce. We may be five years away from viable and cost-effective

electric RIBs, but for operators wanting green credentials there could be a strong incentive to invest in the technology.

INBOARD ENGINES

Inboard petrol engines have seen use on RIBs that operate mainly through a stern drive propulsion system, and there are still installations of this type being used, mainly in the US. However, most inboard engine installations use diesel power, which has advanced dramatically in the past ten years. Apart from the increased efficiency of the counter-rotating propellers, Duo Prop stern drives are far less sensitive to trim than conventional stern drives (stern drives need to be trimmed underway in the same way as outboards).

Modern small, powerful diesels are only a little heavier than comparable petrol engines and much of the development of these boat engines has indeed been spurred on by progression in the automobile industry. Yanmar was a pioneer in offering compact, powerful marine diesels and its engines have been used in racing RIBs with considerable success. Volvo Penta has followed suit and

is in the unique position of offering both engines and drive systems, including its pioneering DuoProp stern drive units.

The use of inboard diesel engines was previously limited to RIBs of maybe 8 metres in length, but advances in diesel design have now allowed RIBs as small as 3 metres to use diesel power. Apart from the diesel fuel being cheaper in many countries and more readily available, the big attraction in the military, commercial and yacht tender sectors where the fuel is compatible with the mother yacht or vessel. For yachts, particularly in the larger sizes that come under SOLAS requirements, special provision has to be made if petrol is carried on board for fuelling the tender, while the requirements for the carriage of diesel fuel are standard for the main engines of the yacht or ship. Insurance companies also prefer diesel to be carried in garages when the tender is also being stored there.

The propulsion market

Diesel engines have a higher torque than an equivalent petrol engine, and this slowed down the application of diesel power in RIBs with stern drives, since the early drives could only handle limited torque. Today, this limitation has been largely removed for diesel engines up to around 400hp so the requirements of most RIBs can be met with stern drive propulsion. However, the water jet is growing in popularity for RIB propulsion for several reasons.

■ A water jet can absorb the full power of the engine even at low speed, so that a water-jet boat has good acceleration and gets on to the plane easily.

↓ A water-jet unit complete
with its built-in intake

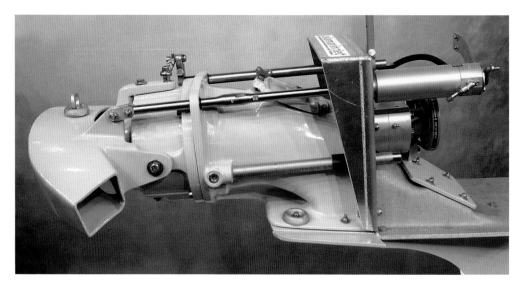

■ The propulsion unit is fully protected for shallow-water operations.

■ It provides good manoeuvrability, with steering control available even when the boat is stopped in the water.

■ It provides excellent stopping power. It is safe for operation close to people in the water.

■ It more or less fits within the dimensions of the hull, and there are not protrusions below the bottom of the boat, so stowage on a mother ship is easier.

■ A jet-powered RIB can be beached with a high degree of impunity, which is great both in the leisure sector and for some military applications. It can also be made to move sideways at low speeds so a bow thruster may not be necessary.

Against the use of water jets are their relatively high cost and the fact that the water entrained within the jet housing counts as part of the weight of the boat and

so detracts from performance. Because the jet unit incorporates both steering, neutral and reverse, it is nice to think that a gearbox is not necessary, but that is not usually the case and certainly a neutral or a clutch is required to be able to isolate the engine from the jet unit. Some water jets incorporate the reduction gearbox into the water-jet housing, while on others it is a separate unit, adding to the weight and complication.

However, compact and integrated small petrol engines and water jets have been developed from jet-ski technology and these are often used on small RIBs. These units are lightweight and do not require the reduction gearbox – or any gearbox for that matter – and they are finding considerable favour in compact yacht tender markets where the tender is too small to accommodate diesel power. With diesel power now being fitted to RIBs as small as 3 metres, the use of petrol/water-jet units may be dying out, except where sporting performance is required.

The propulsion market is expanding rapidly with new ideas and concepts, and there may be application on RIBs for pod drives, although these fixed units are not suitable for smaller RIBs that are launched from trailers. The extra fixed draft is likely to rule them out for yacht tenders as well, and they are probably not the best solution for cruising RIBs where draft can be important. So despite their widespread use in the powerboat market, pod drives are likely to remain a rarity in the RIB market, except perhaps for the larger models.

Larger-sized RIBs can also use surface drives where the propeller operates in surface-piercing mode to great efficiency (a surface drive RIB is easily recognised because of the distinctive rooster-tail wake thrown up by the surface propeller). There are larger RIBs with surface drives such as those from FB Design, where the drive is an integral part of the overall hull design. Their propellers are mounted on fixed shafts that extend out from the lower transom and once on the plane only the bottom blades of the propeller are in the water and doing useful work. In this mode there is no appendage drag from the propeller shaft, brackets or drive leg, which is what offers the higher efficiency, with surface propellers offering perhaps a 15– 20 per cent increase in top speed compared with a conventional drive system. Surface drives are only likely to be used where high performance is the over-riding criteria of the design.

While the focus is on the engine, it is vitally important with all these options that the engine systems are installed with a high degree of integrity. The movement of a RIB at sea can put high stress on all its systems, such as its fuel, cooling and electrical systems, and these must be installed to very high standards if they are going to produce reliability. We will cover this more in the next chapter on maintenance, but a modern engine is only as reliable as its support systems.

Summary of engine types

Two-stroke outboards	*Lightweight; higher fuel consumption; advanced electronic control; wide range of power outputs*
Four-stroke outboards	*Heavier; moderate fuel consumption; advanced electronic control; wide range of power outputs*
Petrol inboards	*Potentially dangerous fuel; lighter weight; electronic control on modern versions; higher fuel consumption*
Diesel inboards	*Heavier; good fuel consumption; no electronic systems; very reliable; compatible fuel*
Electronic diesels	*Heavier; excellent fuel consumption; complex electronic systems for control; very reliable; compatible fuel*

THE ENGINES AND PROPULSION of a RIB play a crucial part in the operation and safety of the boat. Lose propulsion and you are virtually dead in the water, and will need someone to come to your assistance. Engine and propulsion manufacturers do a great job of developing reliable units and they have come a long way from the sometimes erratic machinery of the early RIBs. RIB builders in general do an equally good job of installing the engines and systems, and these days you expect your engine to start and you expect it to keep going. However, it will only do this if you play your part and look after the machinery with regular service and inspections. So what are you looking for when you give your engines and systems a check, both during regular servicing and before you go to sea?

MAINTAINING THE ENGINE

The actual engine of a RIB these days will very rarely break. Engines, whether they are inboard or outboard, are tested to destruction by the manufacturers and I cannot recollect over the past 20 years ever having the actual engine break at sea. There have been times – quite a few of them – when the engine has stopped at sea, and there is nothing quite so daunting as the eerie silence that pervades everything when that happens. It can be like the portent of doom because you are virtually helpless in the water.

However, when that happens it is much more likely to be one of the systems that supports the engine, such as the electrics, the fuel supply or the cooling that has gone wrong, and this is where your regular checks and maintenance can reduce the risks.

Outboard engines

The outboard engine's strength is that it is supplied as a complete tried-and-tested unit – many of the systems, or at least parts of them, are incorporated into the engine, although it does still rely on the outside fuel supply and some of the electrics to keep it going. For commercial and military operators one of the benefits of the outboard is that you can have a spare available so that if you get into problems, you can simply change the engine, and Barrus has developed an easy-change bracket that allows an outboard to be changed in a matter of minutes.

Today, outboards are remarkably water-resistant and in most cases you can play a hose over the engine, even with the hood off, and it will keep running, provided you don't stick the hose up the air intake. This is a measure of how the outboard has developed in recent years, and if the outboard does stop for any reason the first thing to suspect is the external connections rather than the engine itself.

PREVENTING THE MOTOR FROM COMING LOOSE Having said this, the outboard motors on RIBs can come in for considerable physical abuse. The motion of the boat can be quite violent, so one of the main things to check at regular intervals is the mounting brackets and fastenings on the transom. Smaller outboards up to 20 or 30hp are simply clamped on to the transom or mounting bracket with the clamping screws, which is adequate. A metal plate is fixed to the transom to spread the load of these clamping screws as they are screwed up tight, and often the mounting bracket where it butts against the transom on its rear side will have little serrated edges that bite into the timber of the transom and help to prevent sideways and up and down movement of the engine, where the transom clamps are the only thing locating the engine. Even on the smallest outboard it is important that you check the tightness of the clamps, certainly every time you use the boat, and then perhaps every half an hour or so when you are at sea. These clamps will only be satisfactory when they are fully tight and any slight play that is allowed between the mounting brackets and the transom will start to magnify until the whole engine can become loose. Just in case you don't notice this, and to guard against the possibility of the engine leaping right off the transom, it is normal practice to have a securing chain between the engine bracket and the transom, which will at least prevent you losing the engine altogether if it does jump off. It shouldn't get to this stage, but it does happen, particularly when you are looking forward and concentrating on the approaching waves or other traffic on the water and the engine clamping bolts are the furthest thing from your mind. That security chain can also serve the purpose of reducing the chance of theft if it is padlocked in place.

On larger outboard motors, the engine is not designed for quick and easy removal, partly because it is too heavy to carry around easily, but equally because it needs to be bolted rather than clamped onto the transom, to provide the right level of security. The forces involved with a larger outboard are too much for a clamping system to cope with adequately and to demonstrate this fact, clamps are rarely fitted on engines over 60hp. Instead, there are brackets to locate the engine at the top of the transom to ensure that it is at the right height, and then it takes usually four or six stainless steel bolts through the transom to bolt the engine securely into place. These bolts should be backed up by large washers inside the boat to spread the load, and the transom will be stiffened in this area to help spread the stress and strain. The securing bolts should be fitted with lock washers, or locking nuts, and every so often these mounting bolts should be checked for tightness and to ensure that the lock nuts are adequately secured.

FUEL TANKS

Integral fuel tanks Small outboards up to 5hp often have their fuel tank integral with the engine, which means that the fuel system has been tried and tested and will be reliable. With such a system, the only problems likely to develop may be minor leaks in the fuel piping (which should be checked for integrity every now and again) and dirt in the fuel (any excessive amount of dirt which collects in the filter should be regarded with suspicion). It is not easy to ensure that the fuel you take into the tank is clean at all times, but there is a fuel filter in the system usually mounted on the engine itself at a point close to the fuel pump. Where a gravity fuel feed is used, the filter will be close to the carburettor and these filters should be cleaned out at regular intervals.

Portable fuel tanks Where an outboard is supplied from a portable fuel tank inside the boat, check that the tank is firmly secured to the deck and that the flexible pipe that feeds the fuel to the engine is not pinched or nipped. Elastic straps can rarely be secured tightly enough to prevent the tanks moving under the motion of the boat and the best system is to use webbing straps with a ratchet tightener. Secure the tanks really tightly, because it only wants a slight amount of play to get them moving. The advantages of these portable tanks are that they can be taken ashore for refuelling, many have a

fuel gauge built in so you know how much is left in the tank, and they are also designed for the job, so they are usually reliable. The negatives of their use include the sharp edges on the handles, the fact that they are usually made from mild steel (which means that they corrode in a salt atmosphere) and the difficulty of securing them adequately.

Flexible fuel tanks Flexible fuel tanks are a good idea, but because they are built from special rubber that has to be petrol-impervious and quite thick to stand up to surge and physical stress, they are expensive. The tanks come in a variety of shapes, some rather like a carrier bag with a built-in handle, others long and tubular so that they can be secured along the inflatable tubes. The flexible tanks have no sharp edges, apart from perhaps the filler cap. Furthermore, air vents in rigid tanks can allow water to get into the fuel under more extreme conditions, but a flexible tank simply collapses as the fuel is removed and no air needs to be taken in to replace the used fuel. A flexible tank still needs to be secured to give it a reasonable chance of survival and you have to watch carefully for chafe against any of the rigid members of the boat due to movement.

Built-in tanks Built-in metal tanks are now the standard for most RIBs and they are usually fitted under the deck where they are not easily accessible. There may be a deck hatch that gives access to the pipe connection plate – check that everything is tight and there is no sign of leaks here (this should be part of your regular checklist).

Some form of external fuel gauge is useful, so that the crew know how much fuel is left, and a breather pipe also has to be fitted to allow air to enter the tank as the fuel is taken out, or for air to escape as the tank is filled. This should be fitted with fine gauze at the outboard end, which helps to reduce any fire risk from the fumes that could emanate from the pipe, but also to prevent water entering the pipe and getting into the tank.

Further fuel tank considerations With outboard motors there is a need for a flexible pipe between the tank and the motor itself. The end fittings on these outboard fuel pipes are usually a push fitting, which has an automatic seal comprising a spring-loaded ball valve, pressing on to a rubber O ring. This O ring serves to seal the ball valve when the pipe is disconnected and to make the seal when the pipe is connected. A leak through this O ring when the pipe is disconnected may not be particularly serious, but any leakage when the pipe is connected immediately allows air to be sucked into the engine rather than fuel, and the engine stops rapidly, or, much more likely, it won't start in the first place. O rings need careful inspection for damage at regular intervals, and if you suspect that the engine is not getting adequate fuel or starts to misfire the O ring could be responsible, although running out of fuel could produce similar symptoms. It makes sense to carry spare rings on board.

An outboard fuel line is normally fitted with a priming bulb, which is like a small manual pump that sucks fuel from the tank and feeds it to the carburettor. This priming is necessary before starting the engine, and once the engine starts the engine-mounted fuel pump takes over the suction process. You can quickly feel when the priming process is complete because the rubber bulb tends to feel much harder and firmer, but if you keep pumping and the bulb never seems to become hard, you should suspect that the O ring is damaged or that there is possibly dirt in the fuel that is preventing the little non-return valve in the priming bulb from sealing properly.

From the fuel line, the fuel is routed first into a fuel filter and then into a carburettor or fuel injection system. On some installations there may be a fuel filter mounted externally to the engine, often on the transom where it is clearly visible, and this serves to trap any dirt in the fuel and also to separate out any water which might be in the fuel. The glass bulb of these filters provides a ready check for any fuel contamination. The engine-mounted fuel filter may also have a glass bulb so that it can be checked quickly for contamination, but you have to take off the engine hood to carry out the check. The engine-fuel filters usually need a spanner to dismantle and clean them and this can be a tricky exercise at sea because you are usually hanging over the back of the boat and you only have to drop one of the dismantled components to render that engine completely immobile. From this fuel filter onwards there is little you can do about the fuel system, but it is designed to operate as a completely tried-and-tested unit, so the chances of problems occurring beyond the fuel filter are relatively small.

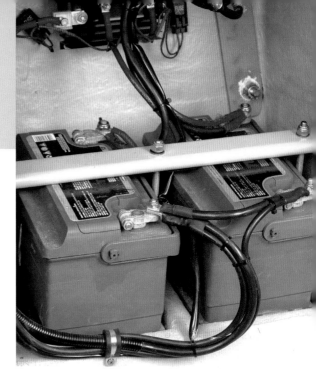

RIB MAINTENANCE

ELECTRICAL SUPPLY The other main component which has to be supplied to an outboard motor is the electrics. For smaller outboard motors up to about 50hp you have a choice of manual or electric starting. The advantage of manual starting is that you do not necessarily need a battery or complex electrical system in the boat if you are using the RIB on day trips only. Most RIBs, however, have a full electrical system and here you rely heavily on the RIB builder to get things right with waterproof connections and well-secured wiring.

The battery The battery itself needs careful stowage and it must be securely clamped or bolted down to a rigid surface to reduce the chance of the slightest hint of movement. Any movement in the battery will mean that the heavy-duty connecting wires will start to move and possibly chafe, and then you have the risk of fire, quite apart from the fact that the engine will stop rapidly without a battery connection. Check at regular intervals that the battery is both securely fastened down and the connections and wires are all secure. A smear of grease on the terminals can also stop corrosion here.

Wiring The wiring connecting an outboard to the boat's electrical system can present problems as it has to be very flexible to accommodate the steering and tilting movement of the engine, while at the same time it is very exposed. In particular, the heavy-duty starter cables have to be of a special type that is fully flexible. The normal heavy-duty semi-rigid starter motor wires found on other engines are definitely not

suitable. The wiring must be protected from chafing against any sharp edges that could damage the installation, and one of the better approaches is to put electrical wiring inside a rubber tube so that it has some protection from the movement of the boat.

Modern RIB electrical systems are normally very reliable but remember that electricity and water do not mix and if they do then the water always wins. If you bear this in mind when installing or checking electrical systems on your boat, there is a reasonable chance that it will survive in the harsh environment in which it has to

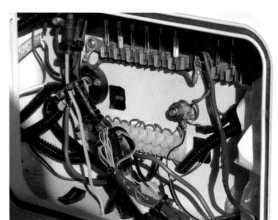

operate. When doing your checks, look out for any signs of chafe in the wiring and for corrosion at the terminals and connections, and if you find it, do something about it because it will not fix itself.

COOLING SYSTEMS The other main requirement for an outboard motor to run is an adequate supply of cooling water. The cooling-water system is built into the engine so there is nothing that has to be done in the installation to make this work. The main thing which has to be understood with this cooling system is that it incorporates a pump in the lower part of the drive housing that uses a synthetic rubber impeller. Rubber impellers are not intended to be run dry, and so while it is permissible to just fire up the engine on dry land to make sure it is going to work, it must be cut immediately, or this rubber impeller gets hot and melts. This pump needs the water that it pumps through the engine to lubricate and cool it, and so as a matter of principle the engine should not be run when out of water unless a hose connection is fitted to supply cooling water.

One problem to which outboard motors can be prone is in getting the relatively fine grid of the cooling water intake blocked. Plastic bags are a notorious hazard in this respect; they wrap themselves around the front of the outboard drive leg, effectively blocking off the water supply. There is not a lot you can do about this except to keep your eyes peeled for debris when you are driving the boat, and try to avoid areas where debris may be a hazard. Clearing any debris from around the outboard is not particularly difficult. Simply tilt the outboard, clear

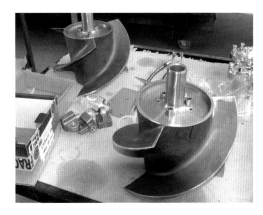

the debris, put the outboard down again and away you go. The main problem is to detect the obstruction to the cooling-water system before it does serious damage to the engine. With electric start engines, there is a warning light or alarm to indicate that the engine temperature is rising, but with manual outboards you probably will not have this luxury, and the first you may be aware of a problem is when the engine starts to falter or stop. By this time there could be serious damage inside the engine because the precision machinery of the modern outboard is very sensitive to changes in its operating environment. The only solution is to be sensitive to the engine's performance and take note of any unexpected changes in engine speed. You can also check the water outlet (which is visible from the rear of the engine) at regular intervals, although the chances are you won't be looking at this when the problem occurs.

DEALING WITH SALT WATER Salt water is highly corrosive, so when operating outboards it is advisable to wash them through with fresh water after each trip. To help you do this there are special fittings that you either clamp around or fit over the water intake. Some modern outboards have this as a permanent fitting. Not only does this flush out the salt water in the engine, but it also allows you to run the engine on dry land where it is much easier to make adjustments and tune it if necessary. If you adopt this procedure every time you come in to shore, you will help prolong the life of the engine. At the same time, take off the hood and check the exterior of the engine, dry it off and spray it liberally with silicone grease, which again will help to reduce the onset of corrosion, particularly around the fittings of the electrical system.

Inboard engines

Much of what has been said about checks and maintenance of outboards also applies to inboard engines, whether petrol or diesel.

The petrol inboard engine is being used less and less on RIBs as lightweight powerful diesels take over, which removes the use of highly flammable and possibly explosive fuel. However, if you have a petrol engine, you need to operate the engine compartment fan for a few minutes before you start it to clear any fumes from the enclosed compartment. It makes sense to open up the hatch anyway to give a visual check around the engine, since it is so easy for the engine to be out of sight and out of mind. On this visual check you are looking for signs of any leakage on the fuel lines and the cooling systems. Leaks on the fuel system may be hard to spot but wiping your hand along the lines and connections will enable you to detect them by feel. On the

> ## Oil checks
>
> *The advent of high horsepower four-stroke outboards has changed the face of RIB engines and the servicing requirements. Instead of mixing the oil and fuel together or having a separate oil container, there is oil in the engine sump and this needs to be checked regularly, preferably every time you go to sea. There is also oil in the lower gearbox, and while this does not need to be checked every time you head out, it should be on a list of regular monthly checks (this applies to both two-stroke and four-stroke outboards).*

cooling system, leaks in the seawater pipes can usually be seen by traces of white salt crystals, but also look for any corrosion on the worm screw clamps – although modern stainless steel clamps will not corrode. Also check for any signs of swelling in the rubber pipes. This is usually the first sign that the pipe is reaching the end of its useful life. While working on the cooling system, check the water intake filters, since these can get clogged up if you operate in dirty water. Also make sure that your seacocks are open before you go to sea and once the engines are running, check that the used cooling water is discharging overboard through the exhaust pipe. Look for any signs of oil leaks around the engine and any signs of corrosion on the electrical fittings.

Most modern engines have flexible mounts that allow a degree of movement in the engine to reduce vibrations. Flexible mounting also means that all the connections have to be flexible, so this may be the first place you see signs of trouble. Check these mounts at intervals, because they do come under heavy stress on a RIB, but such checks may be part of the annual checks rather than every time you go to sea.

With an inboard engine, the electrical system is likely to have a dual battery system where the two batteries are charged from the one engine-mounted alternator, but one is reserved solely for engine-starting purposes and the other is used to supply auxiliary circuits. A paralleling switch will also be included in the circuit, which allows both batteries to be put on line for engine-starting in case the starting battery is low. In this way you can ensure the reliability of the electrical system to a higher degree. Only the highest possible standard of electrical outfitting is tolerable in a rigid inflatable, and this is not an area for making economies.

The auxiliary circuits will be protected with fuses or breakers, but if breakers are used they must be the type that will stand up to the high dynamic loadings of a RIB, and not simply pop out at the slightest excuse. These breakers are much easier to reset than trying to replace fuses.

Although water shouldn't get into the engine compartment, it must be assumed that a certain amount of spray or damp will enter, so connections should be well protected against corrosion by spraying with silicone grease or other proprietary products. All connections should be positively bolted connections, rather than push fit connectors, which have a nasty habit of jumping loose just when you least want them to.

EXHAUST SYSTEMS Normally a wet exhaust system is fitted to a RIB with an inboard engine, and we have talked about the risk of fire and flooding if one of the seawater pipes fails (*see* page 223). To give early warning of this situation you need

a flow alarm in the cooling-water system, which will immediately indicate if the water flow has stopped. Again, the position of the sensor needs to be carefully thought out, because a failure in a hose might not sound the warning alarm since the water is still flowing through the pipe into the bilge. Probably the best position for such a sensor is close to where the cooling water passes into the exhaust pipe, and then it will cover most failure situations.

As far as the engine exhaust is concerned, apart from the problems of failure, the main requirement to guard against is that water flowing back down through the exhaust and into the engine when the boat is going astern or is stopped in a seaway. When going astern the engine exhaust pressure will normally keep water out of the exhaust pipe and the most dangerous time is when the boat is stopped dead in the water. The solution here is to take the exhaust upwards before it runs down to the transom, or at least have the outlet manifold where the rubber section connects in, close to the highest point in the engine compartment, and certainly well above the waterline.

VENTILATION Ventilation is the other important aspect for an inboard diesel engine, and you need to combine a system that allows plenty of air to enter the engine compartment, while at the same time keeping water out. A simple louvered vent is generally all that is required and if it is placed in a protected area around the console, it will ensure that relatively dry air gets to the engine compartment.

Engine checklist

✔ Engine oil level checked
✔ Cooling water checked
✔ Spare oil on board
✔ Fuel filter checked
✔ Seawater intake filter checked
✔ Seacocks open
✔ Loose equipment in the engine room and steering compartment stowed and secured
✔ Battery and electrical switches in correct positions
✔ Belt drive for the water pumps and the alternator checked

→ Hand starting for outboards is practical up to about 40hp

A water trap can be incorporated into the system so that if water does get into the intake it will settle out before finding its way down into the engine compartment. The air intake should be taken close to the bottom of the engine compartment because then the air will tend to circulate around the compartment and help to keep things cool. With experience you will get to know the first signs of engine trouble, and if you manage to detect them early you should have a reliable and trouble-free run out at sea.

MAINTAINING THE PROPULSION SYSTEM

As far as outboards are concerned propulsion is almost entirely through a propeller, but with inboard engines the main choice lies between a stern drive and a water jet. Over a season of use, particularly if the boat is beached or operates in shallow water, the propeller can get worn or damaged. With a painted propeller, the wear is easy to see as the paint flakes off and, although this is not normally a problem, you should look for nicks in the edges of the propeller blades created by striking debris or stones. Unless these are deep, the edge of the propeller can

normally be filed back down to a smooth edge without too much loss of efficiency. If you sense vibration in a drive unit, propeller damage should be the first thing to look for.

With a stern drive, maintenance is similar to that of an outboard, since you have to check the lower gearbox oil level.

There should be no maintenance to water-jet propulsion, except perhaps to check the gearbox oil levels if this is integral to the jet unit. The jet itself may have oil circulation, but often the water-jet bearings are water lubricated. However, if your RIB lies afloat for any time you could face the problem of marine growth inside the jet tunnel. Marine growth can also be a problem with stern drives and outboards if the propeller is not clear of water when tilted. In both cases the growth will cause a loss of efficiency and should be cleaned off as soon as possible, although clearing growth from a water jet could entail dismantling, since access can be very restricted, particularly on smaller jets. Prevention is better than cure and you would do well to store the boat on dry land, but this can be a problem with larger RIBs. If the RIB does lie afloat, as is the case with many commercial and para-military RIBs, running the jet at regular intervals for a short period should keep the growth at bay.

FUEL MANAGEMENT AND ECONOMY

Fuel plays a vital role in RIB operations and it sounds obvious that you need to have enough fuel on board to complete the planned passage, but there is much more to fuel than

that. You may be concerned about operating economically to minimise fuel consumption – whether for economic or 'green' reasons – and you can use the fuel to help trim the boat in certain circumstances. So how can we reduce the amount of fuel that we burn but still get enjoyment from our RIB cruising and effective operations for the professionals?

Calculating fuel use

The main problem with reducing fuel consumption is that on many boats today we don't know how much of it we are using. We know how much there is on board when the fuel tanks are filled up, since the builder's handbook tells us how much the tanks hold, but we need to know how much fuel is going through the engines at any one time and what amount it will take to complete a passage. Of course, you can work it out afterwards by checking what is left in the tanks, but to be meaningful we really want to know what the engines are burning as we go along.

Engine manufacturers' charts show the theoretical amount of fuel the engines are burning at any given rpm, and with larger, more modern engines you can use the computer controls to find out what the real-time fuel consumption of your engine is. Here you get a read-out of how many

litres per hour each engine is burning on the engine monitoring display. That is a useful figure and you can immediately see how, when you open or close the throttle, the fuel consumption of the engine rises and falls. These figures can be quite frightening if you are paying the bills, but they only tell you half the story because they do not relate to the speed of the boat. What you really want to know is not how many litres per hour the engines are burning but how many litres per mile, or miles per litre, you are using. When you have a fuel consumption meter in your car it tells you have many miles you can get to a litre of fuel, but getting this figure on a boat is more difficult. You can work it out from the litres per hour figure by factoring in the speed to know how many miles you have covered in that hour. It is a cumbersome way of getting the figure you want, but without a GPS input in the engine computer it is your only hope.

LITRES PER MILE Assuming that your boat has one of the modern electronic engine displays that show the fuel consumption in litres per hour it is easy to convert this to the much more useful litre per mile figure – simply divide the litres per hour figure by your speed in knots. However, do remember that the main speed read-out on board will come from the GPS, which shows the speed over the ground and not the speed through the water (which is the one you want), so you may need to add or subtract a knot or two to allow for the tide influence.

It can be a good idea to spend some time on a calm day taking fuel consumption figures throughout the speed range of the boat so that you can draw up a graph of fuel consumption per mile. This will be a valuable tool when doing your passage planning, since you can simply multiply the litres per mile figure by the length of the passage to find out how much fuel you will need when running at that particular speed. Then add on a reserve amount – perhaps 20 per cent – and an allowance to get you to an alternative port that could be a greater distance away than your chosen port. Allow for the amount of fuel in the tank that will not be accessible, and you have your minimum fuel quality that you need for the passage. (Do bear in mind that fuel consumption is likely to increase if you have a head wind on the passage and for a planing boat it will also go up if you have extra weight on board.)

Why is this litres per mile figure so much better than using litres per hour? It's quite simple really – for every mile you travel you know how much fuel you will burn or have burnt, and that is the positive indication of whether you are running economically or not. You may have a deadline to keep and need to open the throttles, but if you are just intent on having a comfortable economical cruise, you can set the consumption to suit your mood, or perhaps your pocket.

The litre per mile consumption figures may surprise you. Running at the lowest speed may not prove to be the most economical for a planing boat. You may find that you need to get the boat onto the plane to get the best consumption figure per mile travelled, but at least when you have that litres per mile read-out or calculation, you can see the effect of all the different throttle settings and decide on the one that suits. Having that read-out also means that you can see the effect of trimming the hull and what happens when you adjust the trim with the flaps. You may be surprised to see what a difference a change of trim can make to the fuel consumption per mile. Don't look for an immediate change in the consumption when you make adjustments, because the readings may take some time to settle down after a change.

If you want to be fully in control of the fuel situation, you may need to do trials on different days and in varying conditions to build up a full picture of the fuel consumption.

One important point to remember when carrying out fuel consumption checks in this way is the effect of tide. Since, as we have discussed, your GPS always measures the speed over the ground and not the speed through the water, when travelling with the tide you will get a better mileage, while when travelling against it consumption will appear to go up. These can be valid consumption figures to use when you are cruising because they represent the actual consumption at the time, but when you are trying to find the right trim and balance to optimise the fuel consumption the tide will confuse the issue. Therefore, try to do any fuel trials in non-tidal waters, or at least at slack water.

When thinking about fuel consumption and fuel reserves on a twin-engine boat, also look at what the consumption per mile might be when running on just one engine. If you suffer an engine failure when on passage, you are reduced to running on one engine and that could make a significant different to the fuel consumption (this is one more thing to measure when you are doing those fuel consumption trials). One further thing to remember is that if you are reduced to single-engine operation, it is not a good idea to run the remaining engine at a high rpm, since it will be operating with a propeller that is not matched to the engine and boat speed and will become overloaded. Moderate rpm will help to ensure that the remaining engine keeps going until you get to port and this is not likely to make much difference to your speed.

Fuel reserves

Now that you have your litres per mile figured out and a figure for the number of miles you are planning to travel on the planned passage, it is not rocket science to then calculate how much fuel you will need. The complications set in when you attempt to check how much of fuel you have on board and to calculate what level of reserve fuel should you carry. As we have already mentioned, the boatbuilders will tell you how much fuel your tank holds, but do they tell you how much of that fuel is useable fuel? Almost all fuel tanks have a suction pipe that connects the tank to the engine above the bottom of the tank. It is not good practice to draw from the bottom of the tank, because then there is no space for any water or dirt

in the fuel to settle out. So there could be as much as 10 per cent of the fuel in the tank that is not available for use. That is fine if you know about it, but this scenario brings us to the question of fuel gauges. Today, fuel gauges are fitted on many RIBs using a variety of measuring systems. Whatever the system used, it is vital that you know firstly how accurate it is, and secondly whether or not the amount includes the section of unusable fuel at the bottom of the tank. The tanks gauges that simply show ¼, ½, ¾ and full do not give you the level of accuracy you require and such uncertainty can leave you guessing. Without doubt, the best type of fuel gauge is the sight gauge, a clear vertical tube attached to the tank, where the level in the tube matches that inside the tank. However, with tanks usually located below the deck, access might be impossible.

You should always plan to have a suitable fuel reserve on board before departure. I would hope that you never have to think about using your reserve when on passage, but I like to play it safe and have plenty of fuel on board, even though there could be a speed penalty because of the extra weight. A reserve of 10 or 15 per cent seems to be the accepted level, but I personally think that is too low – at 10 per cent you only have another 10 miles running on a voyage of 100 miles: not much if you have to detour, stop to help another boat or perhaps speed up to get to port early. I would recommend the reserve should be at least 20 per cent, and that should be calculated on top of the distance to the furthest alternative port in your passage planning.

Diesel bug

'Diesel bug' is an organism that can grow and multiply in diesel fuel and which will eventually lead to clogging of fuel lines and filters, and generally prevent effective operation of your engine. The build-up tends to be slow and steady, rather than sudden, and if you clean your fuel filters frequently you may become aware of the problem because of the 'gunge' you find there before it gets too serious. Once in the fuel system, diesel bug is very hard to get rid of and there are various 'disinfectants' that claim to cure the problem, but it is much better to prevent it in the first case, the best safeguard always being to get your fuel from a reliable source.

Reducing fuel emissions

EU legislation will soon dictate that fuel supplied for boats which operate on inland waterways and on recreational craft 'when not at sea' use sulphur-free diesel fuel. Just what is described as 'sulphur-free' is not quite clear at the time of writing, but the sulphur content in fuel does help to reduce the diesel bug problem, so these problems may be on the increase when sulphur-free fuel is introduced. At present, seagoing boats are exempt, but how long that will last is an open question. Another possibility in the future is the use of bio-diesel, and this is also thought to be more prone to the diesel bug. This whole question of safe fuel is a thorny area for boaters and the best solution I can offer is again to get your fuel from a reliable source.

If you want to reduce emissions on a RIB, speed and hull design are two factors where savings can really be made. It's quite simple really – as a general rule, the faster you go the more fuel you will burn and the higher your emissions will be. So one of the easiest ways to reduce emissions is to reduce speed. Your fuel consumption will also rise if you continually open and close the throttle as you might when trying to maximise speed in rough seas. As for hull design, you might get better economy with a catamaran hull and even greater efficiency if this catamaran has the aerofoil lift wing between the hulls. For a monohull, the lower the hull deadrise the more efficient the hull form, but there will be a penalty in the harsher ride. You find that many small yacht tenders have a low deadrise, which is acceptable if they only operate in harbours.

Going green on RIBs has not been developed to any large extent, but that could be about to change. There are a number of alternative fuels such as bio-fuels and LPG that could offer emission savings, but the high cost of conversions has restricted use. Perhaps the best hope for the future will be found in the new generation of electric propulsion systems, with electric outboards now becoming available in higher power outputs that make the planing electric RIB a viable proposition (*see* pages 229-230, for more information).

For future demands for reducing emissions and fuel consumption we may have to live life at a slower pace and adapt to change. To many that will take away the very ethos of RIBs, which is that of a vessel that takes boating to the limits. Perhaps the trend to green boating will start at the professional end of the market, where economy could have a bigger impact on operations.

14 TUBE AND HULL CARE

IN GENERAL, RIBs lead a harder life than most other boats, so both their maintenance and repair are very important factors in maintaining their reliability. The very nature of a RIB and its ability to bounce off quays and jetties and other boats tends to make it the subject of abuse. As we have explored in other chapters, RIBs often operate off beaches, where the wear and tear tends to be exaggerated because of abrasive sand and shingle. Maintenance, in particular, is vital if you are going to get any sort of useful life out of the boat. Knowing how to repair the boat can get you out of trouble when something goes wrong in areas remote from service, such as on board a mother ship. You can usually undertake full maintenance work during an annual check, the main requirements being painting, varnishing and re-gluing any areas that have come adrift. However, it is well worth going through a quick checking routine every time the boat comes back in from sea. In this way you will discover any damage or wear before it gets serious, but perhaps equally importantly you will be secure in the knowledge that the boat is ready for sea next time you come to use it.

'BACK FROM SEA' MAINTENANCE

Washing out the boat

The first thing to do during 'back from sea' maintenance is to wash down the boat thoroughly in fresh water. This gets rid of all the salt water, and can remove grit and other contamination from inside the boat. To do this you need to put the boat into a

position where the water can drain out, and with a RIB afloat this will be automatic, provided that the deck level is above the outside water level (on a trailer, a RIB should drain freely through the stern drains, but you might want to remove the drain plug in the transom, which will allow any water that has accumulated inside the hull to drain as well). Washing down is particularly important if you have been to the beach, because any dirt and grit inside the boat is very abrasive and tends to find its way into the tiniest corners of the boat, particularly between areas where the air tube is attached to the rigid deck. Here it can work away, rubbing the proofing off the fabric and creating the possibility of air leaks. Rather than just washing the boat out with a freshwater hose, it is best to first use a bucket of water with mild detergent, perhaps washing-up liquid, to wash down the boat beforehand. This will remove any grease or other contaminates from the rubber fabric, while hand-washing will make you inspect the tube

↑ Peeling off a patch on a RIB tube show the poor adhesive application

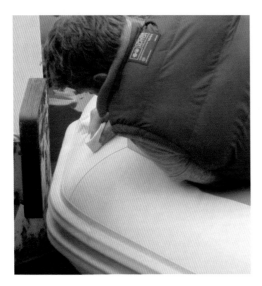

more carefully, which allows you to discover patches or tapes that may be starting to lift on the air tube. Using detergent on the surface of the air tubes could also indicate any air leaks through groups of bubbles gathering round the leak.

Stick to just detergent and water or one of the number of proprietary RIB cleaners for cleaning the boat, but if you use the proprietary ones, check the contents carefully and reject any that contain silicone. Silicone can give the tube a great shiny finish and return it to a close-to-new condition, but it can cause problems if any repairs have to be carried out on the tube. Trying to get that film of silicone off the rubber can be very difficult, and the glue will not stick until it is removed.

Checking fittings and fixtures

Once you have completed the washing-out process, take the time to have a quick look around the boat to check fittings and fixtures. Look inside the console (if there is one) to make sure there is no damp on the electrics, and if there are any exposed connections, a spray of a silicone grease aerosol will help keep corrosion at bay. Any parts such as catches which have to be kept moving should be treated with the same aerosol spray, but don't use it on the air valves in the tubes or other threaded components, because it will tend to attract dust and grit, which may make it very difficult to operate the screw thread (you could also get the silicone on the tube material).

Your routine check on coming in from sea should also include a check on the engine (*see* pages 234–242).

END OF SEASON/OUT OF SERVICE MAINTENANCE

The routine 'back from sea' maintenance should not take more than 10 or 15 minutes, but at the end of the season or when the boat is taken out of service you need to

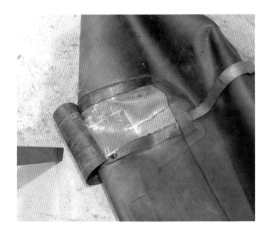

do a much more thorough job. Even so, it should not take more than half a day to go through the boat in detail, or a full day if there is any repair or maintenance work to be carried out.

To do this check, you need to strip down the boat as far as possible so that you can get access to the parts that are not normally visible (it may be possible to remove the console and open up the hatch covers or deck panels).

Varnishing wooden components

Time spent on getting varnished wood back into condition will be repaid in the longer life your boat will get, despite the harsh environmental conditions of salt and sun. If you are varnishing any wooden components, thoroughly rub down the existing woodwork with sandpaper to get a clean, even surface finish. You will need to apply probably four or five good coats of a quality marine varnish (two part polyurethane varnish is the best, and is certainly the most durable) to produce a finish that is going to stand up to a season of hard wear and tear.

Repairing rigid components

Any damage to the rigid components should be corrected by either replacing them or building them up to their original shape. If engine mounting holes in the transom have become elongated because of slight engine movement, the existing holes can be filled with wooden plugs and epoxy filler and then new holes drilled as required. Most minor damage to floors and other components can be repaired by similar use of epoxy filler, which is inserted into the damaged area after it has been cleaned out, and then the surface is ground down to match the original.

With the rigid section of the hull, go over the surface carefully, inspecting every square centimetre of it for chips and scratches. This is best done by rubbing your hand over the surface, whereupon you will often be able to feel the defects before you can see them, particularly if they don't extend right through the gel coat to the laminate underneath. Mark these areas with a waterproof felt-tip pen as you find them, and then look at each one more carefully. Where it is just the gel coat which has been damaged, and you can tell this is the case when you see the same colour right through the scratch or chip, you can simply lightly grind out the cavity with an emery disc in an electric drill or even with emery paper used by hand, and fill it with a matching gel coat, which can usually be obtained from the boat manufacturer. To complete the job, the gel coat insert is then rubbed down flush with the surrounding surfaces using a very fine emery disc and the whole area polished with an abrasive cleaner, so that it matches.

Small chips and scratches of this type can be left in most cases without fear of the damage getting worse, because the gel coat still provides a seal against water getting into the laminate. The touching-up treatment suggested is only really necessary if you are concerned about the cosmetic appearance of your boat.

More serious and certainly requiring attention are those chips and scratches which extend into the laminate. These can usually be a identified as a white or yellowy surface under the gel coat with a fibrous texture. If these are shallow chips or scratches, where only the gel coat has been removed, they can be treated in the same way as described above, but to you do need to grind back the gel coat to a point where there is positive adhesion between it and the laminate underneath. This can be checked by picking at the bond between the gel coat and the laminate with the sharp point of a knife. If the gel coat can be lifted, you will have to grind back a bit further until you find a strong bond. Make sure that the exposed laminate is completely dry (a hairdryer or similar hot-air blower will help here, although take care not to raise the temperature too high). Once the area is thoroughly dry simply you follow the routine above for filling chips.

If the chips or damage actually extends into the laminate, it may require more extensive treatment. Firstly put a straight edge across the damaged area, making sure that it is level with the clean gel coat on either side, and check the depth. If the damage is relatively shallow – perhaps just a millimetre or two – you can probably get away with filling the damaged area with the gel coat without any significant loss of strength. However, if there is any doubt, as could be the case if the damage has been caused by an impact, you will need to grind out the whole of the damaged area, and this includes any areas of delamination between the layers of the laminate, so that you cut the laminate back to a clean, fresh surface. Now you can lay up new laminate inside the ground-out area. It is best to use epoxy resins for this lay-up, because these are stronger than the normal vinyl resins commonly used in the original laminate. After building up the laminate in this way you may need to grind down the surface after it has cured, so that you can lay up the gel coat on top of the laminate and complete the repair.

Much of this maintenance work may be cosmetic, but there is no doubt that it pays to do this annual work on a GRP structure, largely to ensure that water cannot get into the laminate under the gel coat and cause further deterioration.

Repairing air tubes and fabric

As far as the air tubes and fabrics of the boats are concerned, again you must go over the surface with minute inspection, looking for areas where the outer proofing of the fabric has been worn away, where taping and seals may have lifted, and where there is any other evidence of damage or decay. You need to inspect all the usually inaccessible areas, because this is where wear and tear is much more likely. Also check such items as handholds, fender strips, bow rings and transoms. You should not be able to lift any of the joints, seams or patches when you

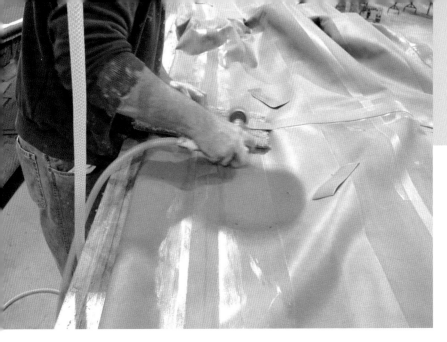

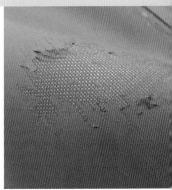

pick at the edge with your fingernail, and if you do find any areas where there is lifting or wear and tear, mark them with a felt-tip pen so that they can receive further attention.

You will probably be aware of whether or not the boat is leaking air during regular use, but now is a good time to check out the air-holding qualities of the boat by painting the air tubes all over with a soft brush dipped in a detergent solution. Inflate the tube hard and then work the solution up into a foam and paint it all over the surface. If there are any air leaks they will soon become evident, because bubbles will form – usually a series of bubbles forming in a particular spot or perhaps along the edge of a seam. These should all be marked so that you can find them once the tube dries off and you can start the repair work. While checking for these air leaks also put the bubbly mixture over and around the air valves to check them for air tightness.

TECHNIQUES FOR ADHESIVE MAINTENANCE REPAIRS Now you have the marked areas which need attention around the boat. If it is just a question of edges lifting, you will need to dry out the affected areas thoroughly and, again, a

hairdryer can be good for this. Separate the affected areas as far as possible, which means opening up a seam until you come to sound adhesive. It is possible to open up a seam or an attachment flange a bit further by careful application of hot air from a hairdryer or hot-air gun into the gap using a fine nozzle. The heat will soften the adhesive and allow you to gently peel it back as you grip it with pliers, and in this way you can be sure you have got back to a sound bond before starting the repair.

To avoid spreading adhesive outside the repair area you can mark it off with masking tape so that the adhesive only goes where you want it to. Now remove any old glue and lightly abrade the surfaces exposed between the two edges of the seam, or the patch and the air tube in the case of an attachment, so that you have a good key for the adhesive. While holding the surfaces apart, firstly clean them with toluene, acetone or a cleaning liquid supplied by adhesive manufactures, then apply the adhesive, making sure that both surfaces are well but thinly covered. Do not apply too much adhesive – only a thin coat is required. There is a mistaken belief that the more adhesive you apply the stronger the joint will be, but it

↓↓ Seam-covering strips have come loose and need gluing back in position

↓↓ A poorly applied patch which is bubbling up and adhesive overlaps the patch

doesn't work like that and the joint is likely to be weaker if anything. Let this first coat dry for some 15 minutes and then apply a second thin coat of adhesive. Once this is virtually dry, after about 10 minutes, you can push the two surfaces together, starting from the back of the seam and working towards the edge to exclude all the air, using as much pressure as possible. It may be better to do this work with the tube deflated so that you can use a small roller to remove any air from the gap, and this will also allow you to apply good pressure to the two surfaces so that they bond properly. After a few minutes you can clean up any excess adhesive with one of the solvents mentioned above. The adhesive will take around 48 hours to fully cure, and you should then have a seam or attachment which is ready for another season's use.

DEALING WITH LARGER FABRIC AND TUBE REPAIRS These maintenance-type repairs are quite straightforward, providing you can get reasonable access to the area. They are not generally critical repairs compared with those which involve an air leak or damage to the fabric. These can be divided into two types that demand a different approach. Firstly there is the small repair, which may be anything from a pin prick to a tear 5cm in length. Then there is the second type, a tear up to around 25cm in length (provided that this doesn't go through any seam in the air tube or cover more than one compartment). Anything outside these two areas of damage would normally mean taking the boat to a repair station where they have the experience and facilities to deal with extensive repairs.

Small repairs are relatively straight-

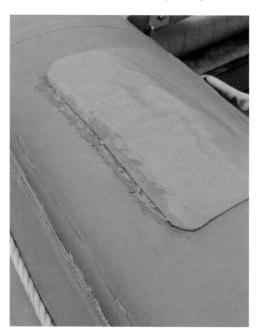

forward and can usually be fixed with a single patch on the outside of a tube alone. Cut a patch with rounded corners using similar material to that of the tube. This can usually be obtained from the manufacturer of the boat, or a service and repair station. If this is the fabric that has neoprene on one side and hypalon on the other, make sure that you use the material the same way round as the way it is used in the boat, which normally means having the hypalon on the outside. Cut the patch to extend 5cm clear of the tear or puncture, so that you have a good overlap, and place it on the tube. Mark round its edge and use masking tape to surround the marked area.

Prepare both the patch and the tube by lightly sanding the surface (you can use mechanical sanders for this job provided you use them with care and don't take too much of the rubber off). It is vital that you get the rubber down to a fresh, clean surface, or the adhesive will not do its job properly. Once you have cleaned the rubber, don't touch it with your fingers because you will transmit grease to the surface and the adhesive won't stick in these areas. Use one of the solvents to clean the sanded areas thoroughly of any grease or other contaminates. Apply your first thin coat of adhesive and again, allow it to dry before applying a second coat. Once this has become tacky apply the patch to the tube using the marked lines as a guide. When you do this make sure the tube is lying on a flat, hard surface and apply the patch with a rolling motion, applying it one side first and then gradually extending the application across the whole area so that air

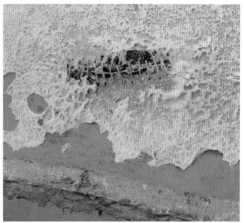

is forced out of the gap between the patch and the tube, and doesn't become trapped as a bubble. You only have one chance to get the patch in the right place because bonding of the adhesive is instantaneous. If you do get it wrong, careful application of heat from a hairdryer will help release the bond, but you will probably have to apply another coat of adhesive and go through the process again.

Once the patch and the air tube have been put together, roll the surface with a small, hard roller, starting at the centre and working outwards. A roller comprised of several discs is better than a solid roller, and the aim of rolling the patch is to both improve the bond between the two components and also to help roll any air bubbles that may have become trapped out from the adhesive area. Pay particular attention to the bonding around the edge of the patch, and when everything looks firm and secure in place, you can then clean up the patch with the solvent that you used before. Allow the patch to cure for at least 12 hours before inflating the tube, and longer if you possibly can.

For larger tears in the inflatable tube it used to be advised to first stitch up the tear with a needle and thread and then apply a patch to the outside. The stitching restores some strength to the area and avoids the need for an inside patch. These days an inside patch is considered necessary in order to give the repair adequate strength, and while it may sound impossible to put a patch on the inside of a tube, it can be done with a bit of careful planning. The first thing is to widen the hole to around 10cm if it is not already this size, so that you can get your hand inside. Now cut a patch which has an overlap of at least 5cm and follow the same procedure as before, cleaning up the surfaces inside the tube and on the patch, buffing them with abrasive paper to get a fresh, clean surface and finally cleaning them with a solvent. Now you apply adhesive to both the inside areas of the air tube and to the surface of the patch, let them become

tacky as previously, and then apply a second coat. Now you come to the tricky part where you have to get this patch inside the air tube. The best thing is to try a dummy run first without the adhesive, so that you know the sort of procedure to adopt, and then slide the patch into the air tube, and press the air tube firmly down on top of it. It sounds easy but is quite a tricky manoeuvre, because as soon as any two pieces of adhesive touch, they will want to stay together, and you can end up with a sticky mess on your hands unless you plan the operation carefully. You can use a thin polythene sheet to cover the adhesive so that it won't stick, and then peel this off before making the final attachment, but when you do this final attachment try one side of the tear first and then the other side so that you can line them up evenly. Once in position, rub the air tube down firmly with the roller to exclude any air bubbles, ensure that the insides of the tube are not stuck together, leave for 12 hours or so and

↓ Using a hot air gun
to loosen up old adhesive

↓ Once the adhesive has been softened the
edges of the old patch can be lifted gently

255

TUBE AND HULL CARE

then try inflating the tube to a pressure of not more than 2psi to ensure that you have a proper bond and air tightness. Now you can tackle the outside of the tube, the technique here being the same as for a small tear except that you will be dealing with a larger patch which will need more careful handling and should be attached at one end and then gradually rolled into position along the length of the tear.

Finally, an owner might be faced with chafe that has worn away the surface rubber or increased porosity over a larger area of the inflatable tube. The basic technique here is very similar to any patch applied to the outside of the tube, but because the size of the patch is likely to be larger than with most repair jobs, you need to pay careful attention to its application. The preparation work is the same, but when you come to apply the patch, apply it down one side first and then gradually roll the join between the patch and the original fabric carefully to

exclude any air bubbles until you reach the other side and the patch is fully attached. It is much easier to get rid of air bubbles during the process of applying the patch than it is after the patch is attached, and any job of this type is really one for two people – one to do the rolling and one to hold the patch so that it can be applied in a controlled manner. Indeed, with most repairs except the smallest, two people can do the job much better than one, and this sort of co-ordinated approach will produce much better results.

Using eye patches on the tube

Pantaenius Insurance says that it has had several claims where RIBs have been moored up using eye patches on the tube as the attachment point, only to have the patch pull away under the strain.

Shipstore's fabric repair recommendations

Below are the repair recommendations from US RIB repair firm Shipstore, which spell out the techniques, risks and dangers.

ESSENTIAL FOR ALL FABRICS AND GLUES

Low humidity and temperature control

■ *Relative humidity must be less than 70 per cent, preferably as low as 40 per cent. The temperature should be between 64 and 77 degrees Fahrenheit (17.8 and 25 degrees Celsius). Never fiddle around with these. Bond strength drops very rapidly with heat or high humidity.*

■ *Take your boat indoors. Don't even think about trying to glue on the dock or near the water or in direct sunlight. We use a specially built, climate-controlled room, and still we don't attempt to work on a rainy day.*

■ *Note: You are using a two-part contact cement. The solvents in the glue must evaporate before assembly.*

■ *When ready to assemble parts, the glue must not be tacky at all to the finger. It must not have spots of whitish glaze. If so, you may have spread the glue too thick, not waited long enough between coats, or a sudden drop in temperature or gust of humid air may have occurred. Someone may have opened the door, or you may have leaned too close and breathed on it. Plan to stay in the room until finished.*

Be safe!

■ *Do not smoke! Glues and solvents are flammable.*

■ *No open flames (e.g. furnace or pilot light when working in a cellar).*

■ *Use in a well-ventilated area. Fumes can be overwhelming. A carbon filter respirator is recommended.*

■ *Accelerator (small bottle) is toxic. If spilled onto your skin WASH IMMEDIATELY with soap and water. If in your eyes, IMMEDIATELY FLUSH WITH WATER for at least 2 minutes and consult a physician. (Accelerator is an isoxcyanate based product.)*

General tips

If using small cans (250ml) mix the entire can with the dose of accelerator. Inaccurate measurement will weaken the glue. The quality of your final bond depends on the proper mix of chemicals.

■ *Once opened, the accelerator cannot be kept. It will oxidise rapidly. Do not economise and try to save it.*

■ *Apply glue with a paint or glue brush with the bristles cut short (12–18mm) so they are stiff. It must be natural hair (i.e. OK for lacquer); bound in metal not plastic; preferably with a wooden or metal handle.*

■ *Old glue must be completely removed – solvent, sandpaper, scraping, grinding with a Dremel tool. Glue will not stick to old glue. Clean it off thoroughly. If your boat has ever been protected with ArmorAll® or another silicone- or petroleum-based product, you* may have great difficulty getting a bond.

■ To find tiny leaks, inflate boat hard. Put some liquid detergent in a bucket of water and with rag or big wash brush, scrub it all over boat. Keep watch for elusive, tiny bubbles. When you find the first leak, keep looking. You might as well fix them all at the same time!

■ Remember, the number one cause of slow leaks is a poorly-seated valve. Unscrew, clean with water only. Make sure little rubber O rings are good. They are the cheapest repair possible.

■ If patching, cut patch 5–8cm larger than tear in each direction and round the corners. Little 3cm circles pasted over a pin hole won't last.

■ Try to get the same fabric used by the manufacturer for your boat. The inside and outside surface may be different. If you can't match colour, sometimes a cleverly shaped patch in contrasting colour can be made to look like decoration instead of a Band-Aid. e.g. arrow, lightning bolt, even a new D ring if in the right spot. We often put one on each side to look like they came with the boat.

■ Inflate boat to apply accessories. Deflate to patch air leaks, even if very small. Air pressure will bubble the patch before the glue sets.

HYPALON-NEOPRENE INFLATABLE BOAT FABRIC GLUING REPAIR INSTRUCTIONS

■ Be sure to follow the instructions above to the letter.

■ Preferred solvent: Toluene (beware: Toluene is much more toxic than MEK. Shipstore don't use it, but Zodiac does in its factory). You may substitute MEK. Methyl Ethyl Ketone is often available at hardware, plumbing or paint supply stores, sold as a cleaner for PVC pipes or lacquer thinner. For non-critical bonds you might substitute acetone. Use acetone for non-critical bonds only.

■ Glue: Shipstore use Zodiac Universal Glue #7097. You can use Zodiac #7097; Bostik 2 part rubber Glue; or Weaver Hypalon glue.

■ Atmosphere: Humidity less than 65 per cent; not in direct sunlight.

■ Temperature: 64–75 degrees Fahrenheit (17.8–23.9 degrees Celsius).

■ Preparation: Gather rags, glue brush; solvent; timer with second hand or stop watch; old glue cleaned off; patch cut out, position noted and marked.

■ Mix accelerator and glue thoroughly, either now or while waiting between the solvent washes below. Accelerator is toxic: keep off skin. Keep mixed glue covered (foil or wax paper) when not using. Pot life is about 1 hour. It may still look liquid, but have lost effectiveness.

■ Abrade/scuff the fabric to remove any oxidation. Use 100 grit sandpaper or a Dremel tool. Do not cut into the threads under the protective coating. You just need to cut through the surface to allow the solvents to penetrate. Weaver davit rubber surfaces have been pre-processed and do not need abrading – rub just the boat fabric. Wipe clean to remove grit and residue.

(continued overleaf)

Shipstore's fabric repair recommendations continued

Solvent washes (two times)

■ *Scrub both sides (boat and patch or accessory) with MEK on a rag to clean surface. Wait ten minutes (time it).*

■ *Mix glue and accelerator while waiting, if not done already.*

■ *Apply one more solvent wash with ten minute waiting time (timed). (You are preparing the fabric for glue adhesion.)*

Glue coating (two thin layers, 20–30 minutes apart)

■ *Apply thin glue layer with stiff brush to both sides. Aggressively work it in with brush.*

■ *Wait 20 minutes (timed). If glue still looks wet, wait longer. Check for no tack with knuckle; no adhesive should stick to your skin.*

■ *Humidity control while glue is drying is critical. Keep door closed. Don't breathe on glue area while inspecting.*

■ *Repeat layer application steps (total of two layers with 20-minute open time between).*

■ *Wait ten minutes after second layer of glue.*

■ *After ten minutes, join the parts with as much pressure as possible. If over ten minutes or if glue has spots of white haze the glue has picked up moisture and you may try to 'reactivate' it; however, this does not work well with glues other than 7097.*

■ *With a clean rag wet the glue surface with MEK but do not rub the glue off (one quick swipe). Then assemble immediately. Press hard. For accessory on inflated boat you can rub it down vigorously with damp MEK rag.*

Press out all air bubbles and wrinkles from the centre to the edges. On deflated boat, rub as hard as possible with smooth tool, e.g. the back of a large tablespoon. For davits and hard-based accessories, deflate boat and press through from other side to make sure of adhesion. Wipe off excess glue with solvent.

■ *Wait at least 48 hours before use. Chemical bond will continue to strengthen over next seven days. Don't be tempted to shorten the process. Shipstore don't release boats to customers for 48 hours to be sure. Don't cut this short: your patch could peel off like a Post-It® note!*

■ *Pressure test if you want to be sure. Blow it up to full pressure. Leave it overnight.*

■ *Enjoy!*

ZODIAC INFLATABLE BOAT FABRIC GLUE AND REPAIR INSTRUCTIONS

■ *Glue procedures for Zodiac inflatables: Strongan (PVC type).*

■ *Be sure to follow the general instructions above to the letter.*

■ *Preferred Zodiac solvent: MEK (methyl Ethyl Ketone). It is often available at hardware, paint or plumbing stores, sold as a cleaner for PVC pipes or lacquer thinner. For non-critical bonds you might substitute acetone. The Weaver Glue Kit comes with a small can of MEK.*

■ *Glue: Zodiac #7097 Universal Glue; Polymarine Urethane (PVC) Glue or Weaver PVCKIT. Do not use Avon Adhesive (one or two part) or Bostik® or other Hypalon or rubber glues. They simply will not work on synthetic* materials. The Weaver Glue Kit can be shipped, Zodiac 7097 cannot.

■ *Atmosphere: Humidity much less than 70 per cent; not in direct sunlight.*

■ *Temperature: 64–77 degrees Fahrenheit (17.8–25 degrees Celsius).*

■ *Preparation: Gather rags, glue brush; solvent; timer with second hand or stop watch; clean off old glue; pre-cut patch, position noted and marked.*

■ *Mix accelerator and glue thoroughly, either now or while waiting between the solvent washes below. Accelerator is toxic; keep off skin. Keep mixed glue covered (foil or wax paper) when not using. Pot life is about 1 hour. It may still look liquid, but will have lost effectiveness.*

Solvent washes (three times)

■ *Scrub both sides (boat and patch or accessory) with MEK on a rag to clean surface. Wait five minutes (time it). Mix glue and accelerator while waiting, if not done already.*

■ *Apply two more solvent washes with five minute waiting time (time each one) between them.*

(You are preparing the fabric for glue adhesion. Abrading these fabrics is not recommended or necessary.)

Glue coating (three thin layers)

■ *Apply thin glue layer with stiff brush to both sides. Aggressively work it in with brush. If it looks too thin, it is probably correct!*

■ *Wait five minutes (timed). If glue still looks wet, wait longer.*

■ *Repeat previous two steps (total of three layers with five-minute open time between).*

■ *Wait ten minutes after third layer of glue.*

■ *Join the surfaces during the next ten minutes.*

If over 10 minutes or if glue has spots of white haze the glue has picked up moisture and you should try to 'reactivate' it. With a clean rag wet the glue surface with MEK but do not rub the glue off (one quick swipe). Then assemble immediately. Press hard. For accessory installation on an inflated boat you can rub it down vigorously with a damp MEK rag. Press out all air bubbles and wrinkles from the centre to the edges. For patches on a deflated boat rub as hard as possible with smooth tool, e.g. the back of a large metal spoon or ladle. For davits and hard based accessories, deflate boat after getting them in place and press through from other side to make sure of adhesion. Wipe off excess glue with solvent.

■ *Wait at least 48 hours before use or removal from the climate-controlled space. The chemical bond will continue to strengthen over next seven days. Don't be tempted to shorten the process. Shipstore don't release repaired boats to customers for 48 hours to be sure. Don't cut this short: your patch could peel off like a Post-It® note!*

■ *Pressure test if you want to be sure. Blow it up to full pressure. Leave it overnight.*

■ *Enjoy!*

Inflation valve repairs

The inflation valves found in inflatable boats are generally very reliable and if replacements are required, it is generally only the insert that needs replacing, which is a straightforward job. Should the whole valve need replacing, this is probably a job for the service station.

All repair work of this nature should be carried out in a controlled environment that is dry and relatively warm. If you try to do repairs on a beach or in the marina you start off with a handicap, and the adhesives do not work well in high humidity or low temperatures. The adhesives used on RIB tubes are generally of the two-part variety, which when they are mixed will have a shelf life of probably no more than a couple of hours; another reason why you need to plan the repair carefully. The RIB builder will recommend a suitable adhesive for your boat and it pays to stick to this, as there is a variety of different tube materials on the market these days. One-part adhesives will work for an emergency repair and are often supplied with a repair kit as they are easier to use, but they are not a good solution for a long-term repair job.

Repairing hull punctures

More extensive damage to the GRP hull of a rigid inflatable can be repaired by an owner who is prepared to tackle the job methodically. Rather like an air tube, if damage has led to a complete puncture of the hull, ideally you want access to both the inside and the outside to produce an effective repair. Cut all the loose pieces of fibreglass right back to sound laminate and

then grind the edges on both sides down to a fine taper. Laminate can then be applied to both sides of the hole, gradually building up the layers and preferably using epoxy resins. On the inside, a generous overlap of material will help to provide continuity and allow you to build up the outside layer to conform to the existing shape in a repair which will be as strong as the original laminate. You will need some sort of backing to provide support for the laminate as you lay it up, and the best material to use here is a piece of rigid plastic sheeting covered with a thin plastic film, which can be fitted on the outside of the hull while you lay up the inside. This will give a smooth contour to the new laminate and it is then a relatively simple matter to grind it down to get a smooth finish.

Without access to the inside, your repair job can be a bit trickier and you have to resort to other techniques. Prepare the damaged area in much the same way, grinding back to sound laminate, but in this case the taper is from the outside towards the inside in a gentle curve, since this is the side from which you will be doing all the work. Now you still need something to support the laminate while it is being built up, and one technique is to again use a piece of rigid plastic for the job. Because a hole is rarely regular in shape it will inevitably be longer one way than the other, so cut the piece of plastic so that it will pass through the hole in its longest direction and then you can turn it round so that it covers the whole area of the hole once it is in position. To hold it in position a temporary wooden handle, which extends through the hole you

are trying to repair, can be applied to the plastic. A few dabs of suitable adhesive can be applied to the plastic to hold it in place against the inside of the hull and then you have a base against which to carry out the repair work. Of course you have to unscrew the handle before you start the repair work, but once the plastic is in place you lay up the laminate against it, gradually extending it over the gently tapered existing laminate in a repair that will be completed by the final coat or two of gel, which is then ground down and polished to blend the repaired area in with the original.

For RIBs carried on board a mother ship, or those used for critical operations remote from assistance, one solution when there is extensive damage is to fit a new tube. This is really only practical when the tube is designed for easy replacement and this would apply to those tubes that slide on using a sail track system. To remove the old tube it is normally necessary to remove a securing plate or fixing at the stern and perhaps one at the bow and then the whole tube should slide off towards the bow. When fitting the new tube it can help the sliding process to apply some detergent along the track, and on a well-engineered system it should take no more than an hour to make the replacement. It is possible to replace a bolted-on tube in the field, but this is a long tedious operation, removing and replacing all the bolts. For a glued-on tube the only solution is to send the RIB to a repair station for the work to be done. Carrying and fitting replacement tubes is only justified when the RIB is critical to the operation of the mother ship, or perhaps when there is a fleet

of similar RIBs where the cost of one spare tube can be justified. By replacing the tube in this way it does mean that any repair work on the old tube can be carried out in the necessary controlled environment.

Coating with antifouling paint

Finally, if you keep your RIB afloat you will want to coat the bottom of the hull with antifouling paint to stop marine growth. If the outboard or stern drive leg is not clear of the water it should be coated as well, but check that the antifouling paint you use is suitable for this (you may have to get a special antifouling paint to coat the sensitive metal parts). The same applies if the tube is in or close to the water where it could attract marine growth. Regular antifouling paints could attack the rubber of the tube and there are some special paints that claim to be compatible. One I have located is Gummipaint, produced by Veneziani in Italy (www.venezianiyacht.it). On a well-designed RIB the tubes should be just clear of the water but of course they will become immersed if there is any movement in the boat on its mooring.

EPILOGUE: THE FUTURE

RIBS NOW COME in all shapes and sizes, and you have to wonder where it will all end. In addition to the conventional form, they now incorporate wheels, tracks and sails, while there are hovercraft RIBs, RIBs that can fly and even RIBs that are not RIBs (the fully inflatable version). They have shrunk to appease the smaller yacht tender market, and expanded to match the growing wealth of the super-rich. There are even unmanned RIBs that can venture into areas too dangerous for crewed vessels. It does seem as though the RIB now meets nearly all the demands of the ocean, and in addition to becoming the '4-wheel-drive of the sea', it has also become a fashion item. Despite its most obvious drawback (it has inflatables that can puncture), the RIB is the boat of choice for so much of the marine market and both the professional and the leisure user have fallen in love with the concept. The RIB may have had a difficult birth, but in its 50 years of existence it has come a long way and is now a dominant force in maritime design.

But what of the future?

The advent of the RIB has transformed tactical military thinking, and there should be further monumental developments in this area to come. Already there are signs of military ship design placing higher priority on the demands of RIB launch and recovery systems, and these new configurations will enable interceptors and boarding craft to be operated in adverse conditions. Together with helicopters, RIBs are fast becoming the military's primary operational tool.

Currently, the military operates RIBs of up to 10 or 12 metres in length, but we could also see larger RIBs as stand-alone vessels capable of operating well offshore over extended periods. The craft's ability to go alongside other vessels at sea will

create a relatively low-cost but effective means of patrolling and enforcing sensitive areas, such as offshore oil and wind farm installations, and for protecting fisheries. In all marine areas the rising terrorist threat is creating a demand for increased patrols, and the RIB is ready and waiting to take up this role.

Larger RIBs that can operate well offshore as stand-alone vessels may also prove useful to the commercial industry. For example, a larger RIB may provide a low-cost alternative to ships used for survey work and safety and standby operations. They are also ideally placed for servicing offshore buoys and lights. There is scope for using larger RIBs as pilot boats and smaller sizes will no doubt expand into the harbour patrol role.

In terms of the RIB's role in the leisure market, it seems that the sky is the limit. They have become larger and more stylish, yet they have proved that they still retain performance when making serious offshore passages. There are always owners who are looking for adventure rather than glamour, so this side of the market is likely to see growth. In a world where rules on what you can and cannot do increase by the day, the ocean is still a place of comparative freedom and RIBs can provide the key to adventure.

All of this points to RIBs becoming larger and larger, and I am no longer certain of where the upper limit lies. The larger-sized RIBs provide a fender and increased stability, although I am not sure that the actual seaworthiness is improved except by hull design, and that could be incorporated equally well into a conventional hull. The larger RIB feels and looks safer, and perhaps

this is the inspiration behind their use, but it is by no means a given that they offer anything in the way of improved sea-keeping.

Where improvements do still need to be made is in ride comfort and control, and this is where we are likely to see changes in RIB design in the future. The crew is now the weak point in RIB operation and although we have looked at 'shock mitigation', the current buzzword in RIB design, at present the focus is on crew seating rather than trying to stop the shock loadings at source. A more holistic solution would enhance the performance of RIBs both in the leisure and professional sectors.

Most RIBs run with their tubes over-inflated, which increases the harshness of the ride to the detriment of crew comfort. In the future we may see systems that allow the pressure in the tube to be regulated when the boat is underway. Inflation pipes leading to each tube section and coupled to a compressor could make varying tube pressure to suit sea conditions a possibility. You might want a softer tube at the bow in head seas to help absorb some of the shock loadings, or reduce pressure on one side when going alongside another vessel so the RIB does not bounce off. The additional complexity might only be justified when RIBs operate in more extreme conditions, but it has always been a boat designer's dream to come up with a form of variable geometry, and this could be one way to make that a reality.

To a certain extent the modern RIB has lost touch with its origins and the design factors that made those early RIBs, such as the transformational type of craft, have

been lost in development. In some modern designs, the designer and builder have to introduce compensating factors such as sophisticated sprung seating to make the RIBs tenable for their crews, when some of those original design features would have done the job. It might pay modern designers and builders to look back at the history of the RIB to find modern solutions.

We are also likely to see an increase in hybrid designs, the STAB concept being

one version of this, where the inflatable tube is only attached to the side of the hull for stability and fendering. Several RIBs in the leisure sector use a hard bow into which the side tubes fit, and this is another method of not only simplifying the tube design and construction, but providing simple hard mounting points for anchors and other fittings. There are many options to explore in this area, particularly in the case of hull design. However, while the larger builders tend to focus on the mainstream where there is a safe and tested market, the RIB industry is still mainly in the hands of smaller builders who do not have the resources to experiment. Maybe the impetus for experimentation could come from the military, which tends to have better resources to test new concepts. There is definitely a need for RIB research projects.

One of the biggest challenges facing RIB design in the future is that of reducing emissions and going green. At present the emphasis is on promoting performance and ability, but the green challenge is coming, and perhaps we can see the first tentative steps in this direction with the first electric RIBs. Marine electric propulsion is still in its infancy, and as far as RIBs are concerned, it is largely restricted to electric outboards. However, these are producing impressive results and when you look at the operating scenarios of many RIBs, electric propulsion could become a viable proposition. Batteries can now be fully recharged in around half an hour and the battery capacity is improving all the time, so viable electric propulsion for many RIB operations is certainly a possibility.

The need to go green may also spur on new hull designs. Catamarans and trimarans are more efficient than a monohull in most cases and there are some interesting new concepts appearing on the market which take this into account. Foil-assisted catamarans are even more efficient than the standard designs, while some hovercraft hybrids already exist, whereby a cavity is formed under the rigid hull and is filled with low pressure air to lift it in the water and reduce resistance. This removes the need for

flexible skirts. There have been flying RIBs and even submersible RIBs, and operators will continue to demand further specialised applications. There are many ideas, but translating these from experimental to practical everyday RIBs could be a major step.

One area of boating that had seemed to escape from the all-embracing arm of the RIB tube was the jet ski, but now even that is being invaded. A Californian university has built a unique jet ski, one that not only incorporates an inflatable tube around the hull to give increased stability, but that has an air propeller so that the craft can operate with minimum draft. This is a research RIB, designed to explore the seabed in the surf zone where it has previously been notoriously difficult to undertake reliable research. This application demonstrates that RIBs are used when nothing else will do the job, and maybe the jet-ski RIB will be the next generation.

This jet-ski RIB was developed to meet a particular operational requirement and that tends to be the way with RIB development – they have evolved as designers and

↓ Ready for lift-off, a hot air balloon
RIB can open up new possibilities

builders gain confidence and new and better materials emerge. However, there is little or no basic research into RIBs, and to a large degree the RIB business is still a fragmented industry without the resources to invest in experimenting with new ideas and concepts. Therefore, one Dutch builder sought funding from other sources to develop his ground-breaking idea. It received funds from the Netherlands Navy to develop the design of a wave-piercing RIB (wave piercing is taken to mean a very fine bow usually incorporating a vertical or forward reach stem so that the hull cuts through waves rather than riding over them).

This concept has been taken one stage further in a co-operative development involving Damen Shipyard in Holland and the Dutch lifeboat organisation, the KNRM, plus the De Vries Lentsch Design team to develop a new lifeboat design. It is based on a RIB, like all modern Dutch lifeboats, but the hull concept incorporates design features that Damen developed for its Axe Bow commercial craft and superyacht support vessels. The Axe Bow, developed in Marin, also features the wave-piercing bow. It is claimed that this gives the hull a better performance in head seas without the loss of other aspects of performance. Tank tests have taken place at Marin in Wageningen to evaluate the performance of the hull design in waves and this new lifeboat design is an attempt to translate this concept into smaller sizes. It is proposed that the lifeboat will have a length of 19m matched to a draft of just 1.10m, since Dutch lifeboats are often called upon to operate in shallow water. Water-jet drive will aid this minimum draft

and the jets will be coupled to a pair of 1000hp diesels to produce speeds of up to 35 knots, making this new design one of the fastest all-weather lifeboats.

The Axe Bow lifeboat has a high vertical stem that cuts through the waves with a minimum of lift, so there is less chance of the hull contouring over the wave, and the pitching is reduced (often the limiting factor in head sea operations). This lifeboat should have a much more level ride and because the hull widens out from the bow into a conventional deep vee hull shape that runs aft into planing surfaces, it will allow for good speed potential. Furthermore, this new design includes a fully enclosed wheel house that makes it self-righting. The KNRM use inflatable tubes that feature a double skin with a foam layer between the skins. The tube has a small diameter at the bow and, like the hull, the tube increases

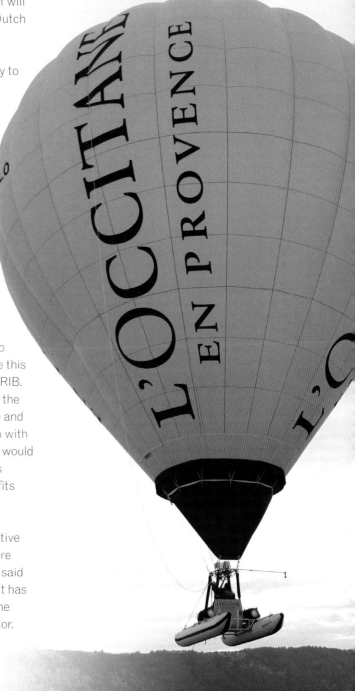

in diameter as it runs aft. The hull itself will be constructed in aluminium, like all Dutch lifeboats.

If this new lifeboat design proves successful in extended trials, it is likely to be adopted by other lifeboat societies.

Wave-piercing hull shapes could be one of the most significant developments in RIB design, but by and large RIBs evolve from past experience or, in many cases, from ignoring past experience in attempts to reinvent the wheel. This could explain why so many of the lessons learned when developing those early RIBs are now ignored and why, too often, modern RIBs have a harsh ride with seaworthiness taking second place to style or convenience in the design. Perhaps the time has come to return to basics, invest in research and combine this with modern materials to reinvent the RIB. It is time for research funding to study the interaction between an inflatable tube and waves and also to research hull design with a view to keeping the hull upright. This would help us to better understand how RIBs operate and how their perceived benefits are derived. The question is, would we come up with a better boat?

Fifty years ago when the first tentative steps towards the concept of a RIB were taken there were plenty of people who said it could not be done. However, the craft has moved inexorably forward and today the RIB is a major force in the marine sector. I am convinced that RIB development has many more miles to run.

THE COMPLETE RIB MANUAL

ACKNOWLEDGEMENTS

There are so many people to thank for their help in writing this book. Firstly, the RNLI, who gave me the chance to experiment and take those first tentative steps into the world of RIBs. There are so many people who were involved in the early development of RIBs and they all deserve credit. It was a co-operative effort that finally came up with a design that worked.

I must thank Charles Dyas, one of the pioneers of RIBs, who introduced me to the world of RIB cruising. Special mention must be made of Fabio Buzzi, the Italian design genius who introduced me to the world of very high-speed RIBs and who gave me the chance to experience driving RIBs right on the edge of performance. We won some very important races together, even share the same birthday, and still discuss RIB design issues today. Then there are the many designers and builders who have allowed me to take their boats to sea, often in adverse conditions, so that I have been able to extend my experience of RIBs.

So many RIB builders have helped me with the photographs for this book, without which it would be the poorer. They have given their time and help willingly and I am so grateful. I wish I could name them all individually but the list is so long.

I must also thank the sponsors of this book: Pantaenius, who have a huge experience of what can go wrong with a RIB through their exposure to the insurance market, and EP Barrus, whose engineering skills have done so much to produce engines that will cope with the harsh environment of RIB driving.

Special mention should be made of John Caulcutt, whose participation in a RIB in the first Round Britain Powerboat Race did so much to get the capabilities of the early RIBs recognised. Also thanks to Johnan Ullman, who has helped with photos and who was a pioneer in the scientific assessment of shock mitigation in RIBs, and to Jaakko Pitjkajärvi, who has allowed me to use some of his spectacular photos. The High Speed Boat Operations Forum is a vital information exchange in the challenging world of professional RIB operations. Thanks also to Jessica Whitelock for the illustrations.

Whilst I have talked to many people about RIBs and their design and development, the opinions expressed in this book are mine. There are many people who may not agree with what I have said, but I like to think that I have experience on my side and the opinions expressed have been developed from hard-won experience in 50 years of working with a wide variety of RIBs. I am beginning to think that RIBs are intent on world domination, particularly when I hear that in Russia alone around 250,000 RIBs and inflatable boats are sold every year. What did we start with those early RIBs?

Power Your Passion!

With a full range of outboard options, you can count on Mercury to deliver the performance you want, the reliability you need and a driving experience that is second to none. From the proven six and four cylinder Verados, the new durable 3.0L, 150hp to the lightweight 3.5hp and 2.5hp fourstrokes, there is a Mercury to suit your demands.

MERCURY

For details of your nearest Mercury dealer please visit
www.mercurymarine.co.uk or phone 01869 363613.

Follow us on Twitter @MercuryEngines

The Power Behind The Brands BARRUS Est. 1917 www.barrus.co.uk

Reliability & Dependability Comes As Standard

Mariner's latest engines lead the pack in offering an unsurpassed level of smooth power, backed by clean, quiet, fuel-efficient running and incredible resistance to corrosion. Add to this an awesome reputation for reliability and you can see why serious boaters choose Mariner.

MARINER

For details of your nearest Mariner dealer please visit
www.marineroutboards.co.uk or phone 01869 363613.

Follow us on Twitter @Mariner_UK

PANTAENIUS YACHT INSURANCE

Pantaenius –
always at
your side!

PANTAENIUS
Yacht Insurance

Germany · United Kingdom* · Monaco · Denmark · Austria · Spain · Sweden · USA** · Australia

1 Queen Anne Place · Marine Building · Plymouth · PL4 0FB · Phone +44 17 52 22 36 56 · Fax +44 17 52 22 36 37 · info@pantaenius.co.uk

www.pantaenius.co.uk

*Pantaenius UK Limited is authorised and regulated by the Financial Services Authority (Authorised No. 308688)
**Pantaenius America Ltd. is a licensed insurance agent licensed in all 50 states. It is an independent corporation incorporated under the laws of New York and is a separate and distinct entity from any entity of the Pantaenius Group.